D1518451

"It's time to repot."

HARVEY HERMAN

ISBN 979-8-3299-9496-4

A new life.

I think it was August 30, 2005, nineteen years ago. I began a new life. A life as a caregiver. There has been so much written about being a caretaker, but until you take on caring for another person in life, believe me it is pretty tough to imagine what you have to go through. The day Elaine had her stroke, life changed forever.

It is difficult to understand what all this means until you live it. I decided right up front that "I" was it. No team of people to help my wife navigate life after the stroke. Was it wise? I think so most days. Has it been tough? You bet. You've heard all the stories about caregivers going first. That is the reason I am writing this now as part of my memoir. These last nineteen years, in many ways, have been the best years of my life. The toughest …and the most meaningful at the same time.

Add to it, seven years ago Dementia struck in Elaines life. In a short time it became like living in the movie Benjamin Button. Elaine is getting younger mentally every day. Play a Frank Sinatra song and she knows every lyric of every song but she can't remember if she had lunch 5 minutes after eating. Her short term memory is gone. And, as each day passes she has less and less patience with everything and everybody, especially me. Here's the rub. I set it up that I am the sole keeper and she expects me to be available all the time. I mean all the time. Sounds horrible, right.

So how come during these past years I am painting better than I ever have, and have produced a body of work that even surprises me. With all the complaining about not having enough time to myself, how come I have written a 300 page memoir. I often ask myself, why have these past nineteen years been so productive in the areas of life that mean the most to me. I think that is the clue….the areas of life that mean the most to me.

My wife and my family now take precedent. My priorities have shifted. My painting and writing fit into my wonderful life with my wife and family, not the other way around. Being a caretaker is the most important thing in life.

I am learning the meaning of being "selfless "at the age of 90.
This old dog is learning some new tricks.

"It's time to repot."

Preface

This is what my wife said to me almost twenty years ago.
She was 74 and I was 72. She woke me one Sunday morning
and we talked about the last 45 years together.

"What do you mean by repot?" I asked.

"You know…when a plant grows as much as it can,
you have to repot it."

"What does that got to do with us?"

She quickly replied, "I think we have to sell everything. New York,
the farm in Sheffield, and the apartment in South Beach, and start all
over again."

So here we are in Hampton Bays…everything was sold in six month
and we have been loving living here for almost 20 years. How many
people would do that at our age. Really. That has been the story of
our life together.

Madonna is not the only one that can reinvent themselves. I realized
that as I wrote this memoir. Time-after-time we have *"repotted."*
And here we are in our nineties and again we are creating a new life
everyday.

Prologue

When I sat down to write this memoir I had no plan. Just started by writing those events in my life that I thought others might find interesting. It was more or less a diary. The stories do not follow chronologically. I wrote them as they came to my mind. As I wrote, it was almost as if I became an observer of myself. I started to see that sometimes an event helped to shape others in the future. Sometimes it would make sense, other times no sense at all.

After writing a couple hundred pages I kept on revealing two particular themes...

Family is a passion truly worth pursuing. It is a valuable lesson so many of us take for granted. Each family member has made their own individual mark. Together we represent strength, connection as well as individuality. Careers come and go. Family is with you forever. Put your efforts into family. Make it your passion. Life can be so rewarding for you, and for the many people that have helped to make you who you are today.

Aging. There is a fountain of youth. It is your mind and your talents. Learn to tap this source, and you will defeat aging.

I am 90 as I write these pages. My wife and I have a ten year plan. My dad had a great life till he passed at 105. My wife is 92 and still thriving. My brother Stan is 95, plays tennis and his business is exceptional. Each one of us has learned to live a life of passion. To use our talents and take risks... so key to living a fruitful long lasting life.

Enjoy the voyage

"One hot towel."
1939

Harry Alesi reached into the giant silver cauldron filled with fluffy white towels. The smoke filled the barber shop as he took one out and carried it over to the chair and slowly wrapped it around the cherub's face.

He was only five years old…what a ritual.
Every Saturday morning Dad had a shave and a haircut and he took me along. Propped high on the red leather chair my Daddy's barber treated me like all the other adults. First a hot towel to soften the beard…then the mug filled with thick foam…the soft brush covered my face with the white stuff…then Harry pretended to shave me with the back of his index finger…only to be followed by another steaming towel. I looked over to the right and there he was.

Sidney Herman resting in the prone position,
fulfilling his weekly shave.

"You have to start your memoir Poppa."
It was time. In a few weeks I will be celebrating my 90th year on this earth. Sophie, one of my grandchildren and her husband David were pressing me to start the process of recording my rich life. Then my older brother Stan said it was time. He had spent the last three years writing about his life…so exciting and wondrous.
"You have so much to say Harvey…just start, and it will come."

OK baby…a shave with my dad at five…and here we go.

Dad on his horse after a shave

"She's way out of your league."
Madison Square Garden, 1958.
The horse show.

My Dad was riding. He never won…but here he was mounted on this muscular gelding…in one of the most prestigious horse shows on earth. All this excitement and I couldn't take my eyes off the hot red head standing at ringside.

"Look at that redhead Paul."
"Forget it Herman she's way out of your league."
He was so right, but forget the horses, I couldn't take my eyes off this lady. Dressed in a Chanel suit and wrapped in a seal jacket. Her hair neatly combed in a pageboy. Her skin was like a porcelain dolls. I was smitten.
"Go on up…introduce yourself…go on."
"No way…no way."

I left the show that night and headed to my black and white 1955 Chevy convertible. It was raining like a Japanese movie. Tishiro Mifune would shake off his ringing wet cape. Nothing would deter him from the next battle. I was heading home to Passaic, New Jersey. Here I was 25 years old still living with my parents. I rushed to the car, my chariot, and whipped out the key. My baby turned over -and -over…but she would not start. Turns out the wires were wet. Here I was on 49th street. What to do?

My Dad had invited me to an after-the-show party just one block away. All those old horsey people. Never! But it was dry there… and my car was wet. I'll have a drink and by then the car would start. Good thinking Herman. Marvin Rappaport ran a restaurant The Spindeltop in Manhattan. He rode with my Dad and this was his brownstone. I rang the bell and a butler showed me in. I crossed over, picked up a Bloody Mary and headed inside…there she was sitting on the stairs.

Was I dreaming!
I shook my head
and peered over
to the redhead.

Oh my...
there really
is a God.

"She's way out of your league." 1958

Kiss on the neck.
1958

It's a little embarrassing, but I guess you have to include these moments in your memoir. As I write it I wonder if it is even believable.

You see I met my wife Elaine on a rainy night in Manhattan. My Dad had been riding at Madison Square Garden in the horse show. I had seen an incredible red head at the show, but was too much of a coward to approach her. After the show I tried to start my 55 Chevy convertible, but the wires were wet.

Long story short I ended up going to a party with all the old horsey folk. Who was there sitting on the steps…the redhead. I took a deep breath and walked over to her. "Hi, I noticed you at the horse show, would you mind if I sat down." She smiled and nodded OK. No words were exchanged at first, but I noticed my whole body was shaking. Was it nerves, maybe, but more than likely it was "thunderbolt." I was smitten.

Really. I can't remember much except at one point I noticed the beautiful nape of her neck and I kissed her there. Yes, out of the blue I made that move. I can't ever remember doing that before or since. A total stranger and a kiss on the back of the neck? I didn't know what to expect. She turned to me and said, "who are you?" I took her home that night.

The next day, Sunday, I picked her up, after she had been modeling at the Hampshire House. She worked every Sunday to earn extra money. Turns out she was the lead model at Bendels, but because she had a young boy in the first year of a now defunct marriage, she worked all the time. I can't remember how I talked her into going to Passaic, New Jersey after the show. I was still living with my parents at the age of 25. We had glorious sex *(the house was empty).*

On the ride back to Manhattan we talked a lot, and laughed a lot too.

We had a hot dog at Rutts Hut. Another highlight on a very special day. Their Rippers are world famous, and as I write this, I am salivating. In a moment of truth Elaine called the shot. "I can't believe you still live with your parents. If you want to see me again, you have to move to the city."
I answered stupidly…"Manhattan?"

Two weeks later I got my first apartment ever. Twelve West 12th Street. A tiny penthouse studio around the corner from The New School (which I had never heard of before).
This school would end up being one of the major sources in our lives together.

And it all started with a kiss on the neck.

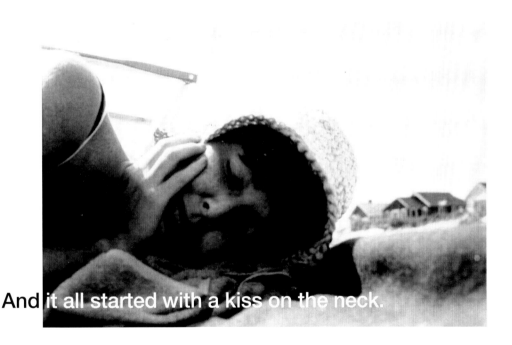

Kiss on the neck. 1958

IG FARBIN INDUSTRIES
1955

Why would a Jewish kid go to work on his first full time job for a Nazi outfit. Well they offered me the best package, and I thought the war was over. I was sure I was going to have to deal with Anti-Semitism...

I graduated with honors from Philadelphia Textile Institute. I was a Textile chemist, and I had my choice of jobs. Really. There was a shortage of Chemists and since the war the textile business was going through the roof. I could have gone to giant companies like Dupont, but my dad convinced me to stay in New Jersey and live at home.

I was a shift chemist at IG Farbin Industries. I worked around the clock. Each week a different schedule. The night shift just about killed me. I was in charge of 10 technicians. Each knew more about chemistry than me, and I was their boss. I dressed in green work clothes with iron plated work shoes. Here's the scary part. All were bald and listen to this... none of them had eyebrows or finger nails and they all had false teeth. It was part of the job. Each of them dressed with a suit and tie and carried a briefcase to work. Then these proper guys would change into their work outfits. We were working with acid all the time, and when they blew the dyestuff up to the filter presses they had to shovel this green dye out of the presses. Most Vat dyes for textiles start out as green. It's part of the Grinyard process. As a side effect, when I took a shower after work, the water was green, even a year after I left the company. I can't believe I did it.

Every day on the job I waited for some one to bring up the fact that of the 1150 people at the plant there were only two Jews. I carried a tin lunch box (like all the other workers) to work each day, and I locked it so nobody could poison me. It was only 10 years since the war and I was committed to having problems. Here's the great part..it never happened. I was invited to dinner by almost every tech who worked for me. They were hard working, caring people.

It was a rude awakening.

I stayed a year and when they wanted to promote me above one of the other chemists, Joe Savoca…I told my boss Doctor Shoen…give the promotion to Joe I am not going to continue being a chemist. He was shocked, and so was I. Four years of college down the drain. Dr. Shoen, believe it or not, called my Dad to try to convince me to stay. My dad was furious. They had offered to pay me almost $1000 per week. That was a small fortune. The average salary of a tech was a maximum of $10,000 per year, and I was still living at home so I would be rolling in dough.

I realized then that the world of chemistry was not for me, and money was not so important.

I needed passion in my life.

Dad had a store in Macy's 34th.

Unions…risks and rewards.
1955

Like I said in a previous story, my first job straight out of college was as a shift chemist for IG Farbin Industries. During the second world war they built tanks for the Nazis, and a lot of other munitions, etc.
Let's not go into why I went to work there.

There was a culture at the plant. Even though the jobs in the plant were mostly manual labor…I discovered that when the workers showed up to work they were dressed in suits and ties and carried briefcases like lawyers. Inside the plant they changed into green work cloths and metal tipped work boots. I showed up in my green outfit and metal tipped shoes every day, even though I was the boss of all of the ten techs. I worked around the clock shifts. The one that was so tough was the 11PM to 7AM shift. It was lonely. And at some times pretty scary. Like I said I was 21 years old and each of my techs had been on the job for at least 10 years. They knew a lot more about chemistry than me.

Something happened about six months into my job that I will never forget. It turns out that the top salary for technicians was $10,000 per year. And this was after they were on the job for quite a while. The company needed more chemists, so they made an offer to the techs. They would pay all the costs for four years of college, and continue to pay them their salaries. How many of the ten do you think took the offer??????? One. Yes just one. Why? I asked a number of the why they turned down this exceptional opportunity.

"They have a tough time firing us, when we are in the union. You are management." Wow this blew my mind. Security was more important than anything in their lives. Risk versus reward. What a lesson to learn. This has stayed with me throughout everyday of my life.

One other event that also was a wake up call.

Try and follow this. As the shift chemist each night the workers in the plant would bring me mason jars with test samples from the giant kettles. Each of the kettles on the first floor contained between 50 and 100 thousand gallons of liquid dyestuffs. They had to be balanced before blowing them up to the filter presses on the third floor. Can't remember all of them, but the most important was the PH test. If the batch was below 7, I would add anywhere from 1000 to 5000 pounds of salt to balance it. A little each time, so that we slowly got the batch to the perfect PH. It generally took most of the 8 hour shifts before blowing the batch. EXCEPT one of the workers seemed to get it right most of the time. He was an expert, I was told. Shift after shift Karl got it right, either the first or second sample every time. I was so impressed. You see, once the sample was OK to blow, Karl was finished for the night. One night I decided to watch him do the sampling. Perhaps I could help the other guys. I watched from the balcony. He drew his sample from the kettle and went behind the wall. I stepped around to watch as he tampered with the sample. Yes, he had a set of test tools similar to mine in the lab, and he tested the sample and added a few teaspoons of salt and some water until the PH was balanced…then he brought it up to have me check the sample. Unbelievable.
It was hard to believe. What should I do? It was 2AM.
I couldn't call anyone. I couldn't blow the batch till it was right. I did a naive, stupid thing…when Karl came up with sample, I told him what I had seen him do. He denied the whole thing. I asked him to go home, and I asked another worker to sample his batch.

What happened the next morning was a real lesson in life. The Forman showed up at 6AM with my boss. I won't go into it all…but the result was I was docked three weeks pay, and Karl was cleared of no wrong doing. The union protected him. I had no right to ask him to go home. I had to reach his Forman and he could talk to Karl. Unions were so powerful in the fifties and sixties. That changed many years later. But what a lesson at a very early time in my life.

Thank you Karl.

From Chemistry to Advertising
1958

Many people asked me why did you pick advertising.
I always say that I didn't pick it...it picked me.

After college and my short stint as a textile chemist I was not sure what to do. One day I was sitting with my brother Stan and we started to talk about what could be next. He casually said..."you are good with people and you like people, why not some business that will fit those skills?"
Why not PR or Advertising? *Sounds right. Why not?*

I got the Agency listings in NYC and circled a bunch that seemed to have the kind of accounts I would like. Made a lot of calls. Over the next few months I must have gotten seven or eight appointments. All pretty good...no job offers. Wrong background. Over and over.
Turns out I went to another horse show and got into a conversation with a complete stranger. His name was also Harvey. Combed his hair in bangs like Napoleon.

"What do you do when you're not at a horse show?"
"I'm looking for a job in advertising."
"I own an agency, come to work for me."
"Your kidding, right?"
"No come in tomorrow." (It was Saturday)."
"You mean Monday."
"No I mean tomorrow."
"What will I do."
"You'll be my slave, and I will teach you the business."
"What will you pay me?" "Pay? OK $50 a week."

That's how I got my first job in advertising.

Slave? You bet. Harvey had me doing everything. I worked six and seven days a week. Got that $50 check every week.
When they asked me to bring the mechanical over to Clairol,

I went into the Art Director's office…"Walt, what's a mechanical." I bought Walter Lefman sandwiches and he taught me Art Direction. Did the same deal with a copy writer. Got to work on a few accounts at night. Finally six months into the job I went into Harvey and asked for a raise. "Get us an account and I will give you a bonus." Within six months I was making almost $450 per week, and Harvey said he had taught me as much as he could and I was making too much money… "Hey dummy…open your own company."
So I did. The Promotion Centre.

Opened a tiny office at 678 Lexington Avenue. In order to get business I got 50 beautiful red delicious apples. My then girlfriend Elaine, my brother Stan, and his partner Gene helped me package them in a white gift box and wrapped them in tissue paper with a simple message…"fresh ideas ready for picking." I made one mistake…sent out 50 and 18 people responded.

I was able to meet with 4 or 5 of them, and they each gave me a project…Van Raalte Stockings…got Andy Warhol, a young guy just starting in the business to draw illustrations for some packaging. Wish I had kept that artwork. Herald Tribune gave me two jobs. And, American Airlines gave me an intercontinental brochure…I titled it "From Sea to Shining Sea" which they copied for the advertisements with Doyle Dane. Yes Doyle Dane, the agency that turned me down. It seemed too easy.

I got five accounts. Van Raalte, Herald Tribune, Heritage Furniture, Beaunit Textiles (got to use my textile background there) and American Airlines. When I finally got around to following up some of other 18…one guy said…"where have you been…the apple is rotten."

One of the apples went to a very good agency…Nadler & Larimer. The president of the agency, Arch Nadler asked me to come to the agency.

At the time I had no idea that Arch would become my mentor.

Arch Nadler
1961

He drove up to the restaurant in a vintage Rolls Royce. This gentle giant, he was 6 foot 4, smiled as he approached the table. "Thanks for meeting me here Harvey, so glad to meet. I had to find out who would send out such a great promotion. I loved your apple mailer." Arch had developed a wonderful ad agency after working, I think, for IBM for years. We had a great lunch, and he offered me a job. Up to now I had done projects for clients, but not as a full service agency. Arch told me that I would be great working with the "big picture", and some day I would have my own Rolls. Very tempting. We kept in touch over the next two years.

In the meantime, a wonderful art director, Bill McCaffrey contacted me. I had gone to a few Art Director meetings, and we hit it off immediately. He was a partner in a great agency De Garmo. He persuaded me to bring my business to the agency and they would give me all their promotional work. Did that. Bill was so creative… I learned a lot from him. Slowly but surely I came to realize that if I wanted to be in the advertising business I had to work for an agency to really get ahead. I think around a year later, I went to work for Arch Nadler. By the way he found out my real passion was painting and he was my first commission. A painting of flowers for $400. He really taught me the business. I loved the guy. I started as a marketing man (MadMan). Eventually I worked on the creative for the clients as well. Accounts like Lionel Toys…Sane Toys for Health Kids. Bob Larimer his partner gave me writing assignments, too. I stayed with them for about two years. What a wonderful experience. I learned a lot about branding and marketing, but I was not ready to open my own agency.

Again…I kept on meeting good people in this business.

Leo Greenland
1967

This cigar smoking man really was so different than Arch. He had developed an ad agency in spite of himself. Here he was with a 40 million dollar agency. He had a secret that he confided in me one night. We went for a drink, and he introduced me to Cuban cigars. By the end of the evening he told me his secret..he had never graduated High School. Unbelievable. He had one of the best small agencies in New York and he worried that he would lose his accounts if they knew. By the end of the evening he begged me to open a promotion company at the agency. I would be a partner. He would make me president of Smith/Greenland/Herman. And, I could do creative for all of the agency accounts, too. I was concerned that he would forget the offer the next morning, but he was sober and really meant it.
How could I say no.

Thinking back on all of this...I realized that I never had a resume. Every job I got was from meeting someone and we liked each other and the next thing I know they ask me to join them. I had to figure there was some luck involved, but I have to admit I made the most of each of these agency opportunities.

Leo was special, but I could not stand his partner Marty Smith. Marty was having an affair with Faith Popcorn, his creative director. She was probably one of the worst people I ever met, except for Martin Landey. Period. She lied and cheated. She took other peoples work and claimed it for herself. A copywriter at the agency, Nina Feinberg, *(a dear friend for many years to follow)* came up with a sensational idea for Johnny Walker Black Scotch. It was the campaign that would catapult that scotch into truly a snob product. She showed it to me before she reviewed it with her boss, Faith.
It was a breakthrough campaign. Later that afternoon...Nina came into my office. Her eyes were swollen from hours of crying. "What up, why the tears." "She hated the campaign for Johnny Walker...she said she was going to fire me." I couldn't believe it.

We had a board of directors at the agency. I was one of the 6 people on it, and so was Faith. All new campaigns had to be reviewed by all of us. You guessed it. Faith showed the campaign to the board and claimed it was hers. I called her a liar in the meeting. Told the board that I had seen the campaign that Nina did before Faith. She lied a Trump- type lie. Turning everything around. I have to tell you I was a very arrogant guy back then. In the meeting, I accused her of sleeping with Marty and that is why she had her job. She was a no talent bitch on wheels. I was sure that they were going to get rid of Faith or me…but they didn't. Leo smoothed it all over. This was how the agency business could be. People would do and say anything for fortune and fame…sometimes.

I stayed on at Smith Greenland for a number of years. One of the great things was I hired my dear friend Charlie Rosner. He was working in Philadelphia and I loved his work…he ended up being my partner in our Agency Herman & Rosner a number of years later. Oh, I almost forgot. Smith Greenland had a gasoline account Flying A for many years. Leo was making a fortune on them, and they were about to fire the agency. The commercials would win all kinds of awards and their business was dying.
They told Leo he was about to get fired if he couldn't turn it around. This was not my area, but I had a great idea and I was sure Faith would claim it for hers…so I went directly to Leo.

"I know how to turn Flying A around Leo." He puffed away as I set up the idea. "Who owns Flying A?" Leo puffed and his eyes lit up as he realized where I was going. "Yes, you got it…let's get John Paul Getty to name all the stations Getty, after the richest man in the world." I then puffed on my cigar…and pretended to be Getty…"Hi I'm John Paul Getty and from now on I am putting my name on all the Flying A stations. I wouldn't put my name on the stations if I wasn't going to give you something special. Here it is folks!"
…Leo shit.

A few weeks later with the campaign all packaged…Leo presented it to Getty as I watched on. He gave me credit for the idea.

At first Getty thought it was too ego driven. "My wife will kill me," he said. Shook his head and then after a few minutes he smiled, you know, that kind of smile when you know the answer…"what if I charged premium at the regular price?" The rest is history. They tested the idea in Philly and it went through the roof. Four hundred percent increase in business in four months. The birth of Getty Oil.

Mr. Getty burned all the Flying A lolly pop signs when he put up his Getty signs. He gave both Leo and I one of the Flying A signs. By the way, many years later someone stole mine but Leo sold his for a lot of money. Say La Vie. Yes those were the days in Advertising …before all those focus groups.

We had balls, and put them on the line. I am so lucky to have been in the business then.

"Fresh ideas ready for picking.

Stan, Gene and Elaine sending out the Apple Mailer.

Martin Landy.
(The worst man I ever knew).
1971

There was another small agency that was hot. Martin Landy Arlow.
I knew Arnie Arlow the creative director of the agency and he introduced
me to Martin. He drove a 1955 Gullwing Mercedes Benz at that time.
And whatever Marty wanted…he got. (Should have been named Lola).
He met me and wanted me to join the agency. I was so successful at Smith
Greenland. He heard all about Getty and that was it. It took him almost
two years and he offered me a lot to join them…but that Mercedes did me in.
Talk about egos. He even let me drive it once.

This turned out to be a big mistake. I helped to double his business in
just two years. He kept on double billing my accounts, and cheating
all of his clients over-and-over. He was a con man personified. We
hated each other. Elaine and I had just bought a giant house in
Hartsdale, New York out of the city. 14 rooms. It was once owned by
the Otis elevator family. I poured money it to that one. Elaine hated
Martin and pleaded with me to get out. "He's going to fire you."

One day Martin called me into his giant office…"Harvey I know we
have been arguing a lot lately, but Arnie and I want to know that we
really appreciate the work you have doing for the agency." He handed
me a check for $10,000. Today that would be about $50,000.
I was blown away. That night I told Elaine the story and gave her
the check. Her response? "He's definitely going to fire you."
Two weeks later my office was empty and I was out.

This was the third time I was fired from my job in the agency
business. De Garmo, Chester Gore and now Landy. You know…
three strikes and your…you know the rest. I finally got the message.
I was too arrogant to work for anyone.

If I was going to make it in the business, I would have to make it on
my own.

Martin Landy 1971

On my own...
1974

When I got fired from Landy I must admit at first I felt like a loser and totally lost.

We sold the giant house in Hartsdale. That was a story. We hated the suburbs. Taking the commuter train everyday. The people were the same. Boring. Almost no culture. We had to get back to the city, New York City. Everybody was leaving the city and going to the lovely suburbs. A good friend of mine had a radio show in the city... John Wingate on WOR. When he found out I was moving back he wanted to interview me on air. It was wild. I told him how boring it was, and that most people seemed the same. Here's what I said on air. "We have next door neighbors. Twins, that married twins. They live in identical houses next to each other, in fact they share the same driveway. That's the suburbs in a nutshell." We shared a big laugh. When I got home...all the bushes between our properties were cut down. Our neighbors had heard the program.

We had no idea of where to move in the city. Luckily again Elaine's Uncle Murray delivered oil to 1010 Fifth Avenue, right opposite the Met and he got us an apartment. Two bedrooms, two maids rooms a dining room and Living room and giant kitchen for $750 per month. A miracle and the beginning of an exciting four years.

I opened another promotion company...Mickey Enterprises. I was going to open an office, but a dear friend, and one of the giants in the advertising business, George Lois heard I was in midair and he called me. Long story short, after a lot of talking George offered me an office and a secretary and the chance to work together while I made up my mind what was next. How could I say no.

That's when I decided that it was time to start questioning if I should stay in advertising. I loved the business, and it had been great for me and the family, but what was next.

Elaine suggested we rent a house in Fire Island for the summer. We went there the first year we met, and it was always a place where we were happy and creative. Good decision.

That summer Elaine and I wrote three TV movie outlines, and a script for one. **Can You Tell Me How to Get to Harlem.** A story about a young black boy brought up in a upper class white neighborhood who gets lost in Harlem. **Documentary Daredevils,** a fast moving series about a family that travels throughout the world shooting documentaries like Wild Mustangs. And **Gemini**…a story about twin detectives, but no one knows that they are twins so they share one life, and can be in two different places at the same time.

I presented all three to Brandon Stodard at ABC. He had produced Roots for ABC and can't remember how I got them directly to him. He contacted me, and optioned Gemini. Gave me $3500. He also liked the others and asked if they weren't sold within the next year, he would like to consider them as well. Elaine said this might open the door to LA.

Then what happened? I needed money and I went back to American Airlines. I pitched them on letting me work on audio video shows for them. They eventually gave me their annual marketing show for all their divisions. I needed a writer and they recommended John Allen. We hit it off immediately. After the show we had dinner one night. He gave me the galleys for a book he had written. The 42nd Year of Helen Prescott. I was blown away.

I optioned the book for $3000. And that became my intro to Hollywood and Elizabeth Taylor. It also broke up my marriage.

But that is another story.

NYCtoLA
1975

In 1975 my wife, who always called all the shots, said it was time for us to go to LA and see if we could get in the film business. I had for the last four years in New York got into directing commercials. I had sold a few scripts to ABC for movies and was back and fourth to LA LA land about half a dozen times. Now that I had optioned The 42nd Year, Elaine said let's "bite the bullet" and see if you can get this movie made. Really! How many wives would do that. Still out of my league.

I was a long distance runner back then. Ran everyday preparing for my first of ten marathons. One day I was running along the water in Venice, California. I waved at all the weight lifters that worked out on the beach.
It also housed a number of drunks who slept it off on the beach that night…As I passed one he smiled and yelled out " Santa Monica Freeway, make a left and keep running." The front of my running shirt said *LAtoNYC* and the back *NYCtoLA.* He got me on that one. I ended up running over 3000 total miles over the years. Enough to run coast to coast.

Yes, I never stopped running, and Elaine made me stop and figure out how we can make this film. Here I was like so many East coast smart guys who was in search of power and fame. I had been directing commercials and felt that this script was very timely. A story about a corporate wife, having an affair with her son's teacher in a marriage that was over…a woman in conflict in her 42nd year. Elaine was so great at casting. She had the second largest casting company in NYC… Herman & Lipson.

"Let's get it to Elizabeth Taylor. It's like the story of her life. She and Richard are on the rocks, and she needs this."

It was a great idea, but was it possible? I spoke to my agent, and they gave me her agent's name. Robbie Lanz…

My three favorites. Elaine, Gin Gin and my 1956 Ford Pickup.

William Morris sent it to her. About a week later the phone rings. Elaine answers. "Honey, it sounds like Jeff, your agent, pretending to be Elizabeth Taylor."
I got on the phone.

"Jeff will you cut it out. It's not funny."
"Is this Harvey Herman…my new director!"

I asked for her number and I would call her back. It was her, and two weeks later I was in Gstaad with the Icon Elizabeth Taylor.

There is only one.
1976

As I left the Beau Rivage in Geneva I wondered what it would be like to meet the person that many had considered one of the most beautiful women on the planet. Elizabeth Taylor had paid for my stay at her favorite hotel in Geneva. Karl, her blond chauffeur waited for me in the stretch Mercedes limo. The smoke from the exhaust seemed to be blowing perfect circles, much like the tobacco sign in Times Square thousands of miles away. I had completed my 5 mile run at 6am that morning.

Normally I did not plan my wardrobe, but this was a special day.

I was tan. I slipped into my Prada black pants and shoes. A beige silk shirt would look great. A black velour top. Black from head to toe, except the silk beige shirt framing the tan. Boy was I trying hard to look great for the lady. When I was a young man I watched all her movies. Who knew that I was on my way to really meet this Icon.

"Can I take your bag Mr. Herman." The limo had a fur blanket. It was really cold so I threw it over my body. "There are Royal Jamaican cigars, your favorite, in the canister, and some orange juice. It's two hours to the chalet and roads are slippery so relax and enjoy the scenery."

So this is how they live. How did she know about the cigars! And, the juice was not from the supermarket. It was fresh blood red from Sicily (I found out later).

As the black Mercedes Limo navigated the snow covered roads I finally noticed the chauffeur. His father definitely was in the Luftwaffe. As I made up a story about her driver I feel into a deep sleep, only to be pulled out of my slumber as the car slipped into a ditch on the side of the road. "Sorry sir...the roads are slippery, but the chalet is just up there at the side of the mountain."

There it was. A picture perfect chalet cut into the side of a ski mountain. The snow pilled up to the first floor and behind on the mountainside, bright colored dots swished from side to side. Wow, if I put it in a movie no one would believe how sensual it all was. My heart was pumping away. What would I say to her for three days?

The house was unpretentious, except for pictures of Elizabeth and Richard with heads of states and famous movie stars. And the paintings. She loved Chagall and Picasso and these were not copies.

Her assistant, Sam Chen, a sultry young lady, lead me upstairs. I watched her body move under her sheer dress. Here I was going to a meeting with this movie Icon and I am salivating over her assistant. Will I ever learn.

She opened a giant oak door and there she stood, silhouetted by the mountain. Stepping toward me, and reaching out her hand… she began to laugh that famous laugh. I couldn't figure it out, was my fly open or what. The figure spoke…

"OK. Which one of us is going to go home and change."

Beat, beat…what should I say! Another beat of my heart in my mouth…she kept laughing while she held my hand. Finally I got it. We were twins. We had both dressed exactly the same, right down to the beige silk shirt. I was in trouble.

This began a five months adventure that would end up being one of the best and worst times in my life. An affair with my movie star. Paramount Studios will make the film. I will direct it. Warren Beatty, Frank Sinatra, George C. Scott…star after star. Doors open . You can't pay for anything when you are with her. Juggle the film and lie to my wife about my affair. Nights at the famous Beverly Hills Hotel. Month and month of trying to balance an affair and getting my first film off the ground.

A write up in the National Enquirer picturing me and Elizabeth sneaking out of the Hotel. I am cooked. My wife leaves me and goes back to New York. Two weeks before principal shooting,

David Picker becomes the new President of Paramount and he cancels every film in the house including ours. I am devastated. How do I tell her? What will she say?

I picked her up that afternoon. She looked so wonderful. A long sleeve white man's button down shirt and jeans. She jumped into my 1951 White Mercedes coupe. Leaned over and gave me a hug and kiss. Her famous purple eyes stared at me with total joy. She was like a child. She kissed me again and I began to wonder if it was real. We drove up Laurel Canyon to the top of the hill overlooking all of LA. The perfect setting, right out of movie. All that was missing was the music.

"Honey, I have bad news… Paramount canceled the picture. I wanted to tell you before you read about it in the Hollywood Reporter."

I explained what I knew. She held my hand as I spoke. "I am not surprised. It was going too smooth. Don't worry I will speak to Robbie and we will get it back on track."

We sat in silence for a few moments. She squeezed my hand and smiled and laughed… "perfect timing my love…Richards left me, and Elaine's left you too…(pause)…**let's get married!**"

Let's stop here. Let's get married…and she meant it..

I am so vulnerable. My wife has left me. My kids are back in New York with her. The film is canceled. I am in LA. What is this all about? Get married to this Icon? Become Mr. Harvey Taylor? A moment of truth for sure. Who was I being? What is my life truly about? What was important to me?

Elizabeth and I sat in the car and talked about all of it for over an hour. She was so supportive, but she truly felt that we could have a life together. The brass ring had turned to tin. I needed time to figure it all out.

Elizabeth went on to another project….A Little Night Music. I stayed out in LA. Directed a mini series Little Vic for ABC.

I cover all that in another story. I was not a happy camper. I missed Elaine and the kids. This was the beginning of my realizing that my family was the most important thing in life and being a famous movie director was mostly ego.

I went back to New York. Elaine did a great course…The Est Training…and I eventually did it too. We got back together. Not the same people who separated. I realized what I almost lost. This was after 14 years of marriage.

The world opened up for me and my family. Amazing.
A great adventure that would some day make a great movie. Maybe.

Photographer: Firooz Zahedi

There is only one. 1976

What does it feel like to be 90!
August 22, 2023

Last night I woke up at 12 AM It was my 90th Birthday, and I wanted to start it off by writing something in my computer. The first thing I noticed was a picture high above NYC…a short but wonderful note from my cousin Lewis…"Happy Birthday Harvey from 33,000 feet above your city." It was 12:01. What a wonderful way to start the day.

I am truly blessed. I woke up next to my bride and best friend of 65 years. Elaine has made my life so special. She taught me to be gracious in every facet of my life. She showed me how to enjoy money. Seems like a small thing, but believe me, it is one of the reasons why my life has turned out to be so perfect.

The phone started ringing at 7:00 AM and continued for the next hour and a half. First Jeffrey Banks, then my daughter Amanda, followed by my dear brother Stan, my dear friend and broker Gilda, and finally my daughter Joss and Mike. Lot's of singing. I followed through with my morning ritual. Popping a few pills to keep me healthy, I think. Shaving, showering, singing. Sliding into shorts and a tee. And then, ironing. Yes ironing any shirt that I had washed the day before.

"Ironing on your birthday?" Her first words of the day. "Give yourself a break." Routine. Perhaps one of the reasons I feel so young. If I keep it going…it helps me realize that life is special, as long as it is productive.

Egg Whites with fresh tomatoes and mushrooms cooked in a tiny bit of olive oil. No butter here. English muffins and turkey bacon. Low sodium V8 juice. We do care what we put in our bodies. We wolfed it down…feeding Izzy and Lola between each bite. Top it off with Elaine's tea and my coffee…now ready for a great day.

Speed walk (more or less) out to the front gate to pick up my "fix"… The New York Times. Have to read it front page to back.

Usually on the outside porch. I had a few things I needed to complete today. One was to write at least one story for my memoir (hello I think I'm doing it already). And finish and sign my latest paintings. I have been working on two of them for the past week and a half. One is a soft moment captured with Stan's Hen Swan and her 3 baby signets resting on his point among the water reeds. The Swan let me get within a few feet of her. The colors are so gentle, just like the moment.

And the second is a painting of daffodils. I paint them quite often. They reflect light and at the same time capture the sun to give it such a rich yellow hue. I love them. And this one turned out great. I am signing it on my 90th birthday and giving it to my self as a present.

My brother Mitch and his wife Catherine sang next, and then Sophie and David. What a day. Sophie is such a wonderful chef, among her many other talents, I needed to check with her on the dish I am cooking for my brother Stan and Elaine tonight. Roasted chicken thighs with onions, garlic and other veggies. I love it. It is one of my favorite dishes. Stan will bring over the desert and some champagne. Looking forward to the evening.

A short swim and a steaming hot shower outside will start the afternoon off, after Elaine and I had yogurt and berries for lunch on the outside porch.

The afternoon was so special. Call after call wishing me the best. I did finish both paintings and signed them. Stan showed up for dinner at 6:30. He had rose champagne and a great peach and blueberry pie.

The chicken turned out to be so special. Sophie told me how to keep everything moist and tender. Three kinds of peppers, onions and garlic with a little chicken broth. One hour later…pure ecstasy. We talked for a while about life. It was a perfect way to complete a perfect birthday.

Happy 90th. Feeling very good.

Flying...the first time.
1983

I could truly fill a book on this one. It all started on my 50th birthday, 40 years ago. At breakfast Elaine said the best birthday I could give myself on my half century birthday would be to do something I had never done before. Something outrageous. After all 50 was a special time. Half way there if I was lucky.

I had a lunch with my client, The MTA. I told Alice Boratkin what my wife had suggested and she was hysterical. "What would that be Harvey"?When I got back to the office there was a message from Alice...your first flying lesson is waiting for you at McCann Aviation in Caldwell, New Jersey.

"Alice, thanks so much, but that is impossible. I am afraid of heights. If I am in a tall building I can't even look out the windows." Alice assured me that I would either love it or hate it...nothing in between. Wow was I scared.

When I got to McCann Aviation I sat in the driveway and almost turned around to go home. What was I thinking! Flying. My Dad always said that Jewish people don't fly or fix cars.

What an experience. First they gave me my own log book. Who knew that I would end up filling three of them over the next 40 years. We had ground school for 20 minutes and then out to my first ride in a Cessna 150. A preflight outside inspection followed.

Then my instructor told me to get in. I thought he would take the plane off and I would sit beside him in the right seat. NO! "Get in the pilot's seat Harvey. You are the pilot today." "I am the pilot?...I don't know how to fly, you must be mistaken, I have never been in a small plane before." He convinced to get in the pilots seat. I started to sweat. So frightening.

The pedals are for steering not the yoke. He showed me all the instruments and what they were for. "Don't worry, just do what I tell you to do and you will be flying." We taxied out to the active… runway 22. He worked the radios. He spoke to the tower…"Student pilot on first run…taking the active."

We lined up on the runway. "This is the power, slowly push the power forward and take your feet off the brake…when the airspeed on this dial reaches above 53 SLOWLY pull this yoke back a little… don't worry I am right here in case you fuck up." I turned to him "you must be kidding me." NO…GO… first the power slowly to full. He put his hand on mine and nudged the throttle forward. We were rolling. "Remember at 53 knots on this dial pull the yoke back slowly. Oh my god. 30…35…40…50 pull the thing back slowly.
…all of a sudden the ground disappeared under the plane.
I WAS FLYING.

The next 15 minutes were ones I will never forget for the rest of my life. He landed the plane twice and I took it off (more or less) twice. I was flying and that feeling of freedom and joy only happened a few other times in my life, like when my daughter Amanda was born. Flying can be an experience that opens your mind and body to everything and anything possible.

It changed my life forever.

Flying, 40 years but who's counting?

Flying…the first time. 1983

My life as a pilot.

There are very few specific things that have enhanced my life as much as being a pilot. I started flying when I turned 50. Yes fifty years old. I sat in McDan Aviations Pilot Bay many, many days learning all of the basic of flying. At ground school most of the people were under 20. I hadn't been in school for so long that my brain forgot how to learn. I flunked the first few tests. I was sure this was too little, too late.

All of a sudden it started to click. I got smart. I couldn't get enough. I was going to class 2 and 3 times per week. My partner, Charlie Rosner was baffled…what could be so absorbing. I talked him into trying it. Now Charlie is normally white and yellow around the gills. When he came down after the first time he was literally green.

Charlie walked over to me and handed me his log book.
I asked him if he was OK?
"You trying holding your breath for 20 minutes."

Charlie never went in a small plane again for the rest of his life. That was Charlie.

I soloed in less than 10 hours. Nine hours to be specific. Amazing. Most people take two and three times that. It seems like yesterday that I soled, some 40 years ago.

My instructor had me do a few touch and goes, and after the last one he announced that he had to go to the "John." " Taxi down to the end of 22 and do a couple of touch and goes." He exited the plane." Wait, what are you doing?" I am not ready."

I had become so secure as long as my instructor sat next to me. He had no idea …the tower came over the speaker. "Cessna N8530 take the active, cleared for runway 22." I was screwed. There was a plane in back of me. Just go I told myself. Got on the runway. Lined up, hand on the throttle. "Cessna N8530 rolling" I announced. At 60 knots I broke ground and I was flying. Straight ahead to 1000 feet.

Turn crosswind, then downwind. I was doing it all on my own. All of a sudden I started singing.."**Up in the air junior bird man…up in the air upside down.**" Yes I sang. After two touch and goes I pulled off the runway. There was my instructor with a big grin and a thumbs up. I taxied to the office and tied it down. I was thrilled, he shook my hand, took out a pair of scissors and cut a piece off the bottom of my teeshirt. He wrote on the piece of shirt…Harvey Herman soloed August 20, 1983. I think I still have that piece of shirt somewhere.

We went into the office. There were a bunch of people laughing and singing…"Up in the air junior bird man…I had no idea that the instructor left the mic on so that they could hear me in the office as I soloed.

Talk about moments you never forget

Each one was a beauty.

When I started flying I rented my ride. Within a year I had my instrument rating. I studied for 6 months and went to Newark, New Jersey to take the test that separates the men from the boys. You learn how to fly a plane without visual references. That's why the call it IFR, Instrument for the I. You fly the plane with the instruments. You can fly in the clouds. Amazing. It was a two day test, and most people flunk the first time. I passed by the skin of my teeth. I think I got a 70. I can't remember a time that I was so wiped out. Mentally I was exhausted . I had a Mercedes station wagon, and it was locked. I could not remember my 5 digit code to unlock the car. Had to go to lunch to clear my mind. When I drove the car for the first few turns I thought I was flying so I used my feet with the steering wheel. I was not satisfied with my 70%. What was in that 30% that could kill me?

A few month later I took the test over and got a 97%. I decided it was time to buy my first plane. A plane I could rely on, now that I was flying IFR. No more rentals for me. Each rental with different equipment. Smart decision.

My first baby was a Piper Archer. I found it after 6 months of looking at a bunch of planes. It was in Chicago. It was a few years old. I paid $39,000 for it, and spent another $15,000 equipping it for instrument flying. I had the Archer for eight years. My wife and I actually flew cross-country in that little plane. Over 3000 miles each way. It took us about four weeks. Here's the kicker. Most of the places we stopped were places that Ralph Lauren had an outlet. He would be so proud of us. The top speed in that baby was only 100 knots. I loved flying her. She was so dependable. Elaine loved that plane too.

While I had the Archer I decided to buy a vintage plane also. A Piper Cub. A true classic. You had to hand start her. She had a tail wheel and two wheels in front. Her total weight was 750 pounds including the engine, and there was no gas gauge. She held 14 gallons of gas upfront. A stick with a cork on the end floated in the gas. When the stick disappeared you had 20 minutes to land. It's frame was wooden and fabric covered the frame. This one was a 1946 model with a 65 horsepower engine. You could buy it in any color, as long as it was bright yellow. That's right it only came in one color.

Elaine and I would open the side door and take off after dinner many nights in the country, where I kept the Cub. Great Barrington Airport. We just loved it. Top speed 73 knots. This was real flying. They call it stick and rudder. When I read this passage to Elaine... she said" I must admit I took a lot of chances with you." She sure did.

I've been a pilot for forty years. There are so many stories to tell. Like the time the whole family was flying back from Florida to New Jersey. I had a 40 mile an hour tail wind so I did not stop in Charleston for fuel. As I was about 50 miles from Caldwell I checked the weather. It was fogged in so I called for weather at Morristown. Solid fog...even La Guardia and Teterboro all fogged in. Not forecasted and here I did not have enough fuel to go back to Baltimore. I decided to try Morristown. I told everyone what was up. Josselyne, who was 18 at the time, said..."don't worry Dad, I have had a good life."

My wife was my copilot. The minimums at Morristown were 300 feet. That meant that you could fly in the clouds down to 300 feet to pick up the runway, in this case the ILS 24. If the runway lights were not visible you could not land. You could try again but very rare after two tries could you make it in.

I announced to the tower that I was going to attempt the ILS. They advised me that minimums had prohibited another plane from landing. I advised them I was going to try. I did the whole approach and then made my way down the ILS. Elaine called out the altitude every 50 feet…500…450…400 no runway in site.

I had my hand on the throttle. Minimums were 300 feet.
When you arrive at that altitude…you must go around or leave the airport.
350 ready to leave…300 I start to put the power… Elaine calls out…
"there are the lights"…sure enough how beautiful the ILS and then the side runway lights and then we touched down. I stopped as soon as I could.

We were on the runway, but I couldn't see the exit markers. Just then a car with flashing lights rolled out on the runway. The driver called out "follow me off the runway." We followed the flashing lights and he pointed us where to park. I did my check list and turned the two 300 horsepower engines off. This was the moment I finally realized how close we came to being a statistic. The kids yelled out…" yeah Dad we knew you would do it…Yeah!"

We got ourselves together and made our way to the FBO. There were a dozen people inside and they all clapped. Hand shakes.

One by one the jets that had been circling landed and came in the FBO. One of the jet pilots yelled out. "Where is that Baron pilot?" Me. "Thanks Buddy. Saved my ass."

What a night to remember. A celebration as pilot.

My life as a pilot.

He Did it his Way!
1904 to 2010

I was talking to my Dad last night, that's right he died 14 years ago but I think I talk to him now as much as when he was alive. That may seem a little strange but here's a man who lived till 105 and when I think back on our life together we didn't share much. Oh we talked a lot, but most of it was his telling me what he needed or wanted. Last night I talked to him about my grandchildren and how great they are turning out, and I could be proud without worrying what he would say.

My Dad was a special man. Self educated. I think he only went to a few years of school, and then he went to work. And work he did. He worked until he was 103. My brother Mitch worked together with him for well over forty years. I tried to work with him once, but I quit after less than one month. I guess that's what happens when two people who have strong opinions about almost everything, try to make it together.

I never regretted cutting our work relationship short.
It provided an opening for me to explore what was next in my life. I really grew up in the next few years. Luckily I met my bride of 65 years. She set me straight. I could find a new career. One that would be passionate and fulfilling. And it also made it possible for me to have a healthy relationship with him. But this story is about Dad… not me.

Sidney Herman was amazing. He was the second of eight children. His sister Anna was the eldest, and then there were seven boys. Dad was the lead guy with certain exceptions. Bruno became the man they all looked up to. He made money outside of the Herman Brothers Silk Shop. Although he was one of the youngest he stood out and Dad admired him. Little things like Dad bought a number of Bruno's cars when he was finished with them. The story goes…when my mom passed away, Bruno approached my Dad and suggested that he give him one of his two boys, since he and his wife could not have children. For a short while I was going to Bruno…I can't imagine what my life would have been like with him. He was not a good man in many ways. He ended up adopting a girl and named her Joy. She turned out to be a very troubled person. Anyway back to my Dad.

The thread that held his life together was his ability to have things his way. He was not always right obviously, but he was really consistent. He and Stan got along so well. As I remember my youth I seemed to very often be the one that got in trouble. Not like drugs or booze, but as Dad often put it…I could be the "devil child." He was always so busy with the business. He had a lot of responsibility at work. He was the boss, under his mother of course. Rose ran the show. All of her children kept in line. I think Dad expected that from his kids. He always expected me to go to work with him. It must have been a big disappointment when I didn't. In any case, I believe it all worked out. Stan went on to be very successful in the world of fashion, Mitch ended up being so supportive of him in business and in his life in general, and I love the life that I ended up with.

Which sort of brings me to the end of Dad's life, and why I wrote this story. He passed away in his home in New Jersey. Seems Stan and Mitch went out to get hot dogs for lunch and they got a call from the housekeeper to come home. Dad had finished his lunch and sat down to take a nap and passed away. Just like my Dad said he would. "Have a nice lunch, sit in his chair and take a final nap". Michael, my son-in-law took a picture of him in his chair. He still looked alive. I never saw a picture of a dead man so alive. I still have that picture today. I thought about putting it in this memoir…but I didn't.

At Dad's 100th birthday they played Frank Sinatra singing…
"I did it my way"…my father's theme song.

About Elizabeth Taylor.
1976

Meeting this woman shifted the whole projection of my life.
How come?

Before I met Elizabeth the most important thing was that I become a famous movie director. I thought I really needed that fame.

Imagine if you can meeting Elizabeth Taylor. Having her agree to be in the first feature film you have written and being signed to be her director as well. I say being "her" director because that is how it was turning out. Here I was married 14 years to a supportive, loving, wonderful woman and raising 3 great kids…and all of a sudden I am sucked into her life and life style. A five month affair with an icon you could never even conceive meeting.

A life style that very few people can imagine. Never paying for anything. Getting whatever you want all the time. Traveling in a circle of famous people, most of which were called "rich and famous." Frank Sinatra, Warren Beatty, Richard Burton, Red Fox to name just a few.

$300 dollar bottles of wine for lunch. Every move you make you are surrounded by the press. No privacy. Never going to a public place without a body guard. All this while manipulating a marriage and trying to get your first film off the ground.

It surely was a fast look at the fast lane. So much, so soon. So seductive. I started to believe all the articles written about Elizabeth's new director and eventually the National Enquirer wrote the story about our affair. Where was this all going?

Elaine left me and after doing the EST training she came back for the kids and I was in Hollywood with Elizabeth. Turns out Richard divorces Elizabeth. He was such a cad. He even used Elizabeth's lawyer to draw up the papers. She goes into a tail spin.

The picture gets canceled. David Picker becomes Paramounts new CEO and cancels everything in the house including our film which was 4 weeks from shooting.

When I tell Elizabeth about it, what is her response. "It will all work out sweet heart. I am sorry I know how much the film meant to you… look Richard's left me and Elaine's left you…let's get married."

My kids and wife are back in New York. I am sitting in my Vintage Mercedes Coupe with one of the biggest movie stars ever and she says let's get married.

Why am I sweating? A moment of truth. As I looked out over the city of LA I started to understand a little about what direction my life was taking, and I was not happy. I was pretty lost.

I stayed out in LA for another year or so. Directed a kids mini series Little Vic for ABC. It was nominated for an Emmy. Worked on projects for Mattel Toys, including Barbie. Made pretty good money. Dated a lot of people in and around the movie and TV business.

But the more time I spent away from my wife and kids the less sense my life made. My wife had done a program called EST and she stopped being a victim and got her life together.

I resisted what I considered to be a program that many called a cult, but I finally agreed to try it. Turns out the person that had written the book I optioned for my film with Elizabeth was John Allen He introduced Elaine to the work. If she had not done it, I wonder where it would have all turned out. The circle we call life.

That year I would say I transformed my life and got back on track to follow my North Star. Moved back to New York and my family. Opened my first advertising agency. Wrote a 60 page story about my life with Elizabeth and my baptism in LA LA Land.

I called it…Thank You Elizabeth.

That was in 1975. Here we are in 2024 almost 50 years later and two people have just optioned my story, written a script and intend to turn into a movie this year. It never ends.

Elizabeth and HH in Malibu.

A great family, including Amelia and Alfie.

What ifs?

There are so many places in life that we could ask that question. Well here's one with a very short answer. What if, when Elizabeth Taylor said…" Richard's left me, and Elaine's left you…let's get married." What if I said yes. Well that was in 1976 and here I am sitting in Hampton Bays with my buddy, my best friend, my wife of over 60 years and it's 2024, over 45 years ago. What if I said yes to being Mr. Harvey Taylor or Mr. Elizabeth Taylor. Or something like that. Instead of Mr. John Warner who was her seventh and next to last marriage. I tell you…I would be dead.

That life style would have killed me. That moment was a moment of truth. A shocking reality, that I missed my wife and kids. They call it lots of things. Books have been written about those pivotal moments in life. The Tipping Point. Whatever.
Which way should I turn, and why?

I was alone in LA. I realized that most things that really mattered to me were back in New York City. Life is truly crazy. It's like a merry go round. We get opportunities but how often do we reach out for that golden ring.

I never would have gone to LA if hadn't met John Allen. If I hadn't optioned his book, The 42nd Year. Never would have met Elizabeth. Elaine is back in New York and I am in LA. How did we get back together? Well John had gone back to the East coast after the movie fell apart. I stayed on the West Coast, for over a year or more. Dated every good looking, and not so good looking lady in that city. Directed a TV series for ABC. Little Vic.

In the meantime John Allen calls Elaine and tells her about a course he had taken called EST. She does it and wow…she stops being a victim. Get's a great job. I told her she could not get the kids back unless she got a great job, and an apartment in the PS 6 district for less than $750 per month, with two bedrooms and a doorman. Almost impossible.

Less than a month later she calls me.."I am coming back for the kids." "Over my dead body" I replied. She tells me she got it all done. I don't believe her. Hop on a plane the next day. Sure enough she got it all done.

To show you what a low life I was, I went to check out the apartment on 86th with the broker. Great two bedroom down the block from their school and a doorman for $725. To show you what a schmuck I was at that time, I had oral sex with the broker, in the apartment. What a low life. I did not deserve my wonderful family.

I went back and got the kids and brought them to Elaine in New York City. Elaine told me all about EST. What she got out of it. My retort…"it's not for me, it's for people like you."

I moved to an apartment overlooking the ocean in Santa Monica. Perfect bachelor pad. Again going out as often as possible. Made friends with Don Ameche. He was struggling with life. Out of work. We lived in this complex that was more like a motel, than a rental. Turns out two ladies moved in below my apartment. We made friends. They were very special.

One day they came up to have drinks with me and sat me down. "We never do this Harvey. We are chefs for a very special man Werner Erhardt. He started a program called EST. You need it. You should do it. You will get a lot out of it."

That started me hating these two. It surely was a cult. They would never get me until one day I asked myself where was I going. It was almost 2 years since I turned down Elizabeth and they were the most empty two years of my life. I did EST.

Yes, it was one of the best things I ever experienced. I fought it day after day, It was a four day course. In fact, I got up to leave the first hour of the first day. I raised my hand and said I was leaving…this is not for me. The leader came down to be with me face to face. "Why are you going. Why not share it with the other people in the room.

"Over 300 folks had her full attention. I was sure I was stuck in a cult. Why is she picking on me.

"You won't like what I have to say, but I'll say it anyway. I didn't expect a woman to be leading this program."

Then the shit hit the fan. Women had always been second class citizens to me… and this leader got it. And I got it. A wife and two daughters down the drain. I could see it all coming. It was inevitable if I continued my life with that belief. She got real deep with me… who else were second class citizens to me? Of course homosexuals. I had a brother who was one, and my son Bruce was one as well. Where was this all going. That was just the beginning. The big one was yet to come.

On the third day, there was process that we went through. I won't get into how it all worked but boy did it work for me. You see my Mother had died when I was seven and a half. She was only 37 years old. I loved her so much and she was dying. I knew she was not well but did not understand that in a few short months she would be gone. She called me and my brother Stan in the bedroom one night. And, here's the big one. She tells us if she hadn't had us she would not be dying. She died two weeks later.

Where do I go from here.

You know I had a suffered for years from a dream that I was lying on that bed with my Mom. Wake up screaming. Drove me and my wife crazy. Went to all kinds of therapy. Never shook it. Kept having that nightmare.

Until I did EST. During a process the third day…I had the dream. She accused me of killing her again. This time I stopped and said… "mom I am 42, I am married and I am raising 3 kids, you died for me and I'll die for you and we will be even." They tell me I was out for over 10 minutes lying on the floor. When I woke I felt like I had been washed clean… like being baptized (even though I never was in life).

That's right. I completed that horrible moment in my life and never had that dream again. Yes. Never again. I had completed with my mom and went on with my life

I got so much out of that one weekend that I became a Seminar Leader for that program. Not a Forum Leader, but a person who leads follow up programs after people do The Forum. EST was renamed that later on. Elaine and I put our kids in to EST when they turned 11. It was the best thing we ever did as well. My oldest daughter Joss also became a Seminar Leader and led programs for Landmark for over 30 years.

Why do I bring that all up, because I want you to know how essential these programs became for our family. And, how they have given all of us the tools to have great lives.

As an example, and then I'll drop it…how did Elaine and I get back together. Not easy right. She called the shot as usual.

"Let's have lunch."

A lunch I will never forget. It was at one of our favorites. Japanese Maison upstairs on 38th and Lex. After some small talk she got right to it.

"Do you still love me"?

"Of course I will always love you, but that doesn't mean we should be together."

"OK, how come. Is the sex still good? Are you still passionate about being together?"

"Yes. But I am not sure you are the right woman for me." Wow, how honest can you get. It just came out.

She was not thrown at all. "Why am I not the right woman?" "OK. We both did EST. I will tell you something that always bothered me."

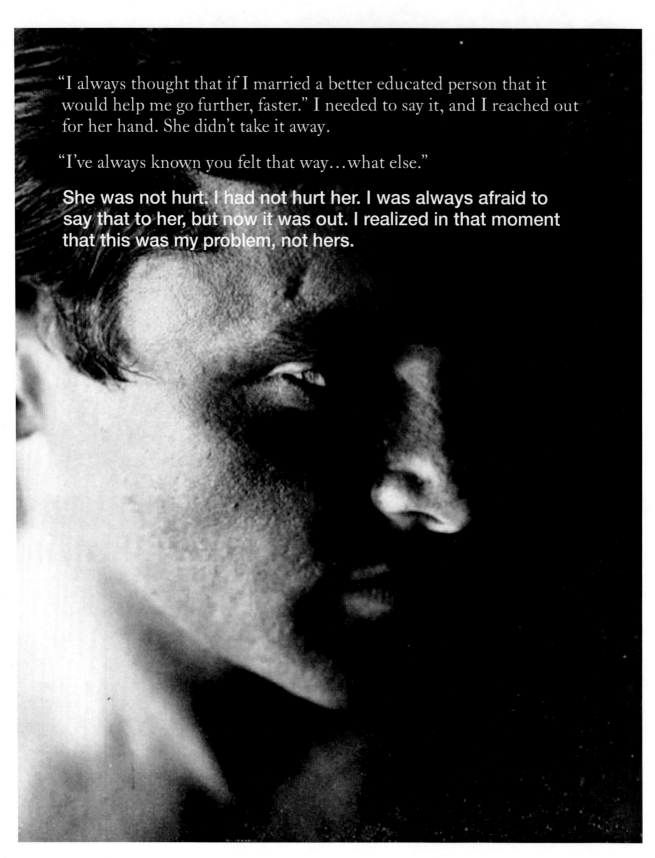

"I always thought that if I married a better educated person that it would help me go further, faster." I needed to say it, and I reached out for her hand. She didn't take it away.

"I've always known you felt that way...what else."

She was not hurt. I had not hurt her. I was always afraid to say that to her, but now it was out. I realized in that moment that this was my problem, not hers.

We spoke for two hours that lunch. The following week I moved back in with her and the kids. From that day on there has never been anything we could not share with each other.

That was around 45 years ago.

Real Estate.
2005

This has been such an important part of my life. The truth is, I am a frustrated architect and I love to invest in properties. It wasn't until we moved out to Hampton Bays in 2005 that I had the chance to use these talents in my life. Where to start?
The name of this memoir is "It's Time to Repot."

One day my wife woke up and she tapped me on the shoulder. "Honey, I think it is time to repot." I was hardly awake. She knew that was the best time to bring up ideas that she knew I would reject. Smart lady. My daughters have told me time-after-time…my first answer to new ideas is usually "no."

I rolled over, shook my head to wake up…"Repot? What does that mean?"

"It means that we have gone as far as we can go, with what we have. Life is good, but all we are going to get is more of the same. Like a plant grows as much as it can in a pot, and it needs a new pot." Give me a break…what does that mean to you?" She responded very quickly…"It means selling everything and starting over."

I am not going to say what I said then, but it was not nice.

Three months later we started a one year project to repot. Sold our home in Sheffield, Mass which we owned for 26 years…our coop in South Beach Florida, and the apartment in New York City. I said I would never, never live in The Hamptons, but it was less than two hours from the city. It was The Hamptons or New Jersey. What else can I say. Yes, it took about a year to get it done. Finding a house on Long Island that we could afford was not easy. We had about one million dollars to spend. I had a big list of "had to be."

Must have at least one acre. Walk to water. Unusual features and a fixer upper so I could put our touch on it. Budget? Less than a million. My brother Stan had lived in Southampton for over 60 years. "Forget it, try Jersey."

After some research we decided we did not want to be right in the hubbub of The Hamptons. We started looking in Flanders, Hampton Bays, Shinnicoch, and a few places in the hubbub. I dragged Stan to about 30 places over the next 10 months. Hated everything. All they showed were ranch houses on less than a quarter of an acre. Might as well been in the suburbs in Jersey. We needed to find a new pot…but it all looked like a dream that would never come true. It looked like as wife said…"never, never land."

I was at the gym around the corner from our apartment in NYC and while on the treadmill, I read an ad in Dan's…the local Hampton's rag, for a house near the water for $999,000. They only showed a shot of the beach. Why not! Called a new broker. Caroline said there was a offer on the house, but would show it to us next Sunday.

It was pouring that day. The kind of rain that the Japanese use in their movies. I had been looking at houses that Sunday all morning with my brother Stan. We both were so frustrated. Stan felt it would not happen on our budget. I called the other broker to show us the house near the water for that afternoon, alone. I met her at the Hampton Bays diner.

Caroline was so sweet. "Are you sure you want to see it in the rain? There is an offer on it."

I said I would follow her. She took us straight up Route 24 and turned on to Red Creek Road. For the next 2 miles I followed her through the Pine Barrens. And barren it was. No homes. No lights. Just lots of trees. I kept flashing my lights to stop her, but Caroline kept going in the pouring rain, turn after turn into what looked like a wilderness. Elaine live here?

Forget it.

We finally pulled down a dirt road. The owner Richard Mander came out." You sure you want to see it in the rain?" He opened the gate and I noticed that the whole property was fenced in. Great for the dogs. He showed me a bamboo forest, two koi ponds and a waterfall. "How far is the beach", It's out the back, but why don't we go in the house first." "No I want to see where the beach is."

Oh my god…a private sandy beach was revealed just minutes from the house. I think a tear came to my eye. I tried not to show the owner how excited I was. "How many acres do you have?" He wiped the rain off his face…" just under two acres." How many bedrooms?" "Four, more or less."

I stopped walking turned to him, the water pouring off my baseball cap…Ok, this is my house. I am going to give you an offer."

"You haven't been in the house, come on. Let's go back to the house. There's a fire and my wife will make some tea. By the way are you married? " Sure" Don't you think your wife should see the house first? My wife! I was so taken by the house, I forgot about her for the moment. She had just had her hip replaced and couldn't come out with me this week.

We went into the house with the broker.."Can I use your phone to call my wife." No cell phones back then.

"Honey I think I found our house!" "You are not going to buy a house without me"she immediately said. "I'll bring you out here tomorrow" I responded.

"In the meantime I am going to make him an offer, and I want Stan to see the place." "I better love it" is all she had to say.

The house was a mess, but the bare bones were there. It was actually two houses connected with a greenhouse. That was so great. And it had an upstairs bedroom that I could use as my studio. But it needed a lot of work. His wife was from the Philippines. Their plan was to buy an island in the Philippines. She served me same tea in the living room in front of a fire. They had an offer out at one million, but they had not returned the papers for over two weeks. I talked to Caroline in another room. We settled on $1,150,000 as an offer. It was as much as I could afford. After seeing the condition of the house I knew we needed at least another $350,000 to get it in shape. Add a three car garage, a pool, and a big back porch. Redo the three bathrooms, paint inside and out, plus who knew what would show up. It was a challenge. I called Stan.

"Stan I found our house, please come over I want to make an offer."
"Harvey I was with you all morning. Give me a break. You have not even sold your apartment. You told me you need to sell it to afford anything out here…besides it's pouring."

An hour later Stan showed up a little pissed. As a side point, remember in the movie The Field of Dreams…Kevin Costner's brother-in-law said…don't sell the property after seeing the baseball team…well when Stan walked into the house on the living room wall he saw a painting…"I know that painting, I know the artist." Turns out the artist indeed had worked for Stan and the Mander's knew him. "You've got to buy this house, Harvey. You are right, this is your house."

I made the offer, one hundred and fifty thousand over the one that was out for contract. " I have to give them a chance to come back with an offer Harvey." We figured it was ours. Elaine came out the next day, and loved it even more than me. We were so happy.

Two days later our broker called. Bad news. The other buyers upped their offer two hundred thousand over ours. We could not believe we lost it. We had gone as far as we could. We lost our dream home.

You know how you visualize something in the future, that is how both Elaine and I had felt about living the rest of our lives out in that wonderful property. We had a few sleepless nights. And then it happened. Our broker called…The owners need to close by May 28th… just 30 days from now. They have to buy the island by that date. The new buyers backed out. If we could close by then it was ours.

I called our broker in NYC, Julie Johnson.
"I need to close on the apartment in the city in 48 hours."
Believe it or not, she had a buyer, at our asking price in one day.
We closed on the house in the Hamptons on May 28th.
Something was just as settled.

That was 19 happy years ago.
We are living in Shangri-la.

Sidney and Evelyn
in LA, LA Land
1976

When the National Enquirer article showing Elizabeth and I cuddling in my white Mercedes came out, the phone rang off the hook. Holly cow... who knew how many people read that "rag." Half of Passaic, really. People I thought had died. So called friends that I hadn't seen in years. Even a teacher from High School. And my father. He announced they were coming out to visit. We had been in LA 6 month, why now!

About 10 days later they arrived. I had no idea what to do with them. Elaine had the genius idea of taking them to Disneyland. I bought over $330 in tickets. We drove all the way down there and Evelyn lasted less than an hour. Her feet hurt. Her back was out. Too many people. On the trip back my Dad said he wanted to talk with me. I did not expect what was coming. I figured he was worried about me and Elaine. As we walked around the block the first words out of his mouth were..."how is she in bed?"

How many days of this could we take. And then it came to me." Let's go look at the movie stars houses in the hills. Evelyn almost had a heart attack. The only reading she ever does are all the movie mags. Now to see their houses in person. Oh my god.

We pilled into the Mercedes and made our way to Homely Hills were most of the stars had homes. Each one so unique. So big. "There's Rock Hudson home." A brute stucco mansion behind a golden gate. "I knew it. It looks just like him. Oh my!" she said. A pink ranch sat on the hillside. A winding driveway with pink flowers completed the perfect picture. "Doris Day bought this home a couple of years ago to be near the Rock, I told her. I think this is when I noticed a tear in the corner of her eye. Jimmy Durante, Jack Lemmon, Gene Kelly and last but not least Ginger Rogers. It was exhausting, but not for Evelyn. I think she had an orgasm as we approached Ginger Rogers.

That afternoon Evelyn called half of Passaic. I must tell you, she thanked me so many times over the years. She remembered every house. Every detail. It made our lives manageable.

©2019 Paul Deetma, Pexels.com

Do you think I made it up?
Oh well that's Hollywood, right.

My 90th Birthday Party.
2023

When my brother Stan turned 90, he had at least a half a dozen parties to celebrate that milestone. I had one, but that one was so special.

My daughters birthday is just 5 days after mine. She and Sophie and the rest of the Saccios put the affair together. You know when about 50 people show up…close friends and family…you realize how special your life is. People came from all over. A special group of 6 showed up from Boston and The Cape. We met on Zoom in a Landmark seminar about 2 or 3 years ago and we meet on Zoom every Sunday… but here's the kicker. We never met in person. They all came down for the party. So special.

The night before I realized that I had not written a speech. I hate to wing it, so I got out of bed and wrote until late into the night.

The speech turned out wonderful. I first acknowledged Joss for the difference she has made in our lives. We adopted her 56 years ago. She changed our lives forever. And then I acknowledged everyone that was there that day for making my 90 years so special. My bride of 65 years. My brother Stan who is so special. We speak everyday. The Wiesenthal's and the Saccios. Both families have enriched my life. I am a proud father and grandfather. Each of my five grandchildren are unique. Very strong and yes very different. My brother Mitch couldn't come. His wife Catherine was recovering from surgery. Over the years we have had our issues, but he was missed.

For Stan's and my wife's 90th Birthday's I painted a collage of each of their lives. For my 90th I painted a pitcher overflowing with beautiful flowers, symbolic of my plentiful life.

It's very rare that life turns out the way mine has. And to see the faces of all the people there that made it possible brought a thankful tear to my eye.

Life is good Herman!

Our wonderful group from Landmark.

Sophie and her husband, David.

The five years.
1958-1963

Elaine and I met in 1958 at a horse show. I knew immediately that she was the one. How come it took me five years, yes five years to get married. The simple answer is I was afraid to marry anyone. I was a baby. I was trying to reconstruct those five years. They happen so long ago, I am still not sure I have it right. When we met I was living with my parents. Elaine was living with her son Bruce at 10 West 74th Street. Like I cover in another story, she insisted I move out of my parents, or she wouldn't see me anymore. I moved to the city in the next few weeks to 12th and 6th Avenue, right around the corner from The New School. We loved that school. I took painting classes from Anthony Tony and Elaine from Hyam Gross. This was the beginning of my passion for art. Before that I played with the idea of being a painter...but now I dove in with Elaine. I was working for Harvey Lloyd advertising...struggling to make a living...that is when I went into business for myself with The Promotion Center.

The next year I moved to the Village on Greenwich Avenue, right around the corner from the famous White Horse Tavern. Elaine and I had so many great times at White Horse and so many other places in the Village. I could have guessed we would have ended up there. But not for four more years. We each kept our own apartments. Even when we started going to Fire Island we rented separate houses. Around two years into the relationship somehow we stopped seeing each other. If I remember...Elaine was worried about Bruce. She wanted a Dad for him and I was not ready.

I met a wonderful illustrator who worked freelance, Salli Rendigs. She was so different than Elaine. Salli came from a very wealthy family from Rochester, New York. I think her grandparents founded Eastman Kodak. Need I say more. I thought she was special. But that passion was not there. In spite of that we spent almost a year together. I learned a lot from that relationship. I realized that I needed that bond that I had with Elaine. At the time, I was to naive to understand what was happening. Elaine and I wanted to be together, and we loved being together. But it still wasn't enough for me to commit to marriage.

Salli met a very talented guy. Robert Benton and they married. Benton became a very special film director and writer. He did Bonnie and Clyde and Kramer versus Kramer, one of my favorite movies, and a number of other great movies. They had a child, and at this writing they are still married and living in New York City.

Over the next 2 years or so Elaine and I got back together and we were inseparable. We antiqued together. I got much closer to Bruce. I went to City College to take film courses. I did a film about us, as a family. Elaine and I studied Art at The New School. Still in separate apartments until…one day I get a call from Elaine…"I found a great apartment at One Sheridan Square in the Village. I am moving in."

"What…without me?
Let's get married." That's how I proposed.

How romantic can you get.

Marriage, finally!
1964

Every Sunday Elaine and I would make breakfast and listen to Ethical Culture. The head leader there was Dr. Herman. We loved the premise. It started from the idea of working with organizations and individuals to be ethical in their lives. Both Elaine and I were moved. We joined Ethical Culture that year. And, when we got married...that is where we got married, by Dr. Herman.

When I told my Dad that Elaine and I were getting married, he was pretty nasty. In fact, very insulting. "Why marry a divorced woman with a child...she's dead wood." My dad never understood strong women. I doubt if he understood women at all. He married my mom because the family introduced him to her. I don't know if he ever appreciated that special human being. I won't go into whom he married the second time, or that he constantly belittled my younger daughter Amanda for wanting to work. The only woman who he loved was my daughter Joss. She made that happen by reaching out to him and his late wife all the time.

When I think back on the time that I introduced Elaine to Dad, I wondered why I wasn't stronger with him. This was the relationship we had over most of my adult life. Rather than confront him, I just let it be. It wasn't until we got married that I shifted that relationship. Actually more confrontational, and Dad hated it.

When I told Dad that we were getting married at Ethical Culture... all he had to say was "make sure they don't have any cross's around, otherwise I am not coming." I believe he said the same thing when Amanda got married in the Burton Estate. There were crosses there but I had them cover them up. Oh well there we go again.

I am not going to bore you by going into the ceremony...it was a day I will never forget some 60 years later...but one precious moment... Bruce was the ring bearer, and when Dr. Herman asked for the rings,

Bruce dropped them on the floor and they rolled under the chairs.
You should have seen all those people crawling on the floor.
Dr. Herman was so great...he couldn't stop laughing.

Our wedding day, May 3, 1964

I remember he said..."I think this is one I will never forget."
Neither did we.

Horseback riding, and more.
1939-1955

Dad put me on my first horse when I was 5. Not a pony, a small horse. I took to it naturally. I loved riding. Dad was like a professional. He has been riding most of his life and now he rode in horse shows. Five gaited horses. Very challenging. Most riding horses are three gaited. Walk, trot and canter. The other two gaits are not natural to a horse. They train them for slow gait which is the front legs trot and the back ones canter. Then the rack is a powerful version of the slow gait. When you are riding in slow gate you urge the horse with your hands, knees and heels to push into a very fast version of slow gate. It is very exciting. When you are in the slow and rack gates you "sit" the saddle. In other words you do not post like in a trot. It is so exciting and when you rack on you are flying but in total control with very little effort. I was an aggressive rider. I loved to push the horse to their very limits. I believe most horses loved that. I could feel when they gave their all. My Dad did not really like it, when I pushed the horses. He was much more conservative, much the way he ran his life.

Dad tried to have Stan and Mitch ride as well. Neither ended up having a love for it like I did.

It got to a time, when I thought I was ready to be in a show. Here's the rub. My father never felt I was ready. Time after time he refused to let me try. So after a while I stopped riding. This happened when I was in my early or late twenties. What a pity. I thought I was so good, and I never had a chance to see if was true. Again…Dad and I were so different. I wanted to take the risk…he never felt I was ready.

This showed up over and over in our lives. I was supposed to go into business with my Dad when I finished school. He did not want me to go to college. Why waste money on college if I was going to work with or for him. When Stan came home from the University of Cincinnati and found out that Dad had put me in a typing class, he went crazy.

Sammy made a friend in Bruges.

The Brothers.
In fashion even back then.

Bruce and his horse, Bill

Horseback riding, and more. 1939-1955

"No way." He convinced Dad that I needed collage...Thank god for my older brother. By the way, I got to be a pretty good typist from that class. I am using that skill as I write this story.

What was it that had Dad feel that I was not ready for most things? I never figured that one out. But I sure didn't give him the confidence like Stan did.

As I look back on our relationship, that pattern kept on showing up.

I was going to Philadelphia Textile. I was in my second year of being a textile chemist. Dad's brother Bruno was partner in a dye house with a laboratory and they hired me in the summer to work in the lab...I thought!

First of all they let me intern for no pay. And second, I got there and they put me in the back ripping rags and cleaning the place. It was a really hard labor. I was young and strong and I did it well.

After two weeks I went to my Dad and asked if he thought I could talk to my uncle to see when I was going to go to work in the lab. He said that obviously they would do it when they "thought I was ready." Another week went by and no lab work for me.

So I quit. Dad was furious.

I went to work in the Borscht Belt at the President Hotel...which is another story. I earned over $1000 per week as a bus boy. At the end of the season I bragged about how much I earned, almost $7000 dollars, Dad shamed me into giving him half for college.

Keep your mouth shut Herman. I guess I wasn't grown up enough for that either.

I sound like such a baby.
I was, until I got married in my late twenties.

Horseback riding, and more. 1939-1955

The year mom died.
1941

She was only 37 when she died. What a waste. I was only seven and Stan was twelve. My Dad told me many years later that he was advised before he got married not to have children. She had a weak heart. Don't know why, but Stan was born and I came 5 years later, and 7 years afterwards she was gone. I was so young, but I remember so much about her.

We lived on Palmer Street in Passaic, New Jersey. I can remember that house so well. You walked in and there was a large living room and a front windowed porch facing Palmer Street. There was a piano in the Living Room. It was like a railroad apartment. Room after room. To the left was a bathroom with a shower and bath and a giant sink. Mom would wash me in the sink. I would watch her in the medicine cabinet mirror. She would sing to me a lot. I remember it so vividly. I loved to watch her, as she soaped my body and rinsed it off with fluffy white small hand towels. It brings a tear to my eyes as I write these memories.

Stan and I slept in the same bedroom to the right of the bath. My first thoughts go to how much I loved and admired my brother. At this time he was twice my age, and he was so nimble and athletic. We had two single beds and between them a wooden chest. Stan would bounce on the bed and do a somersault on to the next bed. He was so great. I had to try it. I bounced up and down and flipped my body over, only problem I never made it to the other bed. I landed on the corner of the chest head first. The giant cut over my right eye seemed to spout out immediately. I started to cry.

Mom rushed in and lucky enough Dad was home. She grabbed a towel and wrapped my head to stop the bleeding. As I remember Dad started to scream at me. They rushed me to the hospital. A bunch of stitches later they took me home. It seemed I was always getting into trouble. My dad called me "a devil."
Dad and Mom slept in the room next to ours and opposite the

kitchen, where we spent most of our time. A large storage room was in the back and a side door lead out to the garage. We didn't have a car yet, but when I was about 5, dad got a pony for me and kept it there. Funny thing the neighbors didn't complain. Dad took all the kids out for rides so I guess that made them happy. How wild was that. It seems so unlike him, right?

Stan had piano lessons and tap lessons. I wonder why not me. We lived there for about 3 years. The lady next door was Mrs. Madison. She would make potato pancakes, known in Jewish circles as latkes a few times a week. Stan reminded me that they were very thin and crusty, and melted in your mouth. From our kitchen we could see into Mrs. Madison's kitchen and get the rich aroma of those tasty orbits. I would run over there and she would ask…"have you been a good boy?" I nodded with a smile and she would wrap two of those beauties in a napkin and send me on my way. Life was so simple back then.

Stan had a few friends that came to the house after school most days. Howie, Eugene and Merty. I always wanted to play with them, but those bullies said I was too young. They built a house in the woods in back of the house with two giant refrigerator cartons. They cut a hole in the middle of each carton, which were massive, and piled them on top of each other, making it a two story house. They placed them in a tree with a small ladder to climb up into them. Straw on the floor. It was cool. Almost every afternoon they were in their house.

"Please let me see the house, please" I pleaded…to no avail. They never let me in. So one day I burnt it down. My dad gave me the strap. I had a red backside for a week.

Those days were so memorable even at my young age. The only times that were hard were sometimes after dinner, dad would yell at mom for spending too much money on food. Money was the big one. We didn't have much, but I can't remember feeling poor. There were always meals on the table. Although we could only afford meat once a week. God forbid you left some on the plate. "People are starving in Europe" he would say. We couldn't leave the table till we ate everything on the plate.

Even though money was always tight, mom made sure we went great places. Like the movies at the Lincoln theatre every once and a while. Don't tell your dad we spent the money she would say. She made popcorn at home, because it was 5 cents in the movies. A giant jar of corn sat on top of one of the kitchen shelves. "Take down the corn, we are going to the movies" she would proudly announce. Tickets were 5 cents then and if you were under 36 inches tall you could get in for free. Luck had it I would crunch over and not be an expense to mom.

In step to the World's Fair

A real highlight happened when I was six years old. Mom took Stan and I to the 1939 Worlds Fair. She dressed us up in the same outfit. Pristine white Worlds Fair tee shirts, white shorts and matching white shoes. I was so proud. The General Motors building was the a giant world of the future. We sat in seats and rode above villages with winding roads, and General Motors cars riding on every one of them. Heinz gave us pickle pins. And we had sandwiches on white bread at the Wonder Bread Pavilion. Here I am eighty plus years later and I can never forget the wonder of it all.

Like I keep on saying…life was rich even without money.

The year mom died. 1941

It all came to an end on Christmas. 1941

My Mom died on Christmas Day in 1941.
The Japs had attached Pearl Harbor a few weeks before.
Our country was at war. What a very sad time.
For some reason I was not allowed to go to my wonderful moms funeral.
Dad told me later that I was too young. Yet, I remember not being there.

Dad was hardly ever home. My aunt Bertha cooked for us, and my Aunt Anna too. Dad's textile business went through the roof. He was selling fabric to the Army and other military installations. He could not manage both Stanley and I. So, we went to live with Aunt Bertha a few blocks away, and Palmer street no longer was our home.

Bertha had two of her own children…Tippy and Marvin. Tippy, or as he was originally named, Sylvan was close to my age and Marvin was a few years older than Stan. My uncle Adolf was a toy jobber. He was strange. I found out why, many years later. My dad came to live with us too. Bertha meant well but it was all too much for her. Four kids and Sidney. It did not work…

I was sent to Brooklyn to live with my uncle Sunny. This was the beginning of a deep and enriching relationship for the rest of my life. Sunny and Elinor took me on as their child. They did not have children of their own yet. Elinor taught me to how to cook. They treated me like a semi-adult. Sunny taught me everything. They rented a small cottage in Golden's Bridge, New York and on weekends we would pile into the car and drive there. Many years later, when I was thirteen, right after my Bar Mitzvah Sunny taught me how to drive his 1931 Model T Ford with rubble seat.

I remember the day like it was yesterday. I was a kid and Sunny handed me the keys to the car. "What's this for?" "Today you really become a man. Today you learn how to drive." Oh my. Here's the thing about my Uncle Sunny, he was an accountant, and when he said something was going to happen…it happened. He trusted me. He encouraged me. He was like my dad at the time. I missed that a lot.

The model T was not an easy car to drive. It had a clutch. No automatics back then. Also the brakes were very bad. You really had to press down hard to stop the car. Yet here I was. I sat in his lap and he showed me how to pull out the choke and push the button and start the motor. "You can only drive here on the road in Golden's Bridge. You understand!."I don't remember much about how I learned, but by the end of the day he was sitting along side of me while I was driving. My legs were not strong enough to brake, so he handled that part for me.

The real beginning of my manhood started that day I learned to drive..

There are so many fond memories of Sunny and Elinor. One happened when I first came to live with them. One afternoon I went shopping with Sunny. We were running short on time, so he asked me to shop at one store without him. "Go over there to that store and ask for a can of Similac. Stay there and I will pick you up."

I was only eight and had never shopped on my own. I held the $5 bill in my hand very tightly so I would not drop it. When I got in the store there was a line and there was a machine to take a number. I asked someone to lift me up to get a number. They handed me one and I waited, and waited.

About 15 minutes later I was still waiting on line Sunny showed up in the doorway. "What are you doing here…this is a pork store." He said it so loud. I was so embarrassed. Who knew that Similac was baby formula. Their daughter Ruthie had just been born. That was Sunny. He treated me tough at times. But it worked.

Another, a few years later Sunny was in the military and he was based in Wilmington, Delaware. My favorite time was at the end of the day, Sunny would often bring home a three foot long submarine sandwich. Loaded with salami and all kinds of meats and cheeses.

It all came to an end on Christmas. 1941

Yes, it was at least three feet long. And Elinor would make donuts from scratch. She had a handheld bottle that held the batter. When she pumped it, out a came a round donut, and she popped into oil that was cooking on the stove. I had to stay clear of the hot oil, but I put the powdered sugar on top when they were cooling.

Three foot long subs and donuts.
Does it get any better.

Sonny. 1935

Elinor at 92

Uncle Sunny with daughter, Susan.
She is a cancer doctor.

The Brothers, again.

It all came to an end on Christmas. 1941

The Boulevard
1942

These memories happened over a number of years.
In the meantime we moved in with my Aunt Anna at 93 Boulevard, in
Passaic. She had three kids, our cousins. Phillip or Fish as we called him
who was about 5 years younger than me. Herbie the oldest. He was a few
months older than Stan. And Nancy, the only girl in the bunch. Beautiful
Nancy. She was about a year older than me. I had such a crush on her.

The house was a five story giant Victorian, situated in the old section
of Passaic. All the houses were part of Passaic's fine past. This was
the wealthy section twenties year previous, but the neighborhood
was running down. Dad could afford this mini mansion, now that
he was cleaning up during the war. Aunt Anna was the oldest of
seven of the siblings in the Herman family. Six boys and Anna was
the only girl. She ruled the roost. In fact she was the only one that
Dad listened to. She was married to Uncle Leon. He was a sweet
man, and a great father to his sons. It was about a year since my
mom had past away, and after being separated from Stan for almost a
year, it was so good to be back together.

The year or so on the Boulevard was a kids dream. All five of us got
along so well. Aunt Anna would manage us. Firm yet loving. She
would sit us down in the kitchen and taught us all how to knit, to
keep us busy. We made scarfs mostly. That was the easiest. We were
a unit. When they would go out at night…lights out at 9PM was
the order. And, every night before we went to sleep we had to take
a bath. With only 2 bathtubs in this giant house it meant we had to
rotate. One night we stayed up too late listening to the program …
The Shadow all together. Only the Shadow Knows. We had to share
our bath otherwise they would catch us up when the came home.
We put Phillip in bed without a bath. What to do next? Stan and
Herbie shared a bath, and Nancy and I shared as well. I was about
nine at the time, and Nancy was 10. This was my first memory of
being aroused. I was so embarrassed yet so inquisitive. We splashed

each other. I spied a peak at you know where. Life doesn't get much better than that bath together, not for a long while. One morning Nancy was cooking us all breakfast and her dress caught on fire. Anna threw a pitcher of water on the flame, and threw her down on the floor to put out the fire. We all started crying. Nancy included. They rushed her to the hospital, and it took many months of healing. She was scared all over her shoulder, and still beautiful. I remember that we all started a new faze in our lives. More independence and an appreciation of love. At least that's what it was for me.

This year or so was very important in my life. Mom was gone. Sunny had given me so much love, and now Aunt Anna and the family made me feel so wanted.

I don't remember much about Dad being there. I was around 10 so this was 1943 during the war. Dad built his business. Over the next few years he opened a number of Herman Brothers Silk shops. Allentown, Easton and a few others in Pa. He even had a textile store in the Macy's on 34th Street. So he was not around much.

However, after just eleven months after Mom died he announced to Stan and I the following…"I will tell you when to call Miss Jacobs, mother." That's how he told us he was getting married. (The Jewish religion said you had to wait one year before marrying again.) I vaguely remember Dad sleeping with Evelyn on the Boulevard and Anna telling him it was verboten.

They married and we moved to a tiny house at 64 Kensington Terrace in Passaic Park.

This was the beginning of a number of very tough years.

Much tougher than a ten year old could ever imagine.

Kensington Terrace was a nightmare. 1942

Evelyn was tough. I think I was about eleven when Stan and I met this woman. She was very big. She loved one thing mostly. Cleaning. She would stay up all night cleaning her silver collection. She would read all the movie mags. No culture. I must admit I really did not give her a chance during the first year. I made her life tough.

The house was small, and carpeted throughout. The upstairs had 3 small bedrooms. One for them, and one each Stan and I. Jumping ahead, when Stan turned a teenager, Evelyn took the doors off each of our bedrooms so that we could not masturbate. Stan, many years later, was on the David Susskind television show and told the story about the doors. It was a show stopper. Evelyn had a fit, she was watching.

Within a year Mitchell was born. At first she was much nicer. She handled my Bar Mitzvah. Picked out my wardrobe, right down to my brown suede shoes. Even bought me a wristwatch. My first. I still have it today, and that was from 1946. And a initial HH gold tie clasp. I was so small, about five feet I had to stand on a platform when reading from the Torah.

And then the shit hit the fan. It turns out that she was overwhelmed with Mitchell as a baby. Stan and I got to be too much for her. Anyway, going back, what I remembered most was how hard it became for her to handle me. I really tried, but she would tell me what to do, and the next thing I knew she started hitting. I became scared of her. She was big and I did not know how too handle it. At first I was very obedient. That didn't seem to help. Most days I ended up being pushed around or hit a lot. Crying didn't help. She mocked me, and told me she would tell my father that I was mean to her, and that I hit her. After a while I told dad. He didn't believe me. He took her side.

Here I am thirteen years old, what could I do?
I told my best friend Kenny about all of this. We had met in kindergarten and he was like another brother. Kenny's dad had a fruit store in Passaic Park. Every day after school we would go down to the store. His dad was so sweet. He would sometimes ask us to stack the fruit on the stands. We could eat as much fruit as we wanted. Kenny's mom was Minnie. That year, Kenny's dad died, unexpectedly. This was a time that was tough for Kenny also. His older sister Alice was so sweet. I loved going over to their house after school.

Kenny wanted to help so he told his mom about my problems at home. Even with her problems she took me in. Every day after school for almost two years I biked to The Berman's after school. I spent many days and nights at their home. This all happen over a period of two years. Stan went away to the University of Cincinnati. And it got worse at home. There was very little peace with her. Evelyn would complain to Dad what a terrible kid I was. He warned me he was going to send me to Military School. And, Stan was not there to protect me anymore.

But it all came to end one day when I was around sixteen. Evelyn cornered me in the front alcove and started digging her nails into my arm. She was hurting me. My arm was bleeding. I pleaded with her to stop. But she didn't. The next thing I knew…I punched her in the side of the head and she went down like a ton of bricks. She was out cold. She was so big I remembered the sound when she hit the floor. I thought I had killed her.

She never touched me after that day.

In the end it taught me that life could be tough, and you had to navigate the bad times. Those few years as a teenager, had me appreciate being loved. I still carry that with me today.

Herman, Berman and Feifer.
1943-2020

I met Ken Berman in kindergarten. My mom dropped me off at school and I immediately took over the Jungle Jim. I got on the top story and played king of the mountain. Some of the kids were crying for their mommies but I loved it. Along came Kenny. He was a little shy at first, but I convinced him to join me at the top. We shook hands and from that day for the next 70 years, more or less, we were special friends.

Passaic, New Jersey was a town of about 59,000. We lived in Passaic Park. A community small enough so that you knew pretty well who lived in each house. Mom walked me to school every day. We went to PS 3. I think it was very safe. Kenny's dad, Phillip or Mr. Berman as we called him ran a fruit and vegetable store on Main Street a few blocks from the school. It was an easy life for most people. We went to the Ahavas Israel synagogue. My Dad and Phillip Berman were on the board of directors of the Hebrew school, and Kenny's moms name was Minnie. All of the Herman's, all of my aunts and uncles and their kids lived near each other. I never had the feeling of not being safe.

Within a year Ken and I would ride our bikes to school. I was so proud. Right after school Kenny and I would get a few other guys and play stickball in front of our houses. We seem to always be outdoors. Ken became like another brother. We did everything together. I think I ate more meals at his home than ours.

My mom and his dad both died within the same year. We were almost 8 years old. Another reason to bond, naturally. We were so different, but we were inseparable. Ken Berman was much more down to earth. I was more a romantic dreamer. Jumping ahead, when we graduated high school we planned a trip across country after our first year of college. He never went, I did, twice. He went to Wharton School of finance at University of Penn to be an accountant. I went to textile school to go into business with my dad.

You would think we would grow apart, but we got even closer as the years went on. In college he wrote to me almost everyday about his first romance with Sandy. It ended in marriage. I think he was a virgin until then.

Around our teenage years George Feifer entered our lives. Talk about different. He had been at Julliard, playing classical music, before his parents split up and moved to Passaic. His mother was a diehard New Yorker and their life was filled with concerts, opera and theatre. Mrs. Feifer was about 4 foot eight, and drove a giant Buick. She sat on cushions and had blocks put on the brake and gas so she could reach them. George had a sister…Leila. She was a real ballet dancer and about five years older than us. George never bought his own clothes. His mom ordered everything over the phone from Brooks Brothers in New York City. My clothes came from Wechslers in downtown Passaic. Amazing, Georges mom would order six white button down shirts, four pairs of chinos. White bucks. The same sweater in every color they came in. And socks…my god…he had them in every color and white by the dozen. They had money, and good taste.

George would practice the piano everyday, and when he was around sixteen he got into arguments with his mom over her seeing a guy she wanted to marry. In order to get even with her he stopped playing the piano, forever. What a fool. But that was George. He was brilliant, yet had no common sense. He knew what was best for all of us, except himself. Yet, for some reason he became part of Herman, Berman and Feifer until he died two years ago.

I know I am jumping around, but it was because of George that I got laid for the first time. He had a girlfriend in NYC. Beverly Blazer lived at 20 East 36th Street. One night George begged me to drive him to New York to meet Beverly. He was too young to drive and I just turned 18 and had a jalopy. A 1941 Pontiac that I paid $150 for. You guessed it. George was first and Beverly was my first. Pretty big deal. I didn't know what I was doing, but Beverly helped me through it all. No more virgin here. I remember the night like it was yesterday. I assume that you never forget the first time…right?

George had gone to a couple of different collages until he ended up at Harvard. Graduated top of the class. He went on to become a writer. He was an officer in the Navy. He started to write for the New York Times. They sent him to Russia. He wrote the famous story when Krushev took his shoe off at a trade show and threw it at some US diplomat. And here's where it took a curious turn. I am pretty sure George became CIA or KGB. He lived and wrote in Russia. Married a Russian woman.

His first book was a best seller The Girl From Petrovka. Goldie Hawn stared in it. He wrote three books on Okinawa. He wrote the book about the hostages taken by Iran. In all I think he wrote 16 books, and all of them were published. And, George remained a know it all fool. He constantly criticized me for being in that gross business called advertising. "Dear boy, why do you waste your life on such nonsense." When he moved back to the states with his Russian wife and two wonderful kids…Gregory and Alexia he was lost. His wife left him and according to him stole all his money. But we were the closest of friends throughout our lives.

Like I said Kenny married early, right out of college and became a very boring, but lovable man. Had two excellent kids. Pam and Freddie. I still talk to them today, even through Ken died about twenty years ago. He gashed his leg on the edge of a glass table. The doctor stitched him up and told him not to move around for about three weeks. Stay immobile, and Ken listened to that schmuck doctor. I told him to get up and walk around. He didn't. A blood clot went to his brain and killed him. What a waste.

Going back, after I did the EST training and got so much out of it I called Ken and George and asked them to do it. Both agreed to do it together. Ken told me what happened. George walked out the first day after about one hour. Ken said he couldn't shut up…George kept on mumbling about the KGB. I can't stay. The KGB. George called me that day and insisted that he wanted to come over to our house to explain why he left. He came over, took out a pad, and read 23 pages of his thoughts on EST. One hour…23 pages. That was George. He knew everything. In the end it was what made his life so tough. He was so talented but never listened to anyone.

George always wanted to work with me on something. He said he wanted to write a commercial script together about the advertising business. One summer we did it together. It was called Sweet Sal. A black comedy that was really naive but charming. You see this professional tennis player Sal had an unusual or should I say weird thing about her breasts. They contained a liquid that was an aphrodisiac. One drop of her liquid would turn a man or woman on. Her coach found out about it, and went to one of the biggest advertising agencies in the world to package and sell this product. The packaging was in the shape of a breast. You dispensed through the nipple. It's not important to go any further. We wrote every day. George was so disciplined. A run in the morning, shower and then 6 hours of writing. We finished it in 4 weeks. It was wild to work with him. We had so much fun. I could see that when he was writing he was at his best. He listened and made tough decisions easily, but he could not carry that into his relationships in life. What a shame. Even to the very end, his partner of many years Barbara could not deal with his petty complaints as his health started to fail him. He moved to the West Coast to live out his final years with his daughter who is a children's doctor. His kids seemed to turn out really great. Gregory is a writer like his dad. I meet them the day that George was honored by his agent and many friends in a NYC apartment one snowy afternoon. I spoke about our times together and prepared a collage of his life, giving each of his kids a copy. It was so great to meet so many people that knew this man intimately… and the thread of the day was George as a man who found it tough to listen, yet produced a body of work that was his legacy. Very true.

So much about George and so little about Kenny. Kenny and I were close most of our lives. There was a period in our forties that our lives were so different that we spoke, but were not very close.

His life as an accountant seemed so predictable to me. He was a Buick guy, when Buicks were for old folks. He became a bit of a bigot, so we could not talk about the changes in America at that time. Sandy was sweet and very supportive, but she would not talk politics with me. She seemed to be frightened of the black movement. We had less and less to share in life.

When Sandy died, Ken and I became much closer to the end. He married a woman, Barbara that couldn't make her mind up about anything. We stopped going to dinner with them. It was too painful to see her spend a half hour trying to pick out her meal.

When Ken and Barbara got married they lived in the same house that Sandy had designed and lived in with Ken for many years. That was Kenny trying to save money. Anyway, Ken's son Freddie was a builder of houses. He literally did the carpentry, plumbing, electrical...etc. Barbara wanted their bedroom redone, and Ken asked Freddie to do it for them. Nightmare. He never got it done. She kept on changing this design and that design. Freddie spent many, many hours and finally quit.

When Ken died unexpectedly, Barbara and the kids fought over who would get whatever in the house. I finally had to go out there and read them the riot act to settle everything. I never saw or talked to Barbara after that day. The kids still find it hard talking about her.

In writing I find it strange that there is very little more to write about. Here were two relationships that lasted over 70 years, yet they seem now not to be so memorable. I feel a little strange about that...perhaps as I continue to write other events will come up. Perhaps!

Me in 1953 at the Grand Canyon

The showgirl?
1957

When I was out of college and working for IG Farben Industries, believe it or not I think my dad introduced me to Bootsie. Yes Bootsie was the daughter of Murry Orlanis that owned the pony farm on the circle where routes 46 and 23 meet in Wayne New Jersey. My dad kept his gaited horses right next to the pony farm. Murray Orlanis had three kids. His oldest was a daughter he named Bootsie. She was a showgirl in Las Vegas and one day my father and Murray decided it was time I met her. I was twenty-two and dating, but nothing serious. This pony ranch was a big feature for families with kids, especially on weekends. They must have had fifty ponies and their house was right on the corner.

I drove my Black and White 1955 Chevy convertible right to the entrance of the farm. I really remember that day. I walked up the front steps and Bootsie's mom showed me in. She was very sweet. They were all in the kitchen and offered me a drink. As I sat at the table I could see Guy their middle son leading a few ponies and their kids around the track. Murry walked in. A stocky, ruddy complexion man. You could tell he worked outdoors. He was wearing a great denim jacket , jeans and cowboy boots, straight out of central casting. He was very shy. He shook my hand and asked if I was Sidney's son. The shitach began.

The door to kitchen flew open and their she was. Wow. She was a showgirl. Cute as a button. I noticed her large breasts which were exaggerated by her tiny waist. Her hair was drawn back showing off an adorable face. This was my blind date.

I can't remember what we did that night. I think we went out for Pizza and when we came back to the farm she asked if I wanted to see the ponies. I loved horses, especially ponies. The barn was well lite and as I entered a cute mutt barked at me. She petted her and picked Daisy up into her arms. I think it was then that I realized I liked this woman. Even though she was only twenty she was sensual woman and I was a naive boy. It was wild, as I studied her face she really reminded me of my mom. Now I understood why my dad wanted to fix me up with her.

The next few months were spectacular. I saw her almost every day after work and every weekend. I worked on the farm. She and I hit it off. It was pretty serious right from the start. And the sex was pretty special, too. I was a happy guy.

Within six months we we're engaged to be married. Murray suggested I quit my job and come work on the farm with the family. They were so lay back. I remember once Bootsie and I went shopping at the supermarket. She took two baskets. When we got to the toilet paper, she filled up half the basket. Same with soap. Bar after bar thrown in the basket. Two or three giant detergents…and on and on. At first I didn't say anything…finally I asked…"what's up with all the toilet paper and stuff." "Oh we'll use it someday." I was a pretty frugal guy…she was not. But, I figured her for costume jewelry not the real stuff…otherwise I would be broke. She wanted a big wedding. Why not. I invited over a hundred people, so did she.

One day when I was all alone with the ponies, her dad came over to me…"Harvey, please don't put us through a circus wedding…please" He had a small bag and he handed it to me. "There's $10,000 in there. It's all in cash in small bills I will give you another one with $10,000 when you get back from your honeymoon which I will pay for, but please, no big wedding." Like I said ,he was a pretty shy guy. Before I could say anything he told me that he had talked to Bootsie about it and she is OK with it. My wife's OK, too. That night I looked in the bag. All the bills were singles. Every pony ride was a dollar. That bag was filled with ten thousand pony rides. I guess he was serious about not having a big wedding.

What no one knew, that I was having second thoughts about getting married. It was about three months to the wedding. All the gifts started rolling in. My friend Marty Zeldin, the big spender, sent us a giant vintage espresso machine. After all, I was marrying into an

Italian family.

I called Kenny that night. And told him the story. After the call I realized it had nothing to do with Bootsie. I was scared shitless. I was a kid, and not ready to take on what now frightening the hell out of me. Every night it was one nightmare after the other. I had given Bootsie the bag to hold. What the hell was I doing. I finally called her one Sunday when I knew her family would be busy with the ponies.

She was going out with her girlfriends that night so she was making up. This was so strange. She had shaved off her eyebrows. She told me all the showgirls did. She kept her eyebrow pencils in the freezer to keep them sharp, and as I poured out my heart she was painting on her eyebrows. She stopped when she realized I was serious. One eyebrow was finished.
She was great about it. We both cried but I told her I was not ready for this kind of commitment.

After listening for a while and holding my hand she agreed it was best to call the wedding off for now. She was so great about it. As I drove home that evening I had second thoughts. I don't remember how I told my dad…interesting. When I told Marty Zeldin I broke it off I asked where I should send the beautiful giant copper espresso maker. He said we should keep it. Bootsie told me that they used it almost everyday.

They were a terrific family, truth is I was not ready to run a pony ranch in Wayne, New Jersey

My Morris Minor on the way to the Post Office with all of my apple mailers.

Bongo, too.
1957

I told you about Daisy, Bootsie's dog. What a great dog. She would go out at 5:30 AM every morning and take the lead pony out to graze for an hour…the other ponies would follow. Amazing. Here's the other amazing thing my dog Bongo. The day he met Daisy he too was smitten. He discovered sex with Daisy. I don't think he had ever had the opportunity to have sex. He was on his back two legs and on Daisy's back every time I saw them. They were inseparable. They ate together. Played together. She taught him how to take the lead pony out to graze. They were the perfect couple, until…

When we called the wedding off I took Bongo home with me. You got to understand…Kenny and I bought Bongo when we were in High School. We each paid $5 for him. He went through the last year of High and four years of college with me. He was the fraternity mascot. The fraternity mother knitted an Irish Green sweater. One day he went out of the fraternity house with the sweater on, and someone stole it off Bongo's back. Everyone in the fraternity searched the streets that night until they found a guy walking his dog with that beautiful green sweater. Forget what happen to that guy. Bongo was my soulmate.

When I got him home that night from the farm, he cried. Day and night he pined away. He stopped eating. I took him to the vet after a week of crying, and told him the story. Long story short I called Bootsie and told her what was happening. She laughed a crying laugh…Daisy hasn't eaten in a week, and she was crying too. I brought Bongo back and I cried a lot, too. I had to leave her. He and Daisy rolled in the hay. I tried to take him home one more time. Same problem. Back he went to Daisy. He never left the farm. I gave him up. He lived happily ever after with Daisy. Really…true story.

My wife painted the Tannenbaums 60 years ago.

Thirty Years later.
1987

Talking about stories. I married. Had two sensational daughters, and they grew up hearing all about the showgirl I never married...Bootsie. Beautiful Bootsie. I described her bell shaped body so often my kids were going to kill me. I heard she had gotten married six months after we split and had four kids within five years. She lived on in Wayne, New Jersey. Her dads Pony farm was turned into condos and became Meadowland.

One day we were shooting some toy commercials in Fort Lauderdale. I had an agency that specialized in kids commercials. My whole family worked on the spots. I wrote and directed the spots. Elaine casted them and Josselyne, my oldest daughter, was my producer.

Elaine went shopping in one of the stores in the hotel basement. I met her there. As I walked into the store a voice rang out...."I know this man." Oh my god it was Bootsie. The store was called Bootsie's Baubells and there she was in all her glory some thirty years later. She was a "fireplug." NO waist.

Oh how she had changed. As we were talking, in walks Joss...and I introduce her to the famous Bootsie....Joss replied..."Your Bootsie!"

It was like a scene from a Woody Allen movie. She introduced me to her husband. A somewhat fatter fireplug, smoking a big fat cigar. We talked for a short while. When we got up to our room, Joss kept on repeating..."your Bootsie."

I kissed Elaine a lot over the next few days...and I stopped smoking cigars. Really.

The Showgirl, Bootsie with a 19" waist.

Sauerkraut.
1938

I had the best grandma and grandpa Tannenbaum. They lived on Strauss Street in Brooklyn. There are so many stories about these two. They were the most loving people you could imagine. Grandpa was big. He weighed well over 300 pounds. He ran a pickle business. He made his pickles in giant wooden barrels in the cellar of his home. He had a horse drawn wagon that he drove around Brooklyn delivering pickles every morning to all the local food stores. When my dad married my mom he went to work for my grandfather in the pickle business. To this day, I think my dad made the best pickles, pickled herring and pickled cucumbers I have ever eaten.

My Grandma was the most gentle loving human being I have ever known. She had a dog name Dixie. Dixie was the neighborhood prostitute. She had almost 100 puppies in her lifetime. Grandma could not afford dog food, so she would give Dixie a two day old roll dipped in water and milk for her meals. When things were good she would add an egg. When I was there visiting she would send me to the baker down the street to get the crusty rolls for free. Grandma always was cooking. On the stove was always gievala. Chicken skin that was burnt and sat in the fat. We could dip the two day old rolls in the fat if we were good.

One day Grandpa sat me down in the kitchen. I was about 7. My mom was not well so I was staying a few days with them in Brooklyn. The table had a plastic table cloth on it. He placed a giant bowl down and poured about five pounds of sauerkraut that he made fresh that morning into it. Then he poured olive oil on top of it. Cup after cup, followed by a few handfuls of salt and pepper. "Sunny Boy (that's what he called most of the grandchildren) get two bottles of seltzer off the back porch…don't drop them they are heavy." These big blue bottles filled with the bubbly water were so heavy. They had silver tops that you pressed down to get the seltzer out. I could only manage one at a time. Then the ritual began. He dipped his hands no utensils, into the mixture and poured glass after glass of the bubbly, until he finished everything in the bowl. All five pounds.

In between portions he told me how to be a good boy. Why my mommy was sick. To listen to my dad. What it meant to be a good Jew. Why we should help others when we had more. I had never heard anything like that before. I hung on every word. He was gentle and wise. A true Tannenbaum. I was glad to be his grandson.

The Tannenbaum's visiting the Hermans

Sauerkraut. 1938

Who created the greatest?
1937

In 1937 Allen B. Dumont held a meeting for fifty business men in Passaic and Clifton, New Jersey. He was looking for investors for his newest invention. My dad was one of those invited. Of the fifty, not one person invested in the project.

For $5000 investment you could own 1% of the rights to this new technology. He called it television. Many years later my dad told me the story and I wondered how they made the presentation and why he didn't invest.

He said that Allen Dumont, the inventor told them that they could predict that a picture could be taken and sent throughout the world. He took out a tiny screen and he said to watch this postage size screen. He left the room and in a few minutes or so Allen Dumont showed up on the screen from a different room. "Hi I'm Allen B. Dumont… imagine motion pictures of me being able to be received across the globe." Not one could believed him, and what difference would it make? Besides $5000 back then was a small fortune. Right?

Cut to the sixties. The Sarnoff's had bought the whole rights to TV. And, my dad had one of the first black and white 8x10 inch sets in Clifton. He proudly set it up in our finished basement. Tuesday nights were Milton Berle with his Texaco variety show. So many stars from around the world. Sunday nights the Ed Sullivan show. The Beatles, Elvis and so many other groups were introduced. It was all here, right in our woody pined basement on Woodward Avenue.

One night my brother Stan was to be on TV on the David Susskind show. He was a successful fashion designer. He was introducing successful Jewish young men. My mother invited all of her friends. Dad set up folding chairs row after row. Goldberg from Goldberg's Pizza. Mel Brooks, my brother and a few others. The program was very funny. Stan wore a one piece jump suit, that kept on creeping up on his crotch. And then Stan told a story that stopped the show. He said our step mother had removed the doors from his and his brother's bedroom to prevent us them from masturbating. Susskind flipped. My step mother denied it. My father left the room, if I remembered correctly. That show was so successful they repeated over and over. My mother accused Stanley of having them repeat it.

I will never forget that show and my mothers embarrassment. That was the last time my dad had people over to watch TV. To think we could have owned that technology. Really.

How to survive in LA.
1976

It was 1976. I had gone to the coast to become a famous movie director. I will tell the story all about my baptism into Hollywood and my five month affair with Elizabeth Taylor. It didn't quite work out the way I have planned. The movie was canceled a month before shooting. Elaine left me and took the kids back to New York after finding out about my affair. I was alone living in Santa Monica. Going out with a different woman every other week.

In order to make money I had reached out to an ex-client Ed Hamoway who was now marketing guru for Mattel Toys. He introduced me to his agency Ogilvy and Mather and I started shooting promotion films of Barbie and other Mattel toys. Larry Aledort, was their marketing/advertising director for Mattel. We hit it off immediately. Like me Larry was originally from the East Coast and he missed his friends and family there. He gave me so many projects. I did all of Toy Fair for Mattel. Big success one after an other.

When I first went to LA I went to Mattel's agency for promotional work. Forget it. When I worked directly with client, the agency got nervous. One day I got a call from John Martin, the president of Ogilvy. I knew he was going to want to stop me somehow from working on Barbie directly. Maybe he would offer me freelance. John was the perfect Mad Man. He was so slick. He fit in with the Hollywood crowd. Sure enough when we met he got right to the point.

"Why not work free lance for the agency. You can do Mattel and all our other clients. No advertising. Just promotion." We talked for about fifteen minutes how it could work. We agreed on one day a week. That would make it possible for me to work on my movie.

How much? I was ready to offer him $25,000 a year for the one day a week. Many years ago a great businessman told me…always wait for an offer, never give them an offer.

"How would $75,000 per year work for you. About $1500 a week."

A number of years later when John was made president of Ogilvy New York, he took me to a very expensive breakfast at the Regency Hotel on Park Avenue. He had always wondered what my number was that day.

When I told him he almost choked on his Egg Benedict.

Sindy Who?
1980

My dear friend Larry Aledort left Mattel and was offered a great job in Stanford Connecticut with Marx Toys. This was an English company that had become famous for their tin toys in the 50's and 60's. They wanted Larry's expertise on Barbie. The English company had a great doll called Sindy and they had thoughts about having her go up against Barbie for years, but never had the balls to do it.

One day I get a call from Larry. He filled me in on his new job. He wanted to know if I would shoot some commercials for him for their Big Wheel. He knew my wife and kids had left me and he said time to get back to the Big City.

When we met he showed me the line of toys. When he got to Sindy I almost fell off my chair.

"Larry let's bring Sindy to America and have her go up against Barbie. Who better to do this than you and me?" We went out to lunch and when he asked me how would we do it…I started to "wing it." You know…"tap dance as fast as you can."

"I'll go over with a cameraman and shoot all over Europe. Germany, England, Holland, France and Sweden. I'll show kids from all these countries loving Sindy. They will call her their best friend. Then I will shoot kids on the Queen Mary singing their praises of their best friend Sindy, waving the doll as we pass the Statue of Liberty. Sindy is finally coming to America. Don't mention Barbie. Sindy will become the friend every little girl in America will want.

"Can you actually do it? What will it cost?" We spent an hour talking it through. We agreed on a creative fee of $50,000 plus out of pocket costs. If we shot commercials that would be extra. "Can you really do it" he repeated a couple of times. Now the moment of truth. "I can't do this without Bob Butler's approval. He will love it. He is an Englishman. You will love him."

Sindy Dolls!

Bob Butler, my hero!
1980

Bob Butler was as English as you could get. As he entered the room all I could think of was Sidney Greenstreet. A movie legend. He was fat. He was nice fat. He sat down at the head of the table and Larry gave me a great build up.

"Harvey knows Barbie as we'll as me. He has an idea that will blow your mind. It will take Marx Toys to the level you have always talked about."

Butler was a genius. He listened for over an hour and said nothing. Then he asked Larry…"You think we can really do this?" He turned to me and said, "I have wanted to do this for years…I will have to take it to the board in England. No bullshit…can you really make this happen?'

Three weeks later it happened. He got the money and the approval. The only caveat was if after we did the whole film, if he didn't like it… then he would not go forward. He would pay me, but I could not tell anybody about it if they canceled out. He just didn't want to look like a failure. I agreed.

As my wife said later, you were so full of yourself…you thought you could do anything.

I called Bob Steadman. He was my cameraman on a series that I had done for ABC called Little Vic. So happens he was separated from his wife. He had two daughters around my daughters age. He had never been to Europe and was between jobs. He jumped right on it. I had a great idea. I said I would ask Elaine if I could take my two daughters also. We would turn it into a vacation/shoot. Amazing. Elaine agreed.

Here's how it worked. We would hire crew on each location. We settled on Germany, England, Holland and Sweden. Each of those countries sold more Sindys than Barbies. We would travel to the country. Have prepro and casting for two days, shoot two days… have two days vacation and travel the last day of the week. The shoot was for four weeks and then back to America for the big finish with the Statue of Liberty and the Queen Mary. It was exciting, and the children were amazing. Each country was better than the last.

Two cute stories about my kids…
In each country when we landed their was always a limo waiting for us. The limo would take me and my two kids and Bob Steadman and his two kids everywhere for the next week. When we got to Sweden, there as no limo. Instead a Volvo station wagon awaited us. Amanda was about five at the time…"we're is our limo daddy, don't we get a limo?"

Also on our last stop in London, when I went to check out of the Sturbridge Hotel there was an extra charge of 300 pounds on the bill. I pointed it out and said it had to be a mistake. "No Mr. Herman that's your daughters' laundry charge.." Seems the kids wanted to return home with all clean laundry on our last stop. They put in their underwear, their socks and every thing else. They even had their shoes shined.

The last part of the shoot was the best. We couldn't afford to shoot on the Queen Mary as it moved. Also there was all kinds of insurance issues if the boat was moving. Here's what I did. I hired a helicopter and found out when the Queen Mary was coming to America. I shot her passing The Statue of Liberty. Then I got all the clients kids to be shot on a ferry with their Sindys passing the Statue of Liberty, and intercut the same kids singing on the deck of the real Queen Mary when she was docked, it worked. It was thrilling when it was cut together.

When Butler saw it he had a brilliant idea. Every Toy Fair it was excepted practice that you would accept competitive toy companies to see your showroom and you would see theirs. "No toy company can see Sindy. The showroom is closed to the competition. Only accounts are invited. It will be a first. Marx has a closed showroom.

One of 24 commercials we shot the first year.

"Only by invite."

When I talk about success…without exaggeration we were talk of 1977 Toy Fair. We sold more Sindy that year than they ever had in Marx Toy company's history. Larry and I were heroes…which leads me to the next story.

My dream come true.
1979

After the giant success for Marx Toys in 1977 I saw a way to get back to my family in New York City. I called Larry Aledort and told him my plan. I wanted to meet with him and Butler to see if they would make me the agency for the whole Marx Toy account. I thought I had earned it. All the other Marx Toys did better that year because of the launch of Sindy in America. I figured lets go for it.

You have to understand I had no office, no employees. I had always schlepped my work around in a Hunting World carry bag. Marx had a pretty big agency…Marchalk. They had 5 teams servicing the account. Each with an account man and a creative team. They shot a minimum of 25 commercials a year. Their product line was extensive.

Butler and Larry met me at the Top of the Sixes . They had a restaurant on the top floor. We made small talk for a short while. Bob thanked me for the job I had done on Sindy. I was so arrogant at that time.

"Bob, no thank you for the opportunity, and you know how you can really thank me?" "How?"

"I want to be your full service agency for all your products." He asked me if I had an office…I told him the truth. It was sort of like when he asked me if I could do the Sindy film…"do you think you could really do it?" After more conversation he got down to money. "How much will you charge me?" "You won't pay a penny more than you pay Marchalk. By the way how much is that?" Sixty six thousand dollars a month he said without hesitation.

He called the waiter over. It seems there is a tradition in England, when you are taking a giant step in life you always do it while… "breaking it in with wine."

We toasted to the new agency that evening. 1979

Our baby.
1968

Elaine and I had a tough time with pregnancies.
She had five miscarriages.

We started the adoption search. We wanted to get the baby through an agency, no grey market. We went to the Catholic agency. They were not happy that we were married in Ethical Culture. Besides they seem to be to worried about how we would bring the baby up. They never said it outright but they wanted to know if we knew enough about the Catholic religion. Next we went to Louise Wise the Jewish agency. That was a total disaster. Thank goodness we loved Spence Chapin.

They accepted us after one meeting. The process took over 15 months, much longer than a normal pregnancy. I could write a small book how much we learned about the responsibilities of raising children. They met with each of separately a couple of times. They met with both us together around once a month. Elaine had had a child before, but even she felt all they wanted to do is prepare us for raising a child, and how it could effect our lives together. We stopped trying to have a kid during the process.

One Friday afternoon, I got a call. I had come home early from work. The telephone rang. "Hello, this is Spence Chapin, who am I speaking to?" I told them who I was. "We have a baby girl for you. Can you pick her up at noon on Monday?" I was speechless. "A baby girl. How old is she?" "She is three and half months old, weighed 7.2 pounds at birth and besides colic she is very healthy." "Where has she been for the last three and a half months?" "We are way behind on paper work...sorry! Any other questions?" My mouth was dry I could hardly speak. "We will be there on Monday...thank you." That afternoon we were at Saks Fifth Avenue picking up everything you would ever want for a baby. They delivered on Saturday. We had divided Bruce's room in half for the baby. He was not that happy. We had a wonderful apartment at One Sheridan Square in Greenwich Village. Two tiny bedrooms…now made into three. A terrace all around. As I write the story it seems like a hundred years ago.

We arrived at Spence Chapin early. They showed us to a small waiting room with lots of windows. We waited and waited. About a half hour later we heard a baby crying. The crying got louder and louder. The door opened and this woman was holding a screaming little baby girl. She was dressed in like a nylon dress and a nylon print hat. "Are you the Hermans?"The baby was red in the face. She obviously was not happy.

The woman handed the baby to Elaine. "She's got colic but she is really great. She'll stop crying soon. Enjoy her. I have for the last few months."She left and the baby still was screaming. We were waiting to fill out papers. It seemed like an eternity. Joss did not stop crying. Believe it or not I panicked and said to Elaine…
"Do we have to take her?"

When we got to the car, Elaine handed the baby to Bruce and he rubbed her back and within minutes she stopped crying. When we got to the apartment Doctor Leaderman was waiting for us. He came up to the apartment brought her into the nursery and took off all her cloths and held her like a chicken…"you got a good one here." Was he ever right.

Two very important points. About a year later Elaine called her gynecologist for an appointment. He had passed away and we got a new one. Doctor Zuckerman. He saw Elaine and after the exam asked us why she had not removed the large growth in her Uterus… and did we have an abortion at some time?

The first year we were together Elaine had become pregnant, and we went through a terrible abortion. She got sick, really sick. Who knew what the side effects of that horrible time had caused the baby each time to be forced out of the uterus by that growth after three months. Five miscarriages. What I put Elaine through.

Our baby. 1968

Hiccups!
1983

You know by now how much flying has been a passion in my life. Besides the total joy, I believe it has been one of the biggest factors that introduced me to the risk factor of life. In flying you do not take risks, period. You will get away with taking chances often but all it takes is once too often and more than likely it will kill you.

I remember when I got my first license, the teacher handed me my ticket and said.."congrats, this is your ticket to kill yourself."
He was serious.

I have been a pilot for forty years. I have accumulated a little over 3000 hours in the left seat as pilot in command. I have flown singles, high performance twins, taildraggers and even sea planes. Most of the flights have been uneventful. But, three stand out as the exception. Three times in my life as a pilot, I came very close to dying.

Hiccups! 1983

Taking chances never works as a pilot.
2001

We bought an apartment in South Beach, Florida in 2001. I had my twin Foxstar Baron at that times. A true 200 knot plane. Really fast for a single pilot. It was very well equipped for IFR flying. That means I was, and so was my plane equipped and certified to fly in most bad weather. I was at the top of my flying game. So it was natural for us to fly back and forth to Florida. We would leave from Caldwell, New Jersey and make a refueling stop in Charleston at Charleston Executive airport and then fly the next two and a half hours to Opaloca Airport near Miami. It was usually a five hour flight, depending on winds. My plane was pretty fuel efficient. I could fly about five and a half hours without refueling so I could do the trip non stop but I never did. Why take the chance of running dry.

Except one time. I took a chance and it almost killed all of us. Elaine and I, my two kids and our two dogs. We took off from Florida, and as it happened we had a tail wind. Instead of 200 kts airspeed we were flying almost 250 knots. Why not take a shot right through without stopping for fuel. Why not? We passed Baltimore, only 100 miles to go. I waited another 15 minutes and checked the weather at Caldwell. Fog. No visibility to land. OK lets go to Morristown. The same. Teterboro fogged in. Even Kennedy and LaGuardia fogged in. It was not forecasted. Where do we go from here? I checked my fuel. I could turn around and fly back to Baltimore possibly, but I only had enough fuel for about one hour.

I decided to take a shot at Morristown. They had an ILS and I could fly down to 300 feet if I needed. Morristown tower advised that the clouds were down to 200, below landing visibility… "landing not advised" the tower said. I decided to take a shot. I was advised by tower that a private jet had tried an hour before and could not get in. "Thanks, I still want to try." It's up to the pilot so they vectored me to the ILS 24 and we started our decent. Solid fog. It was close to night time and we were in total black as we descended. Elaine knew what to do. I had practiced going through the fog before. She was to call out our altitude every 100 feet. We started at 1500 feet…1400..1000…800 no airport. I kept my hand on throttle ready to go around. 600…400…I figured this was it.. 350 Elaine called…I started to put the power in "The lights, I can see the lights!" Sure enough the ILS lights broke through at 300 feet and we landed. I stopped the plane but I could not see the lights to taxiway off the runway. Just then a airport vehicle with giant lights lead us to the FBO.

When we got inside, the tower started vectoring all the jets that had been circling around that night waiting for a clearance to land. One by one they came in. After a couple of landings one pilot shouted out…"who saved our asses tonight, who was first in?" They cheered for me. It turned out to be one of my best flying events…but it could have gone differently. That was the last time I didn't stop to fuel at Charleston for fuel.

By the way, when my daughter Joss realized what was happening before we landed she said…"It's OK dad I've had a great life anyway." She was 17 at the time.

That's Joss…even today.

No radios, no way!
2002

I had a smaller twin Baron E55. Fast. But I wanted a faster, big one to fly my family back and forth to our apartment in South Beach, Florida. I found one in Wichita, Kansas. A true 200 knot plane, with club seating. It was what was called a Foxstar Baron. Each of the twin engines was 300 horsepower. Special slim propellers. The wings were 18 inches wider on each side than my small Baron. It was a handful. And, I equipped it with twin 430 units. Top of the line at that time. The avionics were familiar, but I really needed some time in this new plane to feel proficient.

I found her in Wichita, Kansas and flew her home solo to Caldwell. That was a scary flight on my own. I was safe, but I needed to learn how to master these avionics. So I scheduled a meeting in Brookhaven Airport on Long Island to learn the equipment.

Small problem, as I flew down from GBR Great Barrington Mass I lost all my electric. I only had a few hours in the plane. Not sure of the avionics and I lost all electric. No radios. Couldn't put my flaps down, except manually. No way to communicate. I was 20 miles from Brookhaven and I decided to take some time up in the air to think this one out. I took the plane up to 3000 ft and took out all the manuals. I could not use the avionics or auto pilot, but I spent the next hour and a half burning off fuel and figuring what to do. It was pretty obvious. I was going to end up landing my new plane on her belly eventually. I tried to manually put the wheels down. My knuckles were bleeding from turning the device that put them down. And when they were half way down, they jammed. I stopped doing that and realized I had to take a few low passes and rock my wings down the runway so they knew I was going to land without wheels. That was my plan, and that's what I did.

I checked the winds and watched the pattern from my altitude circling over the airport. They were using runway 33. This approach took you over the water. I got the plane down to 1500 feet. Pattern altitude was 1000 so I could watch any planes in the pattern. I couldn't slow her down. I had to land at less than 90 knots without wheels otherwise I could catch on fire. I went out over the water raised my nose and to bleed off airspeed. Not too much or you will stall. Lined up on the runway and when I reached the numbers I raised the nose to slow her down and rocked my wings, the tower saw me and gave me a red light, meaning do not land, so I put in full power and took her up to pattern altitude and went downwind. They knew I was in trouble. They cleared the airport. No one was landing. It was all up to me at this point.

I took her a little further out over the water, kept the airspeed up, I decide I needed more practice and I wanted to try to land the plane on her tail. I had a lot of experience flying a tail dragger and I figured I would hold the nose up to bleed off speed. When I was at the right airspeed I would turn off the engines and then put her down like a taildragger, on her tail to prevent damage to the engines. All this was planned on the downwind. I decided to slow her down like I was going to land, but don't land again. Everything lined up, as I approached they tower gave me a yellow light. Good. I would land next time, I did a low pass rocking my wings again. Up to 1000, downwind, base over the water, line her up for landing on 33. The tower gave me a green light. I raised the nose bleeding off speed to about 100 knots till over the numbers then slowly turned off the engines, pop open the door, stay on the centerline, wait, wait, wait until 85 knots…lower the nose and keep her on the centerline. She landed on her tail and I let her settle on the front…we slid for only a few seconds and she stopped. I was shocked. I jumped out, and ran. Nothing happened. A guy came running out. An ambulance pulled up and an airport vehicle came out to spray if there were any flames. Nothing happened. It turned out I had stayed on the centerline and she skidded only 77 feet. I saw my new plane on her belly…but all was ok…Miracle.

It turned out the guy who ran to me was from the FAA. "Are you OK, are you ok lieutenant." I was dazed, why was the calling me that. "I told them you were military, after the first pass." I looked down and finally got it. I have a great collection of vintage military, and that day I was wearing a second world war A2 pilots jacket. The FAA called it an incident not an accident, because it was not my fault and it would not go on my license. One hundred and forty two thousand dollars, and eight months later I would get her back. It seems all the buzz bars in the electrical system failed at once.

They said it was almost impossible, but like I said…that was one day the impossible could have killed me.

No radios, no way! 2002

My favorite.
1990

*With all the planes I owned and flew I did have a favorite. My J3 Cub.
It was a 1946 Cub that was owned by a retired American Airlines
pilot. He has medical issues and had to sell his baby. I had never flow a
tail dragger, but I had flown in my friend Mark Zander's Cub with him
a number of times and always wanted one. One day I was ready Trade
A Plane and there she was in Connecticut. Asking price $11,500, way
below market. I called the guy immediately and got Mark to drive with
me to see the plane. I fell in love. I bought the plane without a mechanic
checking it. I handed him a check. Not a good idea, but two other people
were checking with their mechanics availability so I figured go for it.
Mark flew her home to Great Barrington, and I drove back.*

The next few weeks I flew over to an airport in New York State to
learn how to fly her. We even did spins, which was not required to
get my ticket to fly a taildragger. They are really tough to fly at first.
But they are the best to master you flying abilities in any plane. Stick
and rudder flying is the best. Over the next two years my wife and I
had so many wonderful times. After dinner we would go up and fly
around at about 1000 feet looking at real estate. We would open the
side door and it was as great as it gets flying.

I just remembered one time when I first got the plane I think I had
about 10 hours in her and Zander and 4 other cub pilots invited
me to fly to Lockhaven, where cubs were built. It was a long trip.
About 4 hours from Great Barrington, but I had to go. We all took
off together, but I could not keep up with them. Top speed I think
was 78 knots. We held 12 gallons of fuel and we burned 4.2 gallons
per hour. The first stop for fuel was almost 3 hours out. There is no
fuel gauge in the plane. There is a stick with a cork on the end of it,
and you watch the stick go down…when it disappears you have 20
minutes left to fly. Well those guys initiated me into the Cub world.
The stick disappeared and they were no where in sight. I started
sweating. I started looking around for a flat field to land.

Five minutes seemed like for ever...I saw the airport and landed straight in. When I got on the ground they were all laughing. I thought I was going to die.

One day I decided to redo the plane completely. It was perfect, but needed some cosmetic love. Instead I hired a group that specialized in restoring vintage planes. They were close to us in New York State at an airport called Sky Acres. They needed the plane for a year. The father of the man that ran the shop was the one who had done many J 3Cubs. Walter was famous. They turned my plane into a new plane. Took all the covering fabric off. Replace anything that needed replacing. I even substituted my metal prop for an original wooden prop. When it was finished you could have thought it was 1946 in Lockhaven 6128H was reborn. During the process I checked out all the work, except I did not see it before the final assembly. Big mistake.

It was a beautiful day. Mark Zander gave me a ride to Sky Acres where he hangared his plane. I got into my baby and took off. I couldn't wait to get to Great Barrington to show her off. On the way between the airports was Gus Graffs private grass runway. Let's do a couple of touch and goes before we get home. Gus Graff had given me permission to use his grass strip.

I lined up and landed so perfectly, all of a sudden as I put in the power to take off again I heard a giant thump, and out of the corner of my eye I saw my left front wheel spinning out into the field. I now had one wheel and the axel was going to dig into the grass unless I did something. I pulled back the power, tipped my baby onto her right wheel and held her there as long as I could...then she started to right herself and she dug in and flipped upside down. The tail had dug into the dirt and I was hanging upside down, my safety belt held me in place. I shut the plane off. How do I get down without breaking my neck. I held on to the belt as I let myself down and crawled through the door. My baby looked like an inverted whale on her back. Oh my. I checked myself. Except for shaking I was ok. A neighbor came running by. I went into her house across

My favorite. 1990

the street and called two people...Walter at Sky Acres and the FAA.

Both showed up almost at the same time. The FAA guy went out to get the wheel in the field. No cotter pin to hold it on. He checked the other wheel that was still on the plane. No cotter pin there either. Walter forgot to put the pins on to hold the wheel on the plane, and the wheel had just spun off the plane with nothing to hold it on. The FAA wanted to have me charge Walter, and he would lose his license. Never did. I refused. It took another year for Walter to rebuild my baby, and he paid for the restoration. I ended up flying her for a good 10 more years. She is still at Great Barrington. They now use it for training new pilots. I had a deal that I could fly the plane when ever I was up there, but a lot of time has gone by, and a few lessons would be in order before I would solo her again.

She was the best.
She was perfect before I decided to make her better.
A good lesson.

Harvey and his favorite over Great Barrington Airport.

My favorite. 1990

Baptism.
1975

No I'm not a catholic. I'm Jewish. This is a brief but important story in my life. As you know by now, I wanted to go to Hollywood to become a famous director. In order to make that transition from children's commercial director to film director, one summer my wife and I wrote a number of television ideas and eventually sold one to ABC. Gemini was a story about twin detectives, but no one knew they were twins so they could be in numerous situations at the same time. Perfect fodder for the small screen.

The way I remember it now, after my script…The 42nd year with Elizabeth Taylor fell apart, and my wife and kids left me to go back to New York I really got my taste of Hollywood. Gemini was to be packaged by my agent William Morris. I was supposed to direct it. One day I am reading Variety, and there it is. Alex Cohen will be producing Gemini series…a story about twin detectives. I immediately called my agent…Arthur Axelman at WilliamMorris. What's going on here?

I got a run around for a few days. I had registered Gemini at the Writers Guild six month before. And I had a letter from Brandan Stoddard at ABC saying that they were optioning it from me. They had paid me $3500. All of a sudden it is being done by some else, also a client of Willam Morris. Alex Cohen was a big time New York Tony Award producer. He was famous. I told Arthur. I am going to sue Alex and William Morris. I had the goods. It was my show.

"Don't do it Harvey, you'll never work in this town."

Really! Cut to the finish. They stole my script and story and ABC messed up the show by making it a half hour comedy. Same story that was supposed to be a one hour drama. My name was not attached to it, thanks God. Here's the rub. A few weeks before it aired I got a call from Axelman…"good news Harvey ABC wants you to direct a 6 part mini-series called Little Vic." My payoff.

Some payoff. Danny Wilson was the producer of Little Vic. He did not want me on his show, but you know he had no choice. He told me I was stuffed down his face by ABC. No Herman. No show. I believe it. Truth was I had never worked on a long form before, only on commercials. If it wasn't for my cameraman Bob Steadman, I would have never been able to do it. He taught me everything in a few days.

Danny Wilson was a killer. He hated me in the first place. But he questioned everything I did. I think it was a 24 day shoot in Simi Valley. It was a story about a black(they called them colored at that time) jockey. Lots of horse racing shots. Many big scenes with background. Not an easy shoot. It turned out OK. Finished on time, on budget. Little Vic was nominated for an Emmy.

The last week of shooting I broke my ankle ice skating at night. Wilson was going to kill me. I shot that last week in a golf cart. I had to get back to New York to set the ankle or I was told I would have problems. I needed one last shot. Danny said he would handle it for me. He shot it backwards. It almost didn't cut. We yelled at each other in the editing room in New York. Not a good idea. Danny recut the whole last episode...I was supposed to have the final cut.

What a disaster. I had had enough. I stayed in New York and gave up on Hollywood.

About two years later, I had started my own ad agency and was having such a great time, I get a call from Arthur Axelman. I had not spoken to him since Little Vic. He wanted to take me to breakfast at the Regency Hotel in New York. I figured he had a project for me.
"Arthur I am finished with LA."
We met. He told me William Morris had sold me out.

In a "packaging meeting at the agency one morning they decided to give Gemini to Alex in exchange for William Morris to package the next six Tony Awards." Alex agreed. Arther said he had tried to defend me. "What about Herman?" Forget Herman. He said he left the agency. He was so sorry. I suspected he was fired.

I must admit, Hollywood was like a giant chess game, and I was playing checkers.

Nominated for an Emmy!

Baptism.

How easy can it get.
1979

Like I said, we opened Herman and Rosner Advertising with only creatives. The New York Times did an article when we open.
AGENCY OPENS WITHOUT ACCOUNT MEN.

We opened with Marx Toys which was about 10 Million. Bob Butler bought Aurora Toys the next month and gave us that business too. Now we were billing around 11.5 million based at our offices 110 Park Avenue. We had over 5000 feet and we rattled around with just 5 people. Pretty Amazing. It seemed too easy.

One afternoon Charlie got a call from David Garth. He was one of the most powerful political consultants in the world. He loved Charlie. Turns out that the MTA of NYC had given their agency Doyle Dane an assignment and they hated everything that was presented. Go down there and blow them away. Charlie called Susan, can not remember her last name. She said come down today. Think of some ideas for what she described was a subway that connected with JFK. They called it the JFK Express.

We hoped in a taxi. Great opportunity. I don't remember how it happened but I said to Charlie…we should name the sucker THE TRAIN TO THE PLANE. He loved it. Should we chance throwing it out that way? Could backfire. I loved it. And I made a sound like a Choo Choo train, and Charlie started singing Take the Train to the Plane…take the Train to the Plane. We both were hysterical. We loved it but was it too theatrical for the square MTA?

When we got there Susan showed us into a room with about a dozen people around the round table. Sort of like a movie set. All the divisions were there. Susan introduced us as one of the hottest agencies on record today. She said David Garth had recommended us, and she turned it over to us.

Ladies and Gentleman this is a first for us. On the way down in the taxi we had an idea…we hope you love it as much as we do. We sang the jingle about three or four times. It needed no explanation.

Susan and the group at first just sat for a minute. Then another Susan, Susan Gilbert said…are you kidding. You just made it up? We smiled and nodded. They asked us if we would leave the room for a few minutes.

It seemed like an eternity but they called us back. They all started to sing. Take the Train to the Plane…Take the train to the Plane. Yes, like a movie that's how we got the whole MTA account. About another 5 million. It just seemed too easy. We were voted the hottest agency of 1979 and at the end of the year we were rich in many ways.

We decided to walk back to the agency. Charlie seemed quiet and sad. I looked at him and asked…"what's wrong Charlie. Do you realize we just got the MTA account from Doyle Dane?" He shook his head like no…"do you realize how much work we will have to do."

That was Charlie.
He always thought a light at the end of the tunnel was a train coming the other way.

We opened our agency without any account men.

How easy can it get. 1979

Henry Brofman
1980

Henry Brofman was one of the most famous executives in the USA. He built the most beautiful bronze edifice on Park Avenue in the heart of New York City to celebrate his success and called it The Seagrams Building. He had a reputation for being a brute. For getting what ever he wanted in life.

The phone rang early one Monday at the agency. It was Henry Brofman he wanted to speak to me. Sure I said to myself. I got on the phone and it was a woman. "Mister Brofman would like to meet you at "his building" this afternoon at 3PM if you are available."

We checked back and sure enough it was true. What had we done? Charlie was out of town so I put on a tie and headed over to "his building." What followed next was a meeting that I hesitate writing about. It is hard to believe.

He was a small man in a giant bright office. The floor to ceiling windows were scary. I walked over to look down and had to step back. I was frighted of heights. (Before becoming a pilot). He came in and came right to the point.

"Did you do The Train to the Plane?" He was singing it like on the commercial. I told him we did.

"That, my boy, is making something out of nothing. If you can do that you can create a new wine for Seagrams." I got to tell you I do not know much about wine I told him. "Good, we know too much." He introduced me to his senior marketing man and said he would fill me in. Good Luck and he left. I never saw him again.

The next week a bunch of the marketing guys filled us in. They told us about the kind of vineyards that they had on the Italian Riviera. This had to be a mass market wine made with their grapes. Nothing too fancy.

That was it. We were to test a minimum of 10 concepts every three months. We would pay for all out of pocket. They would pay for the focus groups. The contract was for one year. Thirty thousand per month was the fee. That was a wow.

Charlie was the most prolific art director I ever met. He had such great style. These concept boards were sensational. One board per wine idea. We would work on them over lunch and in the evening. Every month the check would come two days before the end of the month. No wires, but a check. What a windfall.

The focus group was held in a separate office in Seagrams. At least three marketing men would be there. The ideas we did were sensational. One idea just blew our mind, and so it did in each group. Over the next nine months, the same idea came out number one in each group. The marketing people were baffled. They hatted that idea, and asked us to do more traditional ideas.

In the last group we created a wine that was the perfect combination of Italian and French…we called it Mentone. This was a tiny town in real life on the Italian Riviera. Half French, half Italian. Very romantic. It beat out our favorite concept. That was the wine that Seagrams launched later that year. It was a modest success in the marketplace, but we were told that Seagrams was happy.

I was so arrogant back then I told Charlie…"
Let's buy our favorite idea back from Seagrams."

I met with the head marketing guy. This is a meeting I will never forget. He was pleased with the project and thanked us for the work. I asked if we could buy back the idea that we liked so much with our last fee of $30,000. He said no!

When I asked him why…he didn't hesitate.
"You'll probably sell it to one of our competitors and if it is a success it will make us look bad!." At least he was honest.

What was the concept we loved so much?

CALIFORNIA COOLERS.

Charlie and I showed a group of macho guys playing volley ball on the beach and the wine was packaged like beer in a 6 pack. The marketing guys said it would ruin the wine business.

Charlie did the best test boards ever.

Here's the rub, two of Seagram's guys moved to the west coast and brought the idea to a competitor...Bartel and James. They modified it enough so that they couldn't be sued.

It didn't ruin the wine business.

It opened a new venue. The wine cooler market became worth over a billion dollars in the next few years. We were told that when Brofman heard what had happened he fired his marketing guy, and we never got another job from Seagrams.

I tried to reach Edgar a couple of times.
He never returned my calls.

My Apple Mailer. Sent out 80 delicious apples and got 18 responses.
The Promotion Centre was started.

Henry Brofman 1980

Just a few I knew.

Over the forty years I spent in the advertising business I thought it would be good to write down a few that stick in my mind worth writing about. Some were very special, some I wish I had not met and yet all of them influenced my career in the business.

Harvey Lloyd. I couldn't get arrested when I did the rounds at the big agencies. He had a promotion company and hired me as his assistant, or slave as he put it for $50 per week. I learned the basics from this guy, and after about a year and a half with him he told me to start my own company. I wouldn't be happy working for anyone else. Truer words were never spoken.

Arch Nadler. He recognized my talents even before I did. Right from the first meeting he told me I was going to really enjoy this business. He drove a vintage Rolls, and he swore one day I would have one too. Who knew his words would come true. He gave me my first commission as a painter. I worked for him for around two years. He taught me to love what I did in life. Wise man.

Leo Greenland. This cigar smoking boss was somewhat like a father to me. He made me a partner at his agency. He showed me that you could be successful and have humility. He always worried that people would find out that he never finished high. Leo had a grip on life that helped me understand my marriage. No matter how busy we were, he always found room for his family. We did a lot of great work together.

Laurel Cutler. She was the real deal. I met her while on my short stint at Leber Katz agency. I learned about branding and marketing from this genius. She worked as a consultant to some of the top companies in America. She could have bragged about her successes, but she was a real humble person.

Faith Popcorn. A pretend Laurel Cutler. A real fake when I knew her. She stole other peoples ideas and took credit for them. I knew her when she was young. I understand she is still around. Perhaps she learned enough to give back.

George Lois. A real genius. A solid, special friend. One of the creative giants of the industry. He made his initial impact designing covers for Esquire Magazine, but that was just a beginning. I could write a small book about this man. He helped me out so many times, as I jumped from job to job. At one point I couldn't decide if I should continue in the business or move to California to try to get into the film business. He heard through my ex-partner Charlie, that I was in conflict. He offered me space at his agency. "Take time to decide, don't rush." I had free space and a secretary for 6 months. How many people would do that? He kept on saying I shouldn't sweat it…we will work on some projects together. That part never happened.

Just one short story about his advertising career. We pitched the Fuji Film company when they came to the states. I worked with Smith Greenland at the time. We brought 10 people to pitch them. We thought we would overwhelm them.

George Lois was next. He came alone right after us. He was all alone. He got the account with this headline.
FUJI FILM.
FROM THE PEOPLE WHO BROUGHT YOU
PEARL HARBOR.

Yes he got the account. They loved how outrageous he was. By the way they never ran the campaign. He was a frustrated basketball player. Big supporter of the Knicks. He was playing basketball at the McBurney YMCA with his 18 year old son when his son had a heart attach and died. George was never quite all there after that. He just died at 91. He made a giant impact on so many careers, including mine.

Bill McCaffrey. He hired me at DeGarmo. Few people were so private in such a public business. Very talented. I watched as he mentored other to succeed. I took that with me.

Ivan Chermyoff. Great graphic designer. Hired him to do a logo for my client Beaunit. He designed the Chase Manhattan 8 sided blue log. When the client asked him what that meant he said it meant Chase. A man of few words He also did the Mobil logo, and so many others.

Martin Landy. One of the worst human beings I have known.
Arnie Arlow sold out to Marty.
Dick Tarlow married an extremely talented and good person, Sandy Carlson. Dick was a solid copywriter. He made a lot of money in the business with his own agency funded by Revlon. We pitched accounts against his agency…he always won.
He was a sad soul most of his life. I think he mellowed in his later years. Never finished his novel which he carried around and talked about all the time. He passed away this year.

Pushpin Studios. Milton Glaser got the most credit, but **Seymour** and the other folks helped to make them such a valuable source to our industry. Charlie and I loved working with them. They always made our ideas better.

And of course the one and only Charles Rosner.
The best person I ever worked with in any business. By far the best art director. My best partner, and my best friend for many years. l hired Charles out of a small studio in Philly. He was my art director at SGH. I had hired a famous art director Peter Pallazso to be my creative director. He had such great credentials. I couldn't stand him. He felt he was the Pope. He gave out assignments but withheld info, and dolled it out, so he made his position more important. I told him to cut it out and he didn't, so I fired him and made Charlie the creative director. He was young but grew right into it.
The work came fast and was the best work we had done. That was the beginning.

When I moved to Martin Landy/Arlow Charlie came with me, and when I opened my agency I made him a 25% partner. We drew even salaries and even bonuses. In the first year of Herman and Rosner we each took bonuses of $200,000 after taxes. I bought my apartment at 19 East 88th St, and half the cost of a farm and 118 acres in Sheffield, Mass with that bonus. Charlie spent it on a new wardrobe in London. I saw he had a problem with money, and no matter how many times we discussed it, he never changed. That aside, we had a perfect time together for the first two years at the agency. In our mission statement we said something like…The agency Herman and Rosner would be the money source for other important things we wanted to accomplish in life. Charlie was a slave to the agency. Every time I tried other things, like inventing toys for our clients, he complained if I put the same time into the agency we would be successful. I thought we were very successful.

When he got married to Joan it wasn't long before Charles asked to be an equal partner. I knew that his wife, Joanne was pushing him. Long story short I should have said yes, but I didn't. I am not sure even today why I made that mistake. I bought him out according to our buy out contract.

He went on to work for other larger agencies. Even opened his own called Public Sector. He struggled all the time. Never really enjoyed his career. Was always broke.

We remained very close friends for the rest of his life. Elaine and I helped him out financially from time- to -time. When we felt we would not help out any more I called a few of his friends to see if they would pick up the slack. Turns out they all had been helping him for years, too.

He died this year after about 10 years of very poor health. He never provided for the future, so he died broke. To this day I never understood it. I did my best work in the advertising business with that cute, curly haired guy called Charlie.

He is missed.

Barbie.
1974

It is 2023 as I write about this famous doll. She will not die. In many ways she is as big now as when I worked on her back in 1974 and 1975. The new movie has taken her to new heights. However I was there when she was the best known, most successful fashion doll ever created. The Handlers were a wonderful couple. Mrs. Handler had created the doll and named her after her real life daughter. Each product that was created for Barbie was really thought out.

I was hired to work with Mattel back then. I did many promotion films for the client and agency featuring that wonderful young lady called Barbie. She was taken very seriously. When we got position papers, or attended meetings with the agency Ogilvy and Mather we talked about Barbie like she was really alive. She could do this…but never that. Not everyone was permitted to work on her. They had to know the background story and relate to why she was successful over those years. The Handlers made sure that all of us were on the same page if we worked on Barbie. It was really a privilege when you were allowed a Barbie project.

One night I was working late. I think I had not slept the night before finishing up a sales film for Barbie. The sales meeting was either the next day or the day after, so I decided to get it complete that night.

Everyone had left and I had a beer or two. I decided to have some fun. I took some of the out takes of Barbie and Ken. I turned the lady into a lady of the night..that's right Barbie as a prostitute. Heavy lipstick. Low cut sexy dress. Tucked part of a hundred dollar bill down the front of her dress. Ken ended up on top of Barbie at the end of the short film. It almost played like a 30 second commercial. I played it over a few times, and decided to never show it to anyone. I realized what I had done was sacrosanct. What should I do with the footage. I put it in a box and hid it away in the bottom draw of my desk.

A few months later I had a dinner with Joel Rubenstein. He was my client. He worked at Mattel but not on Barbie. He was such a close friend. Did I dare?

"Joel can you keep a secret?"
"About what?"
"It's something I did, but you can't tell anyone…promise!"
"Of course."
 I thought he would love the little film. It was cut like a 30 second commercial…
"Joel want to see a new Barbie commercial?"
I ran the sucker. Joel was drinking something, he almost chocked to death. He backed away to the door.
"Are you out of your fucking mind?
 I am not here. I never saw that. Burn it." He left

I burned the film that night.

Joel never mentioned what happened that night, ever.

Why am I putting this stupid thing I did in my memoir?
Maybe I shouldn't.
But it happened.

Was it a moment of weakness, or a character fault?
You be the judge.

My Baby?
2007

When Arch Nadler drove me in his Rolls Royce for the first time, I was in heaven. That was 1964. He said I was destined to own one someday. Really!

What is a Rolls? Not just a car.
It is one of the few things in life that strives for perfection. The average car takes two days to build today. In 1986 it took 43 days to build a Corniche convertible. The hides for the interior seats and door panels are must be perfectly matched. The wood laminated panels on the doors and dash must come from the same tree. The grill is made by one man, and it is signed on the inside. And on and on. Very few cars are still built like a Rolls.

My next affair with a Rolls Royce was with Elizabeth Taylor in 1976. She had a triple green Corniche. I think it was a 1967. I drove it twice. She told me I belonged in my own. Close but no cigar. They recently sold Elizabeth's Rolls for around a half of a million dollars.

Over the years I kept looking at Rolls. I came close to making an offer on one in Fort Lauderdale, Florida some time in the 90's. I love vintage cars...and have owned many of them over the years. I think I kept on thinking I was not ready for one. Also I thought they might come off a little pretentious. A little?

Around 2004 my wife woke me one morning to tell me "it was time to repot." Our life was so great, and we were not growing anymore. I go into this in detail in another story. This meant we had to sell everything and start over again at the age of 70. Start over again. OK. We sold everything including our wonderful home in Sheffield, Mass.

"We have to live less than two hours from NYC, and let's finally have a place near the water." New Jersey or Long Island. It took well over a year to find our paradise in Hampton Bays.
I realized that I had stopped looking for a Rolls. In fact, we never,

ever saw one in the Berkshires. Not so in the Hamptons. Range Rovers, Mercedes, Ferrari's and even Rolls.

One day I was sunning myself at the pool, (tough life) reading the Sunday Times. There it was in the classified. Rolls. 86 Cornish, triple black for sale.
It was in Southampton, 20 minutes from us. I read it over a couple of times, I couldn't believe my eyes.

Elaine and I got into our car and rushed over to Meadow Lane in Southampton. Right on the ocean. Houses start there at 20 million and up. As we pulled into the driveway Elaine said…"we're in trouble." There my baby stood. She was mine. She was filthy. Hadn't been washed in who knows how long. She was all there. Seemed solid. I checked the oil, to see if it was dirty. These cars hold 12 quarts of oil. The dip stick showed one quart. You could not drive her that way.

"A couple other people are coming over to see her," the owner appeared. He was a slick guy.

"Haven't used her in years. Just got a new one."
He pointed to the garage and there stood a brand new Rolls.

"Take her as is. No inspections," he said.
"Got a Mercedes limo too. Interested?"
"I'll give you a package deal."

I couldn't stand this guy. I was ready to walk. He walked away, and Elaine saw l was ready to walk too.

"Isn't this the exact car you have been looking all over for ten years."
The lady was right as usual.

Why would he sell that Rolls?
Two days after I paid the negotiated price of $42,000 for my Rolls, the guy I could not stand drove it over to our home. I had picked up 11 quarts of oil, and filled that dirty crank case before he drove it over.

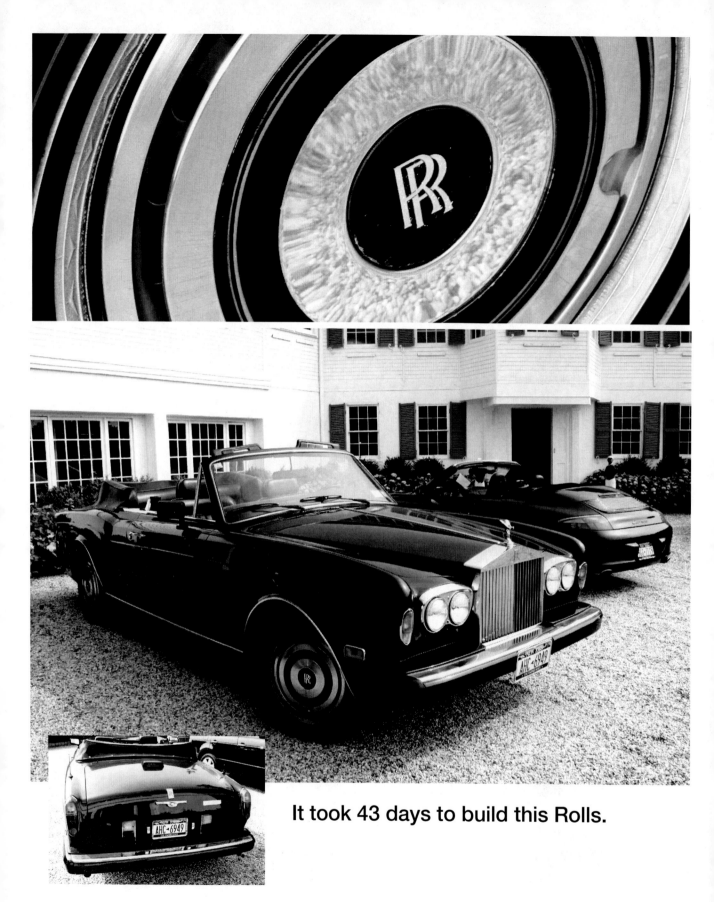

It took 43 days to build this Rolls.

CORNICHE

MANUFACTURED BY
ROLLS-ROYCE MOTORS LIMITED
AT CREWE, CHESHIRE, ENGLAND
DURING   2-86
G.V.W.R.   6184   LBS
FRONT   REAR
G.A.W.R.   3020|3300   LBS
THIS VEHICLE CONFORMS
TO ALL APPLICABLE
FEDERAL MOTOR VEHICLE
SAFETY AND BUMPER
STANDARDS IN EFFECT
ON THE DATE OF
MANUFACTURE SHOWN ABOVE

IDENTIFICATION NUMBER
SCAZD42AXGCXI4713

TYPE OF VEHICLE
PASSENGER CAR

1986 Triple Black Corniche.
They only made 14 that year.

The motor was dirty too. I had never bought a vintage car without having it driven and inspected. He said as is. No inspection. Was I a fool? Time would tell. He insisted he drive it over to house. Why couldn't I drive it. I bought a Rolls without driving it.

I am a romantic. Common sense told me not to do the deal. I did it anyway. He left the car, shook my hand and left. His wife had followed him over in their new Rolls Royce. I couldn't stand how dirty the car was. That afternoon I drove a coupe of miles to the Hampton Car Wash. The guys knew me. I had made a deal for them to wash and wax and steam clean the engine. When Bruno from the car wash saw the car he doubled the price. By the way the car started right up and drove beautifully.
It took them a day and a half to return the car to me. She was beautiful. Not many scratches. I knew I had to put new tires on her. But beside that, I was thrilled until the next day, when I took her for a ride on the highway.

You know Rosser Reeves from Bates Advertising had written the definitive Rolls Royce ad…the famous headline…

At 60 miles per hour, the loudest sound is the tick of her clock.

He was so right. She took off like a dream. I was dropping her off at the best Rolls mechanic on Long Island. They would check her out and return my baby to me. I started to cruise at about 60 for about ten minutes…and then it happened…she stopped. The motor cut out and stopped working. I pulled over and parked as the cars speed by me. What had I done, I couldn't even hear the clock now.

Lucky I had my cell phone. I called John at Hampton Motors. Every one said that he knew more about Rolls than anyone and I told him my story.

"Don't sweat it Mister Herman. I believe I know what the problem is. Let her cool down for 15 minutes. She should start up. You may do that again before you get here, but stay cool." He was right, the car would drive for about 10 minutes and then shut off. I finally made it to his shop.

"She's a beauty. I'll get her running. Go to the office have a cup of coffee and I will call you when to come back." He seemed so confident. That cup of coffee seemed like forever. All I could think about was how much this was going to cost me? Why did I buy her without an inspection? I kept on making myself wrong. About a 20 minutes later John called and told me to come back.

He had pulled her out of the shop. "Let's take her for a ride." I got in and we took off. We headed to the highway. "She rides good…I'll check her over. You should leave her here with me for a day or two." We had been cruising at 60 or more for a good 15 minutes…she kept on driving like a Rolls should. John laughed.

"I'll show you what I did to fix her when we get back to the shop."

He dropped the panel below the glove compartment and an array of fuses filled the panel. "Some fool didn't know what to do. This car only takes fuses. They put in a circuit breaker, thinking it was better. When the circuit breaker got hot, the motor stopped because the breaker blew. No charge Mr. Herman."
That was 10 years ago. My Rolls is the best. It has given me so many years of joy. Just had to replace the shocks and have John check her over every year for service. I can't tell you how many times people have wanted to buy her.

By the way. Two years after I bought the car I was in Southampton. This guy comes over to me. "Is this the car I sold you?" He couldn't believe how beautiful the car was, and he finally asked. How's she driving? I told him the story.

"That son-of-a-bitch at the Shell station."

Our Folly
1969

Elaine and I were trying to have our first child. Over a period of four years we had gone through five miscarriages. We had adopted Joss. That was a wonderful process that took so much longer than a pregnancy and it was well worth it. We felt we would have loved to have a second child together. I think Bruce had left the house. He went to college in Pittsburgh. And Elaine and I did a crazy thing, as usual. She wanted to leave the city and we moved to the suburbs. Hartsdale in West Chester. It would be the perfect place to relax and have the other child she said.

What a house. It was originally built for the Otis Elevator family. I think originally it had much more land surrounding it, but that was sold off. Still it had about an acre of land. That was pretty good for West Chester. To get to this giant edifice, you drove up a driveway with forty Poplar trees bordering on either side. It felt like France. Very impressive. The house itself was a mansion. Big arbor leading to the front door, covered with Wisteria vines. Sixteen rooms in all. Floor to ceiling windows. Fieldstone on the outside. Brazilian wooden floors. Five fireplaces. Two of the fireplaces were walk in. Really. To get upstairs there was a winding stairway like in a Hollywood movie. A two story chapel, with a fireplace, and a lot of bedrooms. The house was in the shape of a U. In the center of the U was a swimming pool. And there was a four car garage.

Why did we even consider this mansion. Elaine saw an ad in the Sunday New York Times. We drove up to see it. Nobody was living in it at the time. She and I walked around he outside and fell in love. Coming from a small city apartment this seemed like Shangri-la. I had a good job in advertising. Why not!

We paid $99,000 for this mansion I think it was 1969 or 1970. No body wanted this monster. The guy who sold it to us, Roger Eustice ran the Joyce theatre in the city. He was a nut. He didn't show up to the closing. We found out why when we got to the house. On the back door were a bunch of summons. He owned everybody in the town of Hartsdale. When he moved in he went around town introducing himself. He went to the cleaner and the local drugstore, and gave them each $500 in cash to open an account with them. Everyone was so pleased to meet this new wealthy neighbor. He lived there for two years and never paid another bill.

The house was wonderful, but we didn't have much money to furnish it. I knew a group of guys that worked free lance in the film business. I made a deal with four of them. Free rent and board in exchange for them to scrape and finish all the beautiful floors, and paint the interior of the house. We had very little furniture from our small apartment so we bought giant ficus trees and grasses and put them in the house, and had lots of pillows made for each room. A few beds and a dinning room table and chairs bought at an auction and we settled in. It took the guys four months to finish, and the house looked terrific.

We hired a woman to come in and clean and help out. She tuned out to be literally crazy. She had five children. None of them lived with her. She said she didn't want anymore children. Elaine told her to wear protection. She said her mother told her to wash out down there after sex with vinegar. It was already too late to save her. When she started to pray to God all day long…she was a goner.

We had a bunch of parties at the house. And we had a 10 foot Christmas tree. We got to know some of the neighbors, so that was good. Except we didn't realize that almost the whole neighborhood was Catholic. It didn't much matter to us, but something kept on happening that blew our mind.

Josselyne was the cutest little 3 year old. During the summer she would go to visit a little girl. The families name was Cardillo. He was a doctor. It was usually so warm she didn't wear anything on her top. She was three years old. We started to notice she had a t-shirt on when she came home. Pretty wild. After this happening a few times I figured it out, and went over to the Cardillos. It was a strange meeting. They were offended that Joss came over "nude" as they put it.

That was strike one.

One day Joss came back from the Cardillos and told Elaine she was not her mother. Mary was her mother and Joseph was her daddy. She was confused and so were we. Strike two.

The final strike …Joss came home one day and said she was not adopted. Only black people adopt.

We stopped sending her to the Cardillos, and we realized that the mansion was great, but the suburbs sucked.

Our next door neighbors were twins. They married twins. They lived in twin houses connect with a common road. To say they were predictable and boring would be a compliment. This was the suburbs.

I took the 6:15AM train to work and rushed to get on the 6PM home. Even had a martini in the bar car. Played bridge and smoked my cigar. I got sucked in. I became one of the guys. Elaine was talking about divorce. She hated living there. "It was your idea I screamed at her." She just shook her head.

After a year of this nonsense we put the house up for sale. It took over a year to find someone as crazy as us. They paid us $125,000. We would have sold it for a lot less. In fact we had two offers at that price, so when one of the people called and started to ask for a sump pump, screens, and a bunch of other things I told him to forget it, knowing I had the other offer in my back pocket. He said ok at our price without all the extras.

After the meeting with this guy, I went into Elaine and told her that he wanted all the stuff or he would not close but he changed his mind when he saw I would not budge on the price…thank God we had the back up offer. Elaine laughed…the other guy backed out earlier that afternoon. She didn't tell me because she felt I would be willing to negotiate if I knew.
That's my sweetheart. By the way Elaine did become pregnant there, but that is another story.

Joss wearing my gas station jumpsuit and my beautiful wife.

Our Folly. 1969

The pregnancy, like no other.
1971

Elaine had had five miscarriages. We move out of the city to the burbs. Here's one of the amazing parts of an amazing pregnancy. Elaine's doctor dies and we get a new gynecologist. He tells us the reason Elaine would lose the babies around three months, is she had a growth in her Uterus and the growth would push them out. Seems her other doctor never picked up on it. If her doctor didn't die there would be no Amanda. Speaking of Amanda, a few month after he removed the growth Elaine got pregnant again.

We got to three months and she was OK. In the fourth month she started bleeding. Rushed to Doctor Zuckerman, our hero. He was a man of a few words. Wore a pony tail and he came right to the point.

"I'm sorry. This is not a good pregnancy. You are not miscarrying yet, but you probably will be back here soon…unless if you want to chance it Elaine must not walk around. She must stay on her back for the next five month…but I would suggest we do a D and C now. Why put her through another miscarriage.? I will leave you guys alone to decide."

And decide we did. We wiped the tears away and embarked on the next five months. They were nuts.

First of all we now lived in a 14 room mansion in the heart of Hartsdale. I made a deal with the nice next door neighbors to give her lunch everyday. I carried Elaine around on my back for five months. Her feet never touched the ground. Zuckie, as we now called her doctor, came to the house to see her monthly. He was great, but around the sixth months he took me aside and said…"this baby is going to be a runt. Don't expect more than five pounds." Scared the hell out of me.

I didn't believe him. Elaine was a "house." She was naturally so thin, from her modeling days. She was a "house." So big. She ate pickles galore. At night after dinner it was a pint of ice cream, with the pickles. She got so heavy, I was starting to get a six pack from carrying her around, but my back was starting to go. At the end of the eighth month Zuckie said it was time. She would have a cesarean.

I will never forget that day. An ambulance to Lenox Hill Hospital. I took Joss by car. We got there very early around 6AM. How would the baby be? How would Elaine manage. I sat in the waiting room for over an hour. Zuckie came out in his green gown.

"She a healthy baby girl. 7.2 pounds. Your wife is a trooper.
I cleaned up inside. If you want another you can go for it. Congrats.
Elaine's resting. Give her another hour. The baby is in an incubator because of the cesarean. I will roll her down to you a little later.
I have another one to deliver. See ya." He left.

Amanda is a miracle.
No runts here!

Amanda and Gin Gin

Speaking of Amanda.
January 12, 2024

She is now 53 and she has two great kids of her own. She is married to…"who's Irving" for 32 years. She traveled throughout Irv's career in the air force. She put her career aside to raise the kids and did a superb job for many years. Irv ended up being a pilot for Jet Blue. He is flying for them for eighteen years. He is a captain and just started flying overseas. His first flight is to Paris today.

About two years ago Mandy felt it was time to get back into the business. She had a great start 20 years before, working for Robert Redford in Quiz show, and two other movies. She had done work in locations. She was very good at it…but family came first. Now it was time to get back to her career.

My son-in-law Michael has been propmaster for Law and Order for over 20 years. He got Mandy a shot at locations on Ray Donovan and that kick started her work in the business. That's Mandy…give her an opening and she will make it work.

I remember when she wanted to go to Occidental College on the West Coast. Tough school to get into. We took her out for an interview. It was a long shot, but two hours later she had pulled it off. Her interviewer came out shaking his head, who is this woman. She had aced it and got in. That is Amanda.

Back to her new career. She did locations for a few shows and then her big break. I am not too clear on how it happened, but COVID came along so people stopped going to office to work. Thousands of offices became empty, wasted space in the city. A company was formed to help to fill the void, and they loved Amanda's background of locations and production. They hired her to fill those empty spaces. Hundreds of thousands of square feet.. I think it was first called Atlantic Pictures, but now it is called Backlot. Look it up on the web. They started in 2019, and have grown by leap and bounds. Here we are four years later and Amanda has played a major role in making them so successful.

As you can tell I am proud of my daughter.

Amanda and her best, Sami and Max.

Elaine's Eye!
1979

We have always loved hunting for vintage cloths and antiques. That's why we loved Massachusetts so much. We would usually be one of the first at any outdoor show. We went to them all. Even when we moved to The Hamptons we ran to show after show. Our house in Sheffield was filled with antiques. We will tell you more about that house in another story.

We became very friendly with Ralph Lauren's brother Jerry and he introduced us to his vintage buyers Doug and Bob Mellet. Every time we would go to a show Mellet would say.. "You go to the left, I'll go to the right." It was inevitable, they would pick out most of the same items as Elaine. Mellet had a much deeper pockets than us.

I have to say this…we taught Mellet a lot and we learned a lot from him. He loved my Breitling Watch collection. I had been buying them in England for years. I still own many of these fabulous vintage watches. Most are from the 50's, 60's and 70's. He started buying them in England, and the prices went up so much I could not afford them anymore. Same thing happen with Enamels. The Brits loved to wear small animal pins on their outerwear going back forever. They were all sterling silver with enamel animals on the front. Dogs and horses were their favorite subjects. Every time we went to England to a show we would pick up a few. So eventually Elaine had a very special collection. One day Bob saw her jacket with a few pins on it. That was it.

We went to England to Portebelo about three months later. No more pins. The same with Byrmanse. No more enamel pins. Ralph's buyer had attacked the markets and bought them all. An average pin was about 18 pounds, or $20. He sold them in the stores for $150 per. Same with the watches. We stopped going to shows with them.

Elaine had an eye. She loved outerwear jackets and vests. She knew a lot about denims. Watch for the big E in the Levis logo. She could spot the best fishing and hunting jackets. To this day we still have about fifty or more of them. And military became my thrill. I have owned and worn so many second world war military jackets. My favorite the A2 pilots jacket worn only by the pilots. The rest of the crew wore other jackets. The A2 in good condition today is worth many thousands. I proudly still own and wear two of them in perfect condition. I sold a number of them to Ralph over the years. Mostly bomber shearlings with fur collars.

And when we sold our house in Sheffield Doug from Ralph Lauren bought so much of our blue furniture that ended up in Ralph's tents on his ranch in Colorado. So nice to see it all in articles over the years.

Elaine eventually opened her own vintage store in Sheffield, Mass. Three Little Indians. That too is worth a separate story.

When it comes to eyes Elaine's got most of them beat.

There was only one!
1948

I always wanted a dog. Grandma Tannenbaum let me play with Dixie all the time. She was a German Shepherd. I grew up with her. I so looked forward to the trips to Brooklyn on Strauss Street. I was so, so small, even for a four and five year old. She would let me ride on her back. She slept on my shoulder at night. I would feed her two day old bread from the baker around the corner. I was so proud to pick up those rolls which were put away for Grandma. A touch of milk and warm water to soften the roll. If I was good, Grandma would let me put an egg in her food. She was my introduction to having a pet. My own dog.

I can't remember why I never got a dog when my mom was alive. I will have to ask my brother Stan why we never were allowed to have a pet. It probably had to do with money. I made up my mind that someday I would have a dog of my own. It didn't happen until I was in my last year of High School.

My best friend Ken and I had often looked in the window of the pet store in Passaic. Nothing fancy. The dogs were all mutts. The window was filled with torn yesterdays newspaper, and if we were lucky there would be a litter of new babies ripping up the paper and rolling on top lop of each other.

I remember it was after school on a Friday. That is when we usually could stop by to see the puppies. There he was. A little white furry ball. Running up and down. There were at least five others in the litter, but I couldn't take my eyes off of this guy. All of a sudden he stopped, looked at me and came over to the window and licked the window where I stood. That's the way I remember it.

Bongo cost $10 dollars. I had five singles from my newspaper delivery. Ken had five dollars also. The owner threw in a small bag of dog food and a tin bowl if we took him that day. We did. It was cold out. I tucked our new found love into my jacket. We had to take the bus home. I was afraid that they would kick us off, but Bongo stayed so still. I could feel his warm body. I was in love. All the way home to Passaic Park we now tried to figure where we would keep her? We started to panic. Neither of us had thought this new edition through.

Who would keep her? Ken said his mom would never let him keep him. I had a basement. I would keep Bongo down there until I had the guts to tell my parents. We named him Bongo after the song… Bongo, Bongo, Bongo I won't ever leave the Congo…oh no oh oh…

When we got home we sneaked into the basement and took a couple of towels to make a bed for Bongo. Ken and I played with him and then I heard someone enter the house upstairs. The moment of truth. Bongo heard them too…and of course he started to bark. Within minutes she came down the stairs…"what's going on here." It began. I begged. I pleaded. "Wait till your father comes home."

We made a deal with Evelyn. I negotiated Bongo's life. We would split the time every other week. I would keep him in the basement except when I had to walk him. A strange thing happened. Evelyn was always afraid of Bongo but my dad fell in love with him. Unbelievable. He fed him and walked him some evenings after dinner. I remember walking with him a few times. My dad told me all about a dog he had when he was my age. His mother would not let him keep her.

Bongo was home.

One Smart Dog!
1952

I took him to college with me. I joined a fraternity...I was a Sammy and Bongo became our mascot. The fraternity house was a giant Victorian three story house on Tulphehoken Street in South Philly. My room was on the third floor. Bongo was loved by all. He got to know everyone in the fraternity.

In fact this, will blow your mind...if anyone from the house came in Bongo would not bark. He would run down the winding stairs to greet them with his wagging tail and loving kisses. However, if a stranger came in, he would bark and stay on the third floor landing. Scared the hell out of some of the new people. He was our guard dog.

One of the mothers knitted Bongo a Kelly green sweater with a white strip around his neck one winter. When we would walk him he would wait until you put it on him. He would also go out on his own. The neighbors all knew Bongo. One day he went out with the sweater and came home without it. Someone had stolen Bongo's Kelly green sweater.

Everyone in the house swore they would find the culprit. It was a few weeks, but Bob Sarafan, one of my fraternity brothers, saw this guy walking his dog with Bongo's sweater. I am not sure what happened to the guy. Bob would not talk about it...Bongo got his sweater back that night, and the world was all good again at the fraternity house.

The Philadelphia Inquirer wrote a story about Bongo and his Kelly green sweater that week.

Bongo graduated with me. Really. The school gave me a certificate and one for Bongo, too.

Bongo was a legend in Philadelphia.

Fire Island

One Smart Dog! 1952

Bongo belongs on the farm.
1956

Bongo really remained a puppy for many years. He was always kissing and hugging. He was full of piss and vinegar. Until I met Bootsie.

Oh yeah, things changed when I met Bootsie and Bongo discovered sex.

When I was 22 I fell in love with Boots Orlanis. She was the daughter of Murray Orlanis. She had been a show girl in Las Vegas. They owned and operated a very famous pony ranch in Wayne, New Jersey. I loved horses. My dad had put me on a horse, not a pony, when I was only five years old. I was a natural. I fell in love with the pony ranch too.

Almost every day after work I went to see Bootsie on the pony ranch. I helped out on the ranch. I cleaned the stalls and rode the ponies too. And Bootsie and I grew together.

Talking about growing together. Bongo met Daisy. Oh my. From the second they met they were in love. Bongo discovered Daisy and sex at the same time. You would see them on the farm attached to each other. They were inseparable in every way. I started leaving Bongo there with Boots. ran the farm. She took the lead pony out to feed and all the other ponies would follow. Then an hour later she would take all the ponies back in. She earned her grub, and she taught Bongo how to do all the chores on the farm including taking the lead pony out. They were smitten. Sort of like a married couple.

Talk about marriage, Boots and I got engaged to be married. Three months before we were to tie the knot I chickened out. I was scared shitless. I was really a baby and I acted like one. Boots was so great about it all. She said I should take some time, and we would see where it took us. It took me home for good. And, of course Bongo came home with me.

I remained single, but Bongo did not. When I got him home he was miserable. He cried all the time. He would not eat. I brought him to the vet and he gave me the bad news. " He's a farm dog now. He belongs with Daisy." I fought it for a few days. He would not eat. He started to lose weight. He was miserable. I finally called my ex fiancé and explained Bongo's plight. Wow. Boots said Daisy was miserable too. She moaned all day long, and refused to do her work on the farm.

I brought Bongo back to the pony ranch. He rushed across the field to Daisy. It was wonderful to watch, but as I stood there watching them play together I came to the realization that my many years had come to an end with Bongo. I cried all the way home that day, and I pined away for quite a while. He was mine. How could this end this way.

I never went back to the farm. I heard through a friend that Daisy and Bongo lived on for many years together. Boots met a great guy about six months later, they married ,they had four kids and stayed together until Boots died just four years ago.

I didn't get married then…
but at least Bongo did.

Cathy Hutchinson
September 27, 2023

Today is an important day in the history of America.

A woman at the age of 24 stood up against our ex-president Trump. She was Mark Meadows assistant and she was there when all of the world stood and watched our democracy being challenged.

She has told it all. In her telling we may finally put Trump in jail where he truly belongs. We all ask ourselves what can I do? How can I stop this man from ruining our country? She has stood up to them all, and told the truth.

An inspiration to all of us. A new lease on life.

Thank you Cathy.

Why I Paint.
August 18, 2023

Tonight I watched Scott Woo in another of his Great Performances show, Friday night on PBS.

Last week he dealt with Schubert. Tonight Mozart.

Each time I listen to him interpret a piece I am reminded of how I work with painting. I am dealing with the essence of what I see. In music it is the same with sound.

He had an exceptional pianist who also was conducting Mozart. The first rehearsal was beautiful yet not profound. Great work is profound, and has a cadence to it. Once he discovered that cadence, that essence… the orchestra mounted a triumphant interpretation of that work.

Koi are moving through a moment in each painting. The job is to capture the essence of that moment. The Hen Swan and her Cignets… proud and responsible. A Canadian Goose launching into the air…a moment of gentle power. Daffodils…capture the light and reflect joy each time you see them.

You could hear it in their musical performances.
I hear it in my paintings, sometimes.

Why I Paint. August 18, 2023

Warren Beatty
1976

I had dabbled with the idea of moving to LA and finally getting into the movie business. A number of trips from New York to the West Coast to test the waters. Each time it seemed I was getting closer. Elaine said it was time. No Fire Island this summer. LA instead.

My brother Stan had a dear friend Helen Fiebelman who had moved out there a number of years ago. She had become a right arm for many studio heads and actors. Her most present position was as personal slave and assistant to Warren Beatty.

He and Jack Nicholson had teamed up to make a black comedy farce which takes place in the 1920's. Nicholson was also a star at that time. Chinatown was a colossal hit the year before. Mike Nichols was directing, and Stockard Channing played an heiress of a sanitary napkin company…she was The Fortune, the name of the movie. Sounded so bad, it couldn't miss with all that talent. The reason I knew so much about the film is Helen wanted me to meet Warren, to see if he would be helpful.

Much of The Fortune was shot on location in New Mexico, but Helen set up the meeting for me when they were shooting in a studio, the famous Forty Acres back lot.

I drove my shiny white 1964 Mercedes coupe up to the front gate and the guard told me where to go. I had to have the right car, you know. It was a small bungalow right off the stage. Helen came out to meet me around noon. Helen was a sweet lady. She was rattled that day. Her hair all messed and a cigarette dangled from the corner of her mouth.

"They are way behind on the shoot. Don't say anything but Mike Nichols is going to kill Stockard. I haven't had a chance to tell Warren about you, but they break in about fifteen minutes and I put out two salads for both of you in the bungalow. He's very nice.

Introduce yourself. I have to run out to pick up Warren's new car. It's the first new car he has ever owned. I will be back before lunch is over," and she ran away before I could say a word.

I looked around the small bungalow. There were parts of storyboards on the side table. Parts of scripts also. Some stills from the shoot. I was looking at them when Warren came running into the room. He was surprised to see me.

"Hello, can I help you"…he said with reserve.

"Hi, I'm a friend of Helen's…Harvey. She told me to tell you that she went to pick up your new car and that she bought both you and I salads and they are in the frig."

"Oh…sure sit down. You scared the hell out of me when I first came in."

"I know Helen said she wanted to be here to introduce us, but you asked her to get the car…sorry."

He pulled the two salads out and we sat opposite each other munching away for a few minutes. I tried to think of what to say. I was really nervous. He looked up from the salad a couple of times, and I thought I should say something.

"What kind of car did you get?"

"75 Mercedes SL convertible. Brown with matching interior and top. Do you know the car?"
"Yes I love that car. I love Mercedes. I have a white 64 coupe 220."
"Great car." He said.

We were bonding.

"How do you know Helen?
"My brother Stan went to school with Helen years ago."
"What's Stan's last name."
"Stan Herman."

He looked up from his salad…"I was with Stan last week."
I am really bonding now, this is going good.

"You were in New York last week?"
"No…Stan showed me a couple houses in Homely Hills."

"Really, my brother Stan's from New York. He's a fashion designer."

"Oh…same name…how do you like that. Stan Herman's my broker."

"What do you do for a living Harv?"
I hadn't been called that since high school

"I'm a children's commercial director in New York, but my wife and I are out here trying to get into the movie business. Helen thought you might be able to help."

Too much, too soon.

He stopped. Looked at his watch…
"I've got to get back to the set. Would you mind telling Helen to come to the set when she comes back." He left in a hurry.

CUT TO ONE YEAR LATER, BEVERLY HILLS HOTEL.

Harvey is at the table in the lounge with Army Archer from the Hollywood Reporter, and Elizabeth Taylor. They are talking about The 42nd Year. Just then Warren Beatty enters. He spies Elizabeth and heads to the table where we are sitting.

"Hello my dear Elizabeth." He leans across the table and hugs and kisses her on each cheek. "You look wonderful. Hear you have a new picture shooting soon."

"Yes Warren. I'd like you to meet my new director of the film, Harvey Herman…"

The next few events happened quickly, but they always stuck in my mind.

Warren Beatty 1976

Saving lives.
1956

I was spending a lot of time with Boots on the pony ranch. Her mom asked me to pick something up for her in the drug store. As I entered a woman pushed me out of the way shouting...

"My baby, my baby she's choking to death....help, help!"

The pharmacist ran out front to the baby carriage, sure enough the baby was choking and turning blue. He picked her up and held her upside down by her legs and turned and handed the baby to me. Before I could say anything he yelled at me...
"Hold the baby like this upside down and run three blocks down to the doctors office. I will call him...run...run..."

I was shocked but I did what he told he to do...I ran and held the baby upside down...she was really blue, but her eyes were open and I just kept running holding her out in front of me. It seemed forever and in the distance a block away this man was waving for me to come to him. I ran right up to him and handed the baby over.

He looked at the baby and while still holding her upside down he slapped her a few times on the back and shook her at the same time... all of a sudden she spit up a red plastic piece and she started crying. The doctor pulled her to his chest and rubbed her back, and he handed her over to me.

"Son-of-a-bitch it's the top of a lighter fluid can she was choking on" as he picked up the plastic from the dirt.

Seemed the mother was a smoker and left her Ronson lighter fluid in the carriage.

The baby did what a baby would do...sucked on it like a bottle.

Saving lives. 1956

Cody, Wyoming.
1955

When we graduated from college, I had a dream. I wanted to drive across our beautiful country. I talked to my buddy Ken Berman and we planned the trip, but when it came down to it he chickened out. We needed a car, so I asked others...finally a close friend from college Mike Merns said he was in. His dad had just gotten him a green 1951 Ford sedan for his graduation and that is all we needed.

We took a number of nights to plan this cross country trip and back. Got the car serviced. Bought two sleeping bags at Sears, and a bunch of other things. We were so excited.

The trip to the midwest was OK. Nothing so spectacular that I could write about. The thing that we had decided is that we would not stay at motels or hotels. We were going to sleep out under the stars in our new comfortable sleeping bags.

The first two nights it poured so we stubbornly slept in the car. When we got to the midwest all other issues came up so that we finally agreed to stay at a pretty ugly motel just outside of Cody, Wyoming.

We stayed in the same room. Tough to finally get to sleep, and in the middle of the night I got up to pee. As I walked across the floor barefooted, I felt and heard crunching with each step. Sounded like I was stepping on corn flakes. I put on the light. Holy! They were water bugs all over the floor. Giant water bugs. I hate bugs. I really hate giant water bugs. I screamed and we were out of there in two minutes and slept in the car.

Cody was a cowboy town. When the sun came up we drove into town and found a little hash slinging diner. When we entered practically every seat had a cowboy eating monster breakfasts and drinking beer at 6 in the morning. They were all out of central casting, with their cowboy boots and cowboy hats. I wanted to offer them money for their giant silver belt buckles. The kind you see at antique shows.

Anyway, two guys got up and we watched them go to their car. I think it was a DeSoto or Plymouth coupe. The big chrome bumper had these guards on them. On one of the guards sat a baby rag doll. So cute. Looked so real. It was real. This baby girl was straddling the bumper, sitting backwards. The cowboys took off. The baby hung on.

Mike and I both ran down the stairs yelling for them to stop. We got in the car and started to chase them. The faster we went the faster they went. We honked and honked…the kid was holding on and crying. We got closer and closer…I was driving. We got within a couple of car lengths…

"Don't get any closer, if the kid falls off we up shits creek" He was right.

We were going over 70 miles per hour. Thank god the road was straight as an arrow. I don't know why but they finally slowed down and we pulled along side…"There's a baby on the back bumper." They stopped and we stopped. One of the cowboys ran out and took the crying baby off the bumper. We never figured out why she did not fall off. Perhaps the wind held her down.

That's how I remember Cody, Wyoming.

Cody, Wyoming. 1955

The fire.
1956

One day I was working on the pony ranch and I smelled smoke. The barn across the field was on fire. The smoke was billowing off the roof. There were many great horses in the barn. I had to do something.

I started to run to the barn.
What would a do when I got there?
I could hear the horses screaming. A haunting sound that would go right through you. The closer I got I planned what I was going to do. Find a blanket .Throw it over the head of the horse when I got into the stall so they couldn't see the fire.

The field was very wide and I got a stitch. I stopped to breath for a few seconds. The fire was now leaping out of the stall windows. Those poor animals. I had to save to save the horses.

Surrounding the barn was a high wire fence. I would have to scale it to get inside the barn. I pulled myself up and over the fence. I landed on my left shoulder.

Over the years had many dislocations. This was just one more. Two people called an ambulance. They put my shoulder back in at the hospital.

Five horses died that night in the fire.

Amanda's first and only marriage.

Our 25th in the country.

The fire. 1956

Second Cross Country
1957

The summer before, I had gone across the country with my dear friend Mike Merns. We stopped in Las Vegas, and I met a wonderful girl in the Sahara Hotel. Sandy Craig was just around 18 years old and she was at the hotel with her dad who happened to do the printing for hotels in Vegas including the Sahara. We could not afford to stay there, but we somehow got into the pool area. Sandy was very beautiful and had a great body. She was alone so I swam across the pool and introduced myself. Long story short we really hit it off.

We spent a few days with her and her parents, and since we were heading to LA they invited us to use a guest room in their home when we got to the coast. What could be better.

Sandy and I got really involved. She was a lot younger than me so I figured it did not have to get too serious. Was I wrong. We stayed almost two weeks. As a side thought…Sandy lived across from a funeral home and while we were staying there they had a spectacular funeral for Carmen Miranda. The next week we left back for New York. Sandy promised she would write.

Sandy wrote to me at least 4 or 5 times a week. I wrote back occasionally. She didn't think she was a virgin when we had sex on the first trip, but so many of her letters kept on talking about how I introduced her to sex.

The next summer I had just graduated from college and I was not going to go to work until the Fall, so I talked Marty Zeldin in to driving his graduation present, a sensational 1955 salmon and cream Chevy convertible across the country to meet Sandy. The trip across was great. Marty had deep pockets so we stayed at nice hotels and eat decent meals. When we got to LA Sandy put us up again.

She was different. In a day or so I felt smothered. She wanted to be with me all the time. She had gotten very serious about our relationship. Marty was wise. "She wrote to you for a year, and now she's putting you up, she want's to get married."

I really felt like a heel. But after a few days, I told Sandy that I was not going to get married yet. It had nothing to do with her. I wasn't ready. She was devastated. She really thought we were going to get married. She told her dad, and he kicked us out that day.

CUT TO ALMOST TWELVE YEARS LATER.
I get a call from guess who. Sandy is in New York City. She had looked me up in the telephone book and to her surprise, I was listed. She always wondered about me and can we have coffee together.

I told her I often wondered how her life turned out. I was married and had just adopted a daughter, love to see her.
What was I doing? No harm. Right. It was just coffee. Right. I was curious. Right. I thought about canceling, but I didn't.

She was staying at a hotel on Sixth Avenue and 34th Street. Can't remember the name. Her dad did the printing for the hotel. What else is new. When I got there I called up to her room. She suggested I come up, she was running late. Oh my. When I got there I rang the bell and she told me to come in.

When I entered Sandy called from the bedroom I will be right out. I waited a few minutes and then she came out in a bathrobe. She came over and smiled. "You actually came. Still a bastard."
What followed is pretty tough to believe.

"You fucked me over all those years ago. Been married twice and divorced twice because of you. You ruined me."

She pulls a gun out of her robe, and her robe came open. All she had on was a bra and panties. I felt like I was in movie. My mind started to race. Should I run? Would she shoot me in the back?

"Scared the shit out you…you deserve it you son-of-bitch, get the fuck out of here."

Our system stinks.
October 1, 2023

Last night I watched a very disturbing movie. TRUTH. It is a true story about 60 minutes and Dan Rather and the truth behind George W. Bush and how he avoided going to Vietnam by getting in the National Guard. The problem was Bush never showed up and avoided serving completely. This was uncovered by a producer on 60 Minutes Mary Maple. However they screwed up and claimed certain documents were real ,when they were not. Didn't change the story. Bush cheated and got away with it.

CBS gave in to Bush's people and demoted Rather, and fired everyone who worked on the story. Outrageous. Rather sued CBS and lost. No truth. The bad guys won again. CBS folded under pressure from Bush and his flunkies. So goes life in the big city.

Not right.

This movie reminded me of a number of situations that I knew about and did nothing to correct them…

William Morris sold me out by taking a story I had written and was to direct for ABC…Gemini. A story about twin detectives that shared a single life. They gave it to another client Alexander Cohen in exchange for packaging a number of Tony Awards. I had it registered at the Writers Guild. Also had a letter from ABC approving the story. When I went to WRA and said I was going to sue ABC, they said you are right, and you probably will win, but you will never work in this city. I gave in. About 6 months later ABC gave me 6 episodes of a mini series to direct. Little Vic. Sold out.

Cliff Robertson was a very good friend. We were both pilots and had the same plane….a B58 Baron. We worked on idea for a movie. A first World War movie about the Americans and the Germans battles in the sky. He told me a story worth repeating.

Cliff wrote and was staring in a movie JW Coop. All about an over the hill rodeo cowboy making a comeback. Columbia produced the movie. David Begelman was then President of Columbia. Cliff was producing as well. He noticed one day that someone had signed his name to a check for $10,000. What was that crazy item. You guess it. Petty cash for Begelman.. He was earning millions but he felt entitled to skim off the top. Robertson called him on it. They fired Begelman. Cliff's career was never the same after that event. People would give him a tough time and some times called him a whistler blower.

Here's the crazy part…Begelman continued to dazzle and defraud throughout his life. They wrote a book about him…INDECENT EXPOSURE about his cheating and willful disrespect of the system. Still he continued his crooked career, until he was found dead in a motel. At least Cliff called him on it.

I was fired from the MTA after seven years of great work, because a rumour started that I had given my brother Stan a project to redesign the uniforms for Metro North and I was getting a kickback. The New York Post claimed it was a multi million dollar contract and my brother payed me off. It was a $15,000 fee. His usual fee would have been 3 or 4 times that. He was one of the biggest career apparel designers in the world and he did me a favor. I made the mistake of not bidding it with 3 vendors and the rest is history.

Here's the thing the MTA never questioned the stories about me. I thought I had so many friends at the account. Many years later I saw Susan Gilbert one of my MTA clients and asked her why she never told me what was going on, and why didn't she go to bat for me. She had no answer.

Today the world is facing Trump and millions of his followers. They will lie and cheat and do anything in order to take our democracy down. We cannot let that happen. Make sure you vote for Biden.

The Berkshires, the Best.
1958 to 2005

We love the Berkshires. We spent close to fifty years there. We raised our kids there. Nothing has ever compared to the joy that we experienced there until we came to Hampton Bays.

Where should I start? Perhaps in the beginning. 1958.

When I met Elaine we were always traveling and exploring new places. I will write all about Fire Island in another story, but also around that time we drove up to the Berkshires, I think to a concert at Tangle wood. We didn't have much money at that time. We discovered some cabins on Lake Lee that we could rent nightly. With the cabin you got a free rowboat, and the Sunday, New York Times. The price...$18 per night. We stayed one Saturday night with Bruce, our son and our dog Corky. It was heaven. I think we stayed off and on at Lake Lee for a couple of years...but we really wanted a place of our own in the Berkshires.

Over the years we had become lovers of Early American antiques. The Berkshires was one of the best sources we had ever discovered. We met a woman Harriet Sossner who had an antique shop in Stockbridge. A wonderful town just a few miles from Tanglewood. She became like a mother to us. Her family owned many properties in the surrounding area. One day I was out in a rowboat with her son Tommy. He told me about a house his mom was selling on the lake.

"Let's go see it...Mom will give you a good deal."

I told Tommy that I was not ready. I had very little money. We rowed across Lake Buel anyway. As we docked our boat , I saw this wonderful red house about 40 feet from the small beach. It had no heat. Purely a summer place. An old tiny barn in the back that had a sagging roof. It needed paint and the screens had many holes in them. IT WAS PERFECT.

His mother wanted $8800.

"Tommy, I have no money to put down."
"Don't worry I have a plan. How much money do you have on you."
I had eight dollars.
"Perfect, here's what we will do. I will tell the bank that we are selling you the house for $12,500 not $8800. This will give you enough money for the down payment."
"Can we do that?"
We did that, and I got the house for no money down. We also used the same attorney for the closing. Bob Donovan. Like we could do that today.

We rented the Lake house out that summer for two months to Arlo Guthries son. We got a call from the sheriff that they were keeping goats in the house. Took us weeks to clean the little pellets all over the place, but once we got them out we rented it to two dentists from New Jersey. The summer rental covered our mortgage costs for the year. We stayed there in the Fall and Spring of the next year. By the way, a local guy jacked up the roof on the barn and fortified the place with cinderblocks. Total cost including labor $154.00.
We love the Berkshires.

The next summer my wife wanted us to leave the city and move to a mansion that she found in Hartsdale, New York. We had to sell the Lake Buel house. We needed $20,000 for a down payment. I was short by $10,000. We offered the house to the dentists for $19,800. They bought it. Payed off the bank and used the cash left to buy our 14 room retreat in the suburbs. As I write this it seems like it never happened, but I promise you it did.

This is where Fire Island came into our lives. We started going there instead of the Berkshires. I will be writing a number of stories about those 4 or 5 summers on Fire Island. They were so special. For a while we thought of buying there but we couldn't stop thinking about the Berkshires and the great times we had there.

So here we were without a place in the Berkshires, living in the suburbs. My career in the advertising started to take off. My salary covered all our expenses and we started to save.

I was just starting my own agency, and I wasn't sure what the first year would look like. It turned out to be a boom. At the end of the year I took a bonus of $200,000. Half for the down payment on an apartment at 19 East 88th Street, leaving another $100,000 for the Berkshires.

We had seen so many places over the years. We knew what we wanted, but couldn't come close. We wanted a vintage house on lots of land. It could be a fixer upper, but it had to have the bare bones. One broker kept after us. Wheeler and Taylor. They had the perfect house in Sheffield, Mass. We did not want to see it because the land was on both sides of Undermountain Road. We had two kids by now…Joss was five and Mandy was two…and two pets. The road was a hazard. Too busy. We did not want to see the property.

Finally my wise wife Elaine said lets look. And we did.
Fifteen minutes in that 1753 home and we were smitten.
This was to be our home for many years to come.

Corky and Bruce

Our 1753 dream home.
1979 to 2005

First of all I have to thank my brother Mitch and my Dad. We could not of afforded to buy this wonderful home without them. I felt that this house would be great for us to share as an investment. They came up and looked at it, and agreed to put up half the money as a loan and they would own fifty percent of the property.

It didn't work out that way. I am not sure of how it all happened. It turned out Mitch and his wife only used the house once. And that turned out to be a disaster. They never said anything to us, but when we went up the next weekend to the house, the water was rotten. It smelled something terrible. We called Perroti the plumber and they discovered that there was a dead deer in the well. Took a few days to clean the water and the well. That's living in the country.

I called Mitch when I got home.
Asked him how his time in the country was.
"Great."
I told him about the deer in the well…
"Oh my god. We took a shower and I was afraid to tell you. I thought I broke something. We couldn't get the smell off for a couple of days."

That was it on the country for Mitch. They never used the house and about a year later, I think, I was able to pay them off.

But back to this unique home.
It was built in 1753. It was the second oldest home in Sheffield. Only two families had owned the property before us. One for over a hundred years, and the Stevens who sold us the home for over a hundred and twenty years.

It was so original. Most of the floors where original. Many of the windows. The doors were over two hundred years old, too. It had three fireplaces and two beehive ovens along side of them for baking bread. The original trivets were still in the kitchen fireplace.

This is where they did their cooking. The kitchen was added many years later. And the kitchen was mostly from the fifties and sixties. Tiny rooms. Very low ceilings. You had to duck when going through most of the doors. Four tiny bedrooms upstairs. A dining room. Living room and a room we turned into a pool room for Joss when she turned 16. A big mudroom and a small porch. That porch became a big one with a stone fireplace. We did a lot of living out there. The house was so special. Every door trim was crooked. The bathroom, all three of them each had a bathtub and a shower all with vintage fixtures. Impossible to find. The two families before us had kept it original.

The land! All 110 acres was so special. Half on the side where the house was and the other half across the road with a swimming pond and stream. Open fields and specimen trees everywhere. We eventually, found a 200 year old deserted barn in New Hampshire and had the Wilkensons take it apart, number each piece of and ship it down to be put next to the pond.

It was a cow barn. I also bought a blue colored 200 year old silo and used that wood for the ceilings and floors in the barn. It turned out to be two stories. Second floor…1200 foot painting studio, the 1200 ft downstairs became Elaine's THREE LITTLE INDIANS antique store. She was way ahead of her time. We used to travel to Santa Fe, New Mexico and we had started to collect cowboy and Indian clothing and housewares. Today we are not allowed to use the phrase Indians, my grandkids advised me. We still have some of those treasures.

Built a pool and a pool house that looked just like the main house. We also built a four car garage out of old wood in the same style as the house with a giant cupola and a deer weather vane on top. The top of the barn had a big storage area. I kept four Vintage cars there.

And last, but far from least we built a one room cottage outside the main porch with a little front porch for the kids. They painted it inside and out. They furnished it with antiques like our house and had a pretend kitchen. They spent many days and some nights in their own little house.

As you can tell from the description…we grew to know so much about ourselves in that home. It's needs. Our treasures. It all fit together.

The house had ghosts. Mister Stevens told us all about them before we closed on the house. Just in case we changed our minds. Here's how we met the previous owner Olin Stevens.

I went up to see the property one more time before the closing. I am not sure, but I think I went with Mitch. It was a cold day, and we had seen the land on the other side of the road. As we approached the house to peek in the windows, a grey haired slight man came out the side door…
"Can I help you?"
"We're the Hermans. We are closing next week."
"Come in. Have a cup of tea. It's too cold."
"Come in this door, we never use the front door."
Right then I started to wonder.

Who was Olin Stevens?
When we first saw the house, in the living room were a number of pictures of this grey haired man shaking the hand of four or five Presidents of the United States starting with Truman.
Happens I was with a client that week, Joe Dockery, who owned land in the Berkshires, and told him I was buying a house from this guy Olin Stevens.
"Do I happen to know him? He is my hero. He designed the sails a boats for most of the America Cup races. He is world famous."

Like I said this grey haired guy called us in for tea. He was a true gentleman. Seemed so kind and concerned for us loving his home that had been in his family for over 120 years. All of a sudden we heard this banging noise in the basement below us. He kept on talking. After a few minutes I couldn't resist…"What's that banging?" "Oh that's the water pump, been doing that for years. You'll get used to it." He told us about the four herb gardens his wife had planted and said he would leave us a map so we could find them.

We asked if he could deliver the house broom clean. He did. Even took all the light bulbs and the toilet seats. Only thing he left was a small round tapestry his wife had done of their dog. We still have it the Hamptons.

The first week we bought a wee Ouija board. Sat in front of a roaring fire in the living room one night and spoke to the ghosts. Really. Liz and Lee. "Stop moving it." "No you stop moving it," my wife and I argued.

After a month of research on the house at the town hall it turns out the original owners were sisters. Liz and Lee Candee. The Candee Sisters had died in that house some 150 years ago. I remember one night I woke Elaine... "Do you hear that?" Some one is downstairs. When I got down I noticed the piece in front of the fireplace had been moved back. I told Elaine and what did she say?
"The sisters didn't like where we put it."

Yes, they moved furniture from time-to-time, but never gave us trouble for the next 29 years.
It was their house.

Painting by Joan Bahm.

Our 1753 dream home. 1979 to 2005

Tradition.
1979-2005

We lived and loved our home for 29 years. When I needed something delivered I would tell them that our home was one house down from the Stage Coach Inn on Under mountain Road. "Oh…the Stevens house." Never got to be the Herman house.

Talk about tradition. Our next door neighbors, the Bartholomew's had lived there for over a hundred years. They had a cattle farm for most of that time. The first day we moved in Ned, the father, came over to introduce himself. His land abutted ours. He had around thirty cows that grazed in the field next to ours. He spent about 15 minutes introducing me to each and every cow. This is Suzie. She has a bit of a cold but it won't effect her milk. Tony is the best boy we've got, except he eats much to much and he's about forty pounds over weight. And on and on…he told me about each and every. To me they pretty much looked like brown and white cows.

"The Stevens allowed us to mow their fields for the hay for the cows as far back as I can remember. In exchange we'll clear your driveway and watch over your home when you are gone.
Is that acceptable?" Ned said.
He reached out his hand for my hand to seal the deal. No paper here.

He looked so hardy and healthy…Ned. Three weeks later he died. Dropped dead after dinner one night. We went to the funeral. Hundreds of people seemed to have loved the man. The next day after the funeral there was a knock on our door. It was Dana, Ned's son. I showed him in and told him how shocked and sorry we were about his dad. He was there for a reason. He knew that his dad and I had shaken hands on the deal a few weeks before. He went through almost the same speech as his dad and we shook hands. That was the spirit of life in Sheffield. Your word was your bond. The lawyers starved in that town.

Jumping ahead to about 20 years later, Dana passed away. Died from the same heart issue as his dad, and he was his dad's age...63. Scary. At his funeral we knew just about everyone there. We were still not natives, but most of Dana's friends accepted us as the New Yorkers, that had learned a little about how to be good neighbors.

I rode them all!

Yes,
she had red curly hair!

Friday night after Thanksgiving.

When pictures of Thanksgiving were painted by Norman Rockwell they could have been painted in our house in Sheffield. Instead they were actually painted in Stockbridge in Rockwell's studio only twenty miles away. Every Thanksgiving our expanded family spent Thanksgiving in our home in Sheffield, without exception. Family and friends participated.
It was a joyous time, year-after-year.

We wanted to contribute to the neighbors in some way. Elaine came up with the idea of celebrating the day after Thanksgiving as well. Invite everyone we knew up there, especially our neighbors. It was pot luck. Just bring one dish. It started with about 20 or 25 family and immediate neighbors and it grew and grew and grew. We celebrated for 25 years in a row, except one. Someone in our family was too sick so we called it off that year. We thought we had reached everyone to tell them it was off but fifteen or twenty people showed up. The largest group we had was around a hundred. What great food. Like the Bartholomew's brought Beth's famous baked beans with bacon and honey. The best ever. Everybody tried to outdo the next person. My ham was good, but not like some of the other dishes. Elaine made two kinds of Lasagna…meat and veggies. And people brought so much wine it carried us over to the next year.

When we left Sheffield our next door neighbor Beth, continued with the event…she had to admit it was good, but never as good as ours.

They still do it. They call it the Herman's Friday night.

That's Ruth, Elaine's mom, in the background.

Friday night after Thanksgiving.

Four of my favorite all time greats.

It's a memoir so I feel that you should know that I have four movies in my opinion that have effected my life in a powerful positive way. They are all very different, yet each in my judgment is the best ever made, in their category. Here we go.

CINEMA PARADISO Who ever loves movies, this is one of the best. It is a movie lovers movie. It won the Oscar in 1988 for the best foreign film. It is a love affair on many levels. The music, the acting, the direction are all perfect. A flash back brings a great film director back to a town where he was trained by a lovable projectionist in the local theatre when he was a very young boy. This movie theatre named Cinema Paradiso is the heart of a tiny Italian town. There is no life without it. The boy falls in love with movies and a young lady. He loses the lady and leaves the town to become one of the leading film directors in Italy. He comes back to his town for the funeral of his projectionist who taught him about love. The grown up little boy is the towns hero. At the end, the movie theatre is torn down and replaced by a parking lot. A simple love story on every level.

PATHS OF GLORY This anti-war movie is the most important one ever made. Stanley Kubrick brings us war in black and white. The brutality. The waste. The soldiers are like pawns for the generals to express their egos . It depicted the French army in such a negative way that although the film was released in 1957 it was banned in France until 1979. Kirk Douglas, Adlolphe Menjou, Ralph Meeker give performances that are impeccable. The futility of war is dramatically riveted into our souls. At the end Kubrick has a scene of a German bar maid singing to worn out French soldiers...she tears your heart out...he manages to restore faith in mankind. Pure genius.

MOONSTRUCK This is one corny movie, and I love it. Norman Jewison turned it into a jewel. I laugh and cry throughout it. Cher is cast against Nicolas Cage...they are an imperfect couple in every way and the movie is stunning. I think they each give their best to this rich movie. When she slaps him after having sex for the first time and says..."get a life" you can so relate to their feelings and it is funny at the same time. Even the music is corny...Dean Martin sings That's Amore. Give me a break. It is a constant reminder of how important family is. I live by that premise. One of the last lines in the movie is alla famiglia... to the family. Love, romance, lots of laughs and family. I guess I am a cornball at heart.

FINDING FORRESTER In many ways this may be my perfect film experience. I learned so much about painting from this one. Gus Van Zant directed. He did Good Will Hunting. The character development is so similar. You feel you know and understand the two leads. First time actor Rob Brown steals the movie from Sean Connery. First time writer Mike Rich tried to sell this script for years. When Connery read it he loved it, it got made.

With the exception of one scene, each scene in this movie is pretty much perfect. In one scene Connery, whose character is fashioned after JD Salinger is teaching Rob Brown how to write. They sit opposite each other on their own typewriters. Connery types, Brown sits and thinks what to write.

"What are you doing?"
"I'm thinking."
"Don't think. Type. Thinking? That comes later."

Any time I find myself thinking about a painting...
I stop...and paint.
So many lines in that movie gave me perspective.
"First draft is from the heart. Second draft is from the head."

I think I have seen it a half dozen times. I still cry at the end.

Four of my favorite all time greats.

Sir Martin Sorrell
1980

When we first met Martin he was not yet a Sir. However, he was one of the most powerful men in the advertising business. Charlie had first met him, and he promised Charlie that someday we would work together. Martin was famous for outdoing the famous Saatchi Brothers. At one time Saatchi & Saatchi was the biggest agency in England. Martin worked for them. They did not get along. They actually got rid of Martin by giving him a Cable company. Not a tv cable company, a metal cable company. Story goes Martin turned that company into another and another and in the end bought Saatchi & Saatchi. He became famous for buying up companies and making them profitable. That is the myth. It's probably true.

One day, my partner Charlie at Herman and Rosner gets a call from Martin. Come over and help him out. It seems he had three advertising agencies in London that he owned and they were not making money. He wanted us to interview each one and take one and make it profitable. Sure!

He set it up in one day. That's right one day. We would have breakfast with one agency, lunch with the next and dinner with the third and then meet Martin for drinks that evening. The most time he would give us.

It was an exciting, exhausting experience. Charlie and I both fell in love with one of the agencies and we felt we knew how to turn it around. The other two agencies were dogs, in our opinion. Too political and set in their ways. We met that night with Martin and told him we could turn Downton Advertising around.

"Of course. Fine. They are the best of the lot. Take either of the other two and we will go from there."
Martin knew what he wanted and we were to click our heels and get it done. In fact, he told us which of the other two we would start with. Stupidly we passed. We were at the top of our game in America

and I think it was my arrogance that had us walk away.
I think I told Charlie, we don't need this guy. Big mistake!

Life is curious.
The house we live in now in Hampton Bays was owned by
Charles Saachi in 1979.

The Brothers: Getting up there!

My story behind the story.
1959

When I got engaged to Boots Orlanis I was working as a shift chemist at I.G.Farbin Industries in Linden, New Jersey. It so happens that one of Boot's uncles was a golf pro in New Jersey. He gave me a set of golf clubs when we got engaged and he said he would teach me the game. Why not. We worked it out that I would meet him after my night shifts, which were over at 7AM. I can't remember what golf course it was, but it was somewhere near Newark. I really got good at the game. He had me play with only three clubs. A driver. A five iron for the middle game, and a putter. Play that game with constant instruction and I got to be a very good golfer in a very short time.

One of the best parts of the game was after we played. We went to a cousins house in Newark. I met Maxine Groffskey there. She was Boots cousin. I never forgot that great house. They had a finished basement with a ping pong table. They accepted me as part of the family. I remember that there was always an abundance of fruit and the frig in the basement, and it was filled with sandwiches and ice cream. Maxine was a year or two older than me, and her family seemed to be a lot wealthier than mine or Boots. She was very nice and a bit of a snob.

CUT TO 3 OR 4 YEARS LATER
SOUTHAMPTON, LONG ISLAND

My brother Stan had been living with his partner Gene in Southampton for many years. I was seeing Elaine at that time but not married yet. I think it was 1959. I was reading a great book Goodbye Columbus. It was this young writer Phillip Roth's first novella. It got great reviews and I couldn't put it down. I remember telling Gene about the Jewish family in Newark, New Jersey. I felt that I knew them, and I remember that basement. He said it was like a lot of Jewish families at that time.

Later that afternoon we were on the beach and I was reading Goodbye. I looked up to see a familiar face. It was Maxine Groffsky. Out of the blue. I hadn't seen her since I had broken off my engagement from Boots. Turns out that Maxine had been quite verbal with me about Boots. She told me outright that the Orlanis family was wonderful, but that I would be "bored to tears" if I married Boots. I didn't break it off because of her, but it didn't help.

I waved at Maxine…she came over and I introduced her to Stan and Gene. We made small talk and then she saw what I was reading. She got startled. She pulled me aside. She was frantic.

"Don't tell me parents, they will kill me. He promised he would never publish it. He promised. That son of a bitch. I hear they are making a movie out of it. I'll die."

Yes, Maxine was Brenda from Goodbye Columbus. Phillip Roth was her lover. We all know Brenda. She was played by Ali MacGraw. Big success.

Maxine turned out to be the Paris editor for the Paris Review and a big time Literary Agent at her own agency. I always wondered if people ever found out that she was Brenda.

I wrote to Maxine many years later to thank her for her advise and council. She never returned my letter.

Bruce
1959 *first meet*

I met Bruce when he was 6 years old. Elaine and I had dated a few times and after the first date she told me about her son Bruce. Elaine had been married for about a year to Marvin Caro and she became pregnant and had Bruce the first year. She got a divorce within the next six months and was raising Bruce totally on her own. Elaine wanted out of the marriage so bad, she settled for $25 per week for child care.
Only problem…Marvin never gave her the $25.

Elaine was working as the head store model at Henri Bendels, She worked 6 days a week, and on Sundays she did fashion shows at Sheri Netherland Hotel to supplement her income. She got off work at Bendels at 5 and headed to her mom and dads building at the Oliver Cromwell on 72nd and the Park.

Bruce got out of school around 3:30, so he walked from school the 2 blocks to the Oliver Cromwell. In the lobby of the building was a newsstand run by a wonderful man, Mr. Fish. Besides running the store he watched over Bruce until Elaine would pick him up… everyday after school. Bruce did not like comics. He loved to read all the daily newspapers including the New York Times at 6 years old. Elaine asked me to meet her at the newsstand one day…she wanted me to meet her son.

Cute! Dressed in a blue blazer with grey flannel pants. He had sandy blond hair that was partially combed. What a cherub. And so polite. He introduced me to Mr. Fish and showed me a few drawings he had done at school that day. I had a two-for. Elaine and Bruce…both so special. I didn't realize how these two would change my life forever.

Elaine had a tiny apartment just one block from her parents. It had a galley kitchen. A tiny bedroom that Bruce slept in and a living room that Elaine used for everything else including her bedroom. The freezer was filled with frozen dinners. That's what they both lived on. There was a TV set in the living room. After he did his homework each night, he was in bed before 9. Elaine read to him every night when she put him to sleep. TV was acceptable only on the weekends.

After a few months Elaine allowed me to be part of the program that she had made work for herself and her son. I never slept over. Although when Bruce fell a sleep we had time to be together. I so resisted falling in love at first, but it happened.

Bruce 1959 *first meet*

Fire Island and the Berkshires. 1959

When Elaine and I started going out all the time, she cut back her work so we could spend time together with Bruce on weekends. Money was pretty tight on my end too, but we went away almost every weekend.

We discovered Lee Lake Cabins in the Berkshires. It was about half hour from Tangle wood. They would rent you a tiny cabin with a kitchen and we had two beds set up. Included in the fee of $18 per night was a rowboat and the Sunday New York Times. Bruce and I would row out, swim off the boat and read the Times. It was so much fun. We also discovered a fast food place that had just started in Mass. Friendly restaurant had the best fresh fast food at very reasonable prices. The best hot dogs. Bruce loved hot dogs when he was young. Wouldn't touch them when he grew up.

We also discovered a favorite place. Fire Island. We rented rooms for the weekends in the beginning. Bruce was so fair. We would dress him from head to toe and put up an umbrella, and he still would scorch. Funny to bring this up here, but when we adopted Joss the folks at Spence Chapin one day asked Elaine and I if there was anything that we would want in our child, and I said we would like a child who had a dark complexion, so that we could spend time in the sun. Thank heavens…who knows if we would have gotten Joss.

We loved our weekends on the island. When we had Joss and Mandy we spent so much time on this very safe place. No cars so the kids were pretty much on their own.

Elaine and I were not married for five years. During those years I learned a little bit about parenting. Elaine had a simple way of being with Bruce. He was her best friend. Because of the way my dad brought me up, I thought raising your children you had to have all the answers.

Tough being a friend and the boss at the same time, right.
In the beginning I watched but didn't learn much.
I thought my way was the best, of course.

Fire Island and the Berkshires. 1959

Married finally
1959

Paul Weintraub was there when I saw the redhead for the first time.
It was only appropriate that he be my best man, and Bruce was our ring
bearer at 11 years old. Why did I finally agree to get married?

I get a call from Elaine one day. She is so excited. "I found the perfect
apartment in the Village, and I am moving in."
She had never lived in Greenwich Village before. We were taking
painting classes at the New School and our favorite restaurants were
in the Village. I was living there for almost five years right around
the corner from the famous White Horse Inn.

"What do you mean. Where is it? Without me?"

One Sheridan Square was our dream home. Right in the heart of
the Village. Down the street from The Bagel. Around the corner
from O Neils our favorite steak house and so many vintage clothing
stores that we were into. The apartment was on the top floor. Two
small bedrooms. A giant living room and a terrace that went all
around the apartment. It was actually the roof and they built these
two apartments on it. The rent was $330 per month. A little out of
Elaines budget.

"Why don't we move into together and split the rent." I said. "In fact
how would you feel about getting married?"

That's how I proposed. As my wife said, "who would turn that
down." A married woman with a divorce child as my dad called
Elaine..."dead wood." And we were in love with each other and the
apartment. The kicker..Bruce loved the apartment too.

We got married at Ethical Culture. Mostly family and friend. Doctor
Herman married us. No relation. When it came to Bruce giving
us the rings, he was so excited that he dropped both rings off the
pillow. You could hear them rolling across the floor. It was hysterical

watching us crawl around the floor. That was the highlight, except when we kissed.

60 years married!

Here we are 60 years later and still love kissing and being together. She is a friend beyond friend

Had a wonderful luncheon at the Sheri Netherland Hotel across the park. I remember that day like it was sort of yesterday.
Happy, happy day.

The apartment
Not big enough
1959

Here's a dilly. When Joss came we were in trouble.
We only had two bedrooms. So what did we do?
We cut Bruce's bedroom in half, of course.

Joss's room was a sliver. About 6 or 7 feet wide. Bruce's was a little bigger. In any case it was the beginning of the baby getting most of the attention.

Bruce put up with it for a while and then when Joss was about 4 months old, we had this little carrier to carry her around. I suggested we put her on the table when we all ate dinner together. Very thoughtful. When Bruce came in and saw our new "centerpiece" that was it.

"I've had it." And he went into his room to read rather than join us for dinner. A wake up call. We had more than one child. He was 12 and he needed Elaine's and my attention for real. I have to admit even though we were pretty young, we got the message.

From that day on, Joss fit into our family not the other way around.

Corky, Elaine and I at One Sheridan Square.

Joss walks the hallway for her adoption day. 11 months after getting her.

The apartment *Not big enough* 1959

Beyond stupid.
1959

The first few years our marriage and Sheridan Square were pretty perfect. Really. Elaine took to raising Joss and Bruce and I adjusted to our family life together, most of the time. I left out a detail, though.

When Bruce was about 9 Elaine and I were suspecting that he was leaning towards being gay. So, we had him tested in a clinic in Brooklyn. They confirmed our feelings. Even though Marvin, Elaine's ex had little to do with his son, she felt he should know. What a mistake. Marvin flipped out. He got this Park Avenue Doctor who supposedly was an expert on the subject to see Bruce.

"If he's a homosexual then I am too," he told Marvin. This started a long lasting battle with her ex. I thought I handled pretty well. Boy was I stupid.

Without realizing it I was somehow afraid of this whole homosexual situation. My brother Stan was a homosexual and now my son was one also. Why couldn't I just be accepting of it all.

When Bruce was about 15 he told Elaine and I that he was definitely gay. Again, I thought I was handling it. Until around 16 Bruce came to me and asked if he could bring home a friend. I told him bring him home , but no sex. Do not bring that into the house. I can't believe that is how I handled it. It drove a wedge into our relationship. I am trying to remember what happened with Elaine and I. It could not have been good. It lasted that way for months, I believe. Until one day Bruce and I had a terrible argument. I was beside myself. I stopped and screamed at him..

"What do you want from me. I am lost. I am not your father. I feel like I'm doing everything. Nothing is working. I am doing my best to make you happy. It is not working. What do you want from me?"

He stopped and looked at me and said without any anger...

"All I want from you, is to be there when I need you. That is all I want from you."

I stopped. He stopped. I reach forward and hugged him. After a little he hugged me back. I can honestly tell you from that moment on, I stopped knowing and started listening to see what he needed. I know it may be hard to believe…from that moment on, the pressure was off. I did not have to figure out how to be with him.

Bruce went on the next year to the University of Pittsburg. He studied theatre, English and writing. After college he moved in with a wonder man…Steven Spector. He came out and wrote a play that he co-produced with Sheri Felt, off Broadway. He picked up background bits in some movies, including Woody Allen's Annie Hall. And, he ended up teaching theater at the Walden High School. Here's the freaky part…Amanda was going to New Lincoln School and it merged with Walden and Bruce became Amanda's teacher in theatre. That gave her the background to be in film, which she is in today. She was there for him at the end when the marks on his face started to show up from his Aids at the age of 37, and Bruce wanted to continue working.

Through it all Bruce had the most wonderful dry sense of humor. He was so bright. So quick to respond. One time we were walking up Madison Avenue and looking in the store windows. This was one of our favorite walks in the world. Bruce and Tony were furnishing their new brownstone on the upper West side. We stopped at a Art Deco store on 72nd Street.

"My God. Look at those chairs. Tony would love them. Let's go in and find out how much they are."

The snooty guy came over to Bruce…Bruce asked…
"Can you tell me how much those two chairs in the window are?"

The guy went into a long winded description of the two chairs. Who designed them, where they came from and on and on. Bruce was so patient, finally he interrupted him.

Beyond stupid. 1959

"Wonderful, can you please tell me how much they are?"

"The price is $12,500 for the pair."

Bruce smiled went over to look at the chairs and finally asked, "Do you happen to have two more, we need four of them."

Or how about Christmas. Bruce had such specific taste. We knew what he would love and searched the city for something special. I remember one Christmas we saw this exceptional hand made sweater. Perfect cut. The colors were his favorite and it was a one of a kind. It was very expensive but Elaine said let's go for it.

We had Christmas in Sheffield most years. This was no exception. Local hot cider and lots of sweets. Everyone opened their gifts. Finally Bruce opened his. Oh my he held it up...he smiled...

"I love the color. It's sensational."
I asked. "Do you really love it."

"Oh yes. I loved it last year too."

Turns out we bought him the exact sweater the year before. That was Bruce.

Beyond stupid. 1959

The final years.
1990

For the next few years Bruce had so special life. It was too short. He died from AIDS at the age of 37. I remember the day I found out. I was on the board of our coop and I was at our monthly meeting. They said that there was someone to see me. When I went out it was the whole family minus Bruce. They were all crying. I think it was Joss or Amanda who said that Bruce had Aids. Back then there was no cure and it was terminal usually within months.

The next year is a blur. I probably would love to forget it. Bruce was living with Tony Hammer, a wonderful man. He took care of Bruce as the end approached. He did not want to be in the hospital. They lived in a 4 story brownstone on the West Side. In the beginning Bruce seemed so normal. We went out to dinner very often. He started to lose weight. Then he began to lose his balance and energy. Then it all changed. He became bed ridden within the next month. He had to go to the hospital. Elaine and I visited with him one time, and that was the last time I allowed her to see Bruce. Within weeks he weighed 80 pounds.

I went to the hospital for the next few days, everyday. The last day I stood at the end of the bed and asked him if he needed anything. He asked me to feel his toes. They were ice cold. He died that night. A shadow of the great man he had been. That disease. No one should die that way.

We buried him in a cemetery in New Jersey next to his grandmother. About a year or two later Tony passed away too. We buried him along side of Bruce. We contacted his mid western Quaker parents. They would not come to the funeral or the cemetery.

They did not have a son.

Elaine and Bruce at 19 East 88th Street.

The final years. 1990

Landmark
1977

December 10, 1977.
Here we are 46 years later and I still remember the two weekends that
I did the EST training, and how it changed my life forever.

EST had gotten a bad rap. It was considered a cult by many. My wife had left me in LALA Land and taken the kids back to New York City. I was still trying to make it in LA. She did the training and asked me to do it. I told her it was people like her that did that garbage. I doubt if there were too many people more arrogant than me. I knew everything. I didn't need anybody.

Cut to almost one year later. I am living in Santa Monica and two wonderful ladies move in downstairs. They were terrific. I made a pass at one of them, and she thanked me, but told me she was a Lesbian and this was her partner. Blind. Yes that was me. Totally narcissistic.

Turns out these two ladies are Werner Erhart's chefs. He's the man who created the EST training. I became friends with my downstair neighbors. One evening we had drinks together in my apartment.

"Harvey. We are not supposed to say what I am about to say, but you know you need the EST training. You are lost honey. You need to get in touch with your life. Do this thing."

Two weeks later I was in New York City doing the training. I'll prove to them that my life is perfect without this bullshit. That's the way I went into that weekend.

I tried to leave the first day. I stood up and said I was leaving because a woman was leading it. That was the start of my transformation. Something weird happened. I started to listen. Person after person talking about how their lives were fucked up because of others. Sounded very familiar.

My mother had died when I was seven. She called me into her bedroom two weeks before she died and she said that she was dying because she had me. If she hadn't had me she would not be dying. Two weeks later she died.

I had carried this moment with mom around my whole life. Here I was 43 years old, and I would wake up screaming many nights to get out of the dream as my mom accused me of killing her.

Five years of analysis had not helped. I blamed this incident for every bad thing that ever happened with women. I needed love.

What did I get out of that weekend. Well for one thing, There was one process that we went through lying on the floor. I fell asleep and had that miserable nightmare again. In the middle of the dream I stopped my mom and I said to her…"Mom stop. I am 43 years old. I'm married. Three kids. What do you want from me? OK. You died for me…I'll die for you." They told me I was out on the floor for 15 minutes after the process was over. Never had the dream again. That's right. I gave up blaming mom for so many things in my life. This was the beginning.

After the training my wife and I got back together. Never would have happened. We started a new life together as two new people after 14 years of marriage. This year we will celebrate our 60th year of a beautiful marriage.

I got trained to lead Landmark Seminars with my daughter Joss. I lead them for 17 years. Joss went on to lead and help create the actual courses. It is now called The Forum. Just about everyone in our family did the work, except for my older brother Stan and one of my grandchildren Max.

I realize reading this, if you haven't done The Forum it could sound like …great you got a lot out of it but what is it really all about. Let me see if I can use a few examples to give you an idea of what people get out of these programs.

I flew my family over to Nantucket one weekend. We stopped to get yogurt. When I got to pay ,the guy behind the counter looked at me and smiled…"No charge, Harvey. You don't recognize me do you? You led my introduction to the Landmark Forum."

I was a little embarrassed, but I said no, I did not recognize him. And then he told me a story I never forgot.

While I was a Seminar Leader I lead hundreds of Introductions to the Forum. One night I was leading one and it was over by 10PM and here it was almost 11 and one of the people who came to find out about the Forum was still in the back of the room.

He said you came to the back of the room and said the intro was over…are you going to do it?

I said, "I can't make up my mind."

You said, OK what would you want to get out of doing the Forum if I did it. I laughed and I told you I would like to stop procrastinating. And you surprised me. You asked me if I stopped procrastinating, what would I do? I told you that I would probably quit my lucrative job on Wall Street and open a bunch of yogurt stores.

Another time I was checking out of King Kullen here in Hampton Bays. A lady on the line in back of me had the cutest little girl about 5 or 6 year old. She pointed at me and spoke to her daughter…
"Honey, thank the nice man."
I realized she was talking about me.
"Yes, thanks for asking me to do the Forum. I'm pretty sure it saved mommy and daddy's marriage."

If I didn't do this work and pass it on to others, who knows where I would have ended up. Certainly not with the great life I have today.

My daughter's group, Boy Krazy, had the number 1 record in America.

The tracks of Passaic
1951

I never forgot this one.

Passaic was a town that thrived in the 30's, 40's, and 50's. It was a town that had a railroad track that ran in the center of it. That track probably was put in by the Erie railroad and the town was built around it. It worked back then but the town started to die when we were in High School. It went from a primarily all white community to almost all kinds of ethnic neighborhoods.

My dad and his family had Herman Brothers Shop on Monroe Street. It thrived when I was in public school. I worked there on weekends. My dad and his six brothers, his sister and my grandma all made a living from this wonderful store. I worked in the pattern department. Advance, Vogue, Simplicity, McCalls, Butterick patterns were sold there. Woman would sit around and pick out their patterns and then one of my uncles would show them great fabrics to make the dresses they had picked out. They would pick out matching threads, buttons, and zippers to complete their garments. Really wonderful. They would leave and within a few days they could have a new dress, jacket or whatever. *How great was that.*

Herman Brothers was just one local store run by locals and kept Passaic such a good place to live. Almost every store on every block was run by locals. What happened next killed off the town.

Malls surrounded Passaic. Shopping moved to the malls. Passaic like so many small towns was dying. What could be done, if anything?

Here was a railroad that was not running trains anymore right in the heart of town. Sidney Zion, George Feifer and I thought we had a brilliant solution. Copenhagen and other towns overseas had done it. Build a mall in the heart of town. No railroad...a mall. We did drawings, and spoke to people in Copenhagen. We did a presentation. My dad knew the board that ran Passaic. DeMuro and Cinnamon.

I was in Passaic High with Sidney and George.
We thought this would solve the problems of Passaic.

Left: George Feifer, daughter and friend.
Right: Ken at our 25th wedding.

We showed my dad, and he thought the idea was good but too expensive. I asked if he could get us a meeting with Cinnamon who was a close friend. Month went by. Sidney Zion thought we should take the idea to The Herald News. They were not interested. We showed it to a few of our teachers in school. One thought it was great and he called DeMuro, who I think was the Mayor at that time. A meeting was set and canceled time after time.
Another teacher in school took us aside as a group.
"What's in it for them? The ones who run it want to know what's in it for them? He said something that always stuck with me.

"Boy's in life, you'll find when you can't understand why things are not getting done...follow the money."

What a lesson. Passaic died.

The tracks of Passaic. 1951

What could have been?
1955

I had just graduated from Philadelphia Textile. My buddy Mike Merns and I always wanted to drive cross country. His dad had bought him a 1951 Ford for graduation and we took that buggy across the United States to Los Angeles. I wrote a whole story about the trip, but I remember an event that happened that could have changed my life forever.

Mike's Uncle Mal Kaplan was head of wardrobe at Paramount Studios. One day Mike and I went over to Paramount. It was very impressive. Just like you have seen in many films, when we drove to the front gate a security guard checked the visitors list and he told us where to park. Mal had his own building and his parking space had a shiny new Mercedes convertible in it. What followed was amazing.

Mal was a greying good looking guy. Tanned and impeccably dressed in a white button shirt and jeans and of course a gold Rolex watch. I was just getting into watches and this was the real thing. If you were casting a head of wardrobe at a major studio he would get the part.

He was so nice to us. He showed us through a giant warehouse. Racks and racks of period outfits. Every category you could think of. Everything marked and the pictures they were shooting then were upfront. One I remember was BLACKBOARD JUNGLE. It was with Glenn Ford playing a teacher in the ghetto in New York City in the early 50's. They were shooting that now.

"I'll check to see what's shooting on what stage and if I can get you in," Mal offered. "In the meantime lets have a little lunch in the commissary." When we got there who was sitting at the next table... Glenn Ford and a few others in the cast. I was blown away.

"Harvey, Mike told me all about you. He says you are very creative and that you really don't belong in textiles. Don't think I am too forward, what are you plans now that you have graduated?"

I told him about my job as a chemist that was waiting for me back east. He shocked me. "Come work with me. I am retiring in the next few years and you could end up being head of wardrobe at Paramount." This came out of left field. He wasn't kidding.

"Why me? You hardly know me? He said he needed someone young and smart and I had that New York smarts he was looking for. Mike chimed in. He thought it was a great idea. "Think about it and call me, we can go talk some more"…he was serious.

Wow! I talked a lot with Mike. I couldn't get the answer to why me? I decided to talk again. I went alone. We met in his office and I said… "Mal…you know I am straight."

He laughed…"is that what you thought?"
I was so embarrassed. I had it all wrong.
"No, I thought about it and I thought you would be perfect for the job, and really in less than five years you would run the place."

Talk about running, I chickened out and couldn't get back to Passaic fast enough.

Stand up..Sit down.
1980

After the EST Training I did a course called The Six Day.
Like the title it took place over six days. Very physical and very mental
exercises. Things like zip lines, jumping off of high places, balancing on
beams…all to test who knows what. There were courses at night covering
every subject possible. The basic idea was to get in touch with who you
were, no matter what faced you in life.

On one of the last nights we finally got to something I was looking
forward to. The whole evening was devoted to SEX. We all sat in a
darkly lighted room and the leader started by wanting to know what
our experiences of sex was to date.
So he started asking…
Who had sex with more than one person at the same time?
Stand up. Sit down.
Who had sex with the opposite sex and same sex at the same time?
Stand up. Sit down.
Who had sex with an animal?
Stand up. Sit down.
And on and on, categories I had never thought of.
Here I was. I thought I knew it all when it came to sex.
After the first Who Did this…I was stuck in my seat.
I was not so worldly…
However next to me was a young lady. Maybe 18 or 19: Stand up.
Sit down. Stand up. Sit down. Stand up. Sit down. Stand up. Sit
down. She got up and down, up and down, up and down.
She had done it all…Stand up..Sit down. "Your kidding," I asked her.
She shook her head yes.

Boy, what I didn't know about sex.
Stand up..Sit down.

The family at our 6 day graduation.

My North Star
1942

When I was around 8 I had a problem with pronouncing my s's and th. I had a bad lisp. It was embarrassing. I remember that I had a great teacher at PS 3 Mrs. Thomas. She taught English. One day she asked if I would stay after school for a few minutes. I wondered what had I done wrong. It wasn't that at all.

"You know, Harvey, I think I can help you with your lisp. It would require your staying after school for a few months. I can check with your Mom, if that is OK with you."

I told her that my mom had passed away, but my Aunt Bertha always picks me up. She said she would check with her.

Long story, short in about two months she cured my lisp. I was so thankful. I wasn't sure how to thank her. I decided that I would draw a picture of her. When I gave it to her she was so impressed. What followed has stayed with me for the rest of my life.

She had a conversation with me about following my North Star. "Harvey this picture is very beautiful. You have a special talent. You captured me. I love it. That is a very special talent. You should pursue being an artist in your life. This may be your North Star."

She went on the say that most people have a talent that they should follow, but in life we get too busy. We get distracted.
Follow your art, I think that may be your North Star.

It took me many years to truly understand what she meant by my North Star. But she was so right. I worked most of my adult life in advertising, but I made time to paint. I stopped from time to time, but never gave up on my talent as a artist. Today at 90 I am painting full time, and I have a new studio that makes it possible to paint almost every day. Thank you Mrs. Thomas.

Tante, me at two and a sexy dad.

I am an Artist
2020

When I teach art to young people and also to seniors at the Hampton Bays and Quogue Libraries I prepare name tags for each of the students. After there name are the words…I am an Artist. Before I let them draw or paint we have a discussion about those words. I teach the same course to children from 6 to 11, and seniors above 65.

Most people live their lives with the practice that…someday I will be an artist. Once I have the right lessons and all the tools. Once I have learned to mix colors and textures. Which brushes to use, what mediums to work in, what papers or canvases to use, and on and on. Someday usually never comes. Before we draw or paint or pick up a brush, I tell them that they are an artist now. That's right. We are starting at the point where most people think they might get someday.

Today I declare I am an artist.
Once I declare that, I will do all the things that I must do to get to be more and more of an artist. Let me tell you …most kids buy into it immediately. The seniors fight like hell. All that garbage that they have picked up in life does them in.

Once and a while I get some senior that insists that they cannot and will never be able to paint.

My favorite one was sister Florence. She had been a nun for many years and as she put it…"I was not blessed in the area of art."
When we started working she could hardly follow the simplest of instructions. After the first week she gave in and tried to listen. I kid you not…her work was so innocent and so beautiful. It brought tears to most of the people in the course.
At the end of the 10 week course she was buying all kinds of pads and pencils and paints, and she told me she was teaching a few of the other nuns, but they had to declare that they were artists.

I guess there is a God.

Most people live their lives
with the practice that…
someday I will be an artist.

It only took 40 years.

I can't remember any time in my life that I didn't feel passionate about art.

I can't remember if I got it from my mother or who started me knowing that I was an artist. One of the earliest memories is covered in another story…when I painted a portrait of a teacher Mrs. Thomas who helped me with a speech impediment. It was something I had to give her.

When Elaine and I first met we started to take painting courses at The New School. She went to Chiam Gross and I learned from Anthony Tony. It came so easy. The first time I did fast life sketches in paint I knew that it was an open door to my passion in life. I could capture the moment with a quick gesture. Tony encouraged me. He painted me in class in my style and I did a painting of him in his style. He pushed me to work outside of the school. He introduced me to sketching everything and everywhere. Carry it with you all the time…beauty is everywhere. Capture it for others.

I was in advertising at that time.
I painted Elaine over and over on Fire Island and in the Berkshires. Painted portraits of Bruce. We were in the middle of the Vietnam war. Elaine and I got married in 64. I started painting colleges about that terrible war. Elaine became pregnant with Amanda. And death in Vietnam and life in our lives together emerged as one in my paintings. Kennedy and my wife standing abreast of each other, she as pregnant as a mother could be. He fighting to stop that horrible conflict. It all worked.

So what did I do with this exciting possibly important work? Nothing. Great Herman. I am still proud of it today…it might have taken me to be a full time artist. I guess I did not believe in myself enough. I did however continue painting through the 70's. In fact a number of really good work.

I got busy in my career. Worked for a number of advertising agencies and then started directing commercials..Then off to Hollywood to become a film director. Oh my. Where was painting then?

In 1979 I opened my own agency. That is another story, but I can't remember painting. Elaine did paint from time to time. She painted in the nude in the bathroom. That's right in the bathroom. I do remember painting pictures on the bathroom walls. She requested it and I did it. I also took my sketch book with me as we traveled around the world. And travel the world we did. Elaine insisted that every year we have a travel budget. It was pretty decent. As long I was making money, no problem.

The agency did very well. I broke off my partnership with Charlie Rosner in 1982, and then I must tell you the agency really took off. I put off the painting again. My plan was to have a studio some day, but living in the city made that impossible, or so I decided. I got out of the agency around 1991 and worked on a number of start up businesses. One with Bob Hillman before Warby Parker, believe it or not, we had the first fashion Ready Readers. They raised a fortune of money we handled ours like a cottage industry. Gave it up some time around 2005.

Elaine felt it was time to "repot." Sell everything and start over. And, we did. Moved out to Hampton Bays in 2005. I started painting seriously. No more advertising. And then I had the dream. You should build a full studio off the back of our home.

It took me a year to design it. Another year to get drawings, and a third year to build. I completed it about a year ago. It is perfect, and my work has become pretty perfect too. I now have a website and will be offering my work there. A portion of all the proceeds is going to support The Trevor Project...helping LGBTQ homeless kids, most of whom are trans.

It took 40 years, but who's counting.

It only took 40 years.

So much in Sweden
1977

When shooting the Sindy film for Marx Toys, one of the countries that we traveled to was Sweden. So many important events happened in that country.

I had never been to this part of the world before. It was summer and what I could not get used to was the length of sunlight each day. There was only about 2 or 3 hours of darkness, the rest of the day was daylight.

It was a nocturnal world. Weird. It meant that most people there sleep very little. That helped to understand what seemed to be a curtness or the very short sentences of the people. It made them feel cold to me.

As I describe more fully in another story, we only spent seven days in each country. Travel. Settle in, pre pro the first day with a pick up crew, except for Bob Steadman, my cameraman. Location next day. Shoot two days and the next two days vacation with my daughters and Bob's two daughters, too. We were both separated from our wives then. Travel the last day.

Sweden was our next to last country, so we had the shoots pretty well organized. When we arrived at each country a limo would pick us up. My kids got used to that luxury right away. Especially Amanda. When we landed in Sweden there was no limo, just a stretch Volvo. "Where's the limo" out of the mouth of babe. She was six at the time.

We got to the production office and "thunderbolt." The production manager for the shoot blew me away. She was beautiful. Blond. Middle age like me, in her forties. We were going to spend the next week together. How was I going to handle this, without screwing up, again. Yes, Elaine and I were separated, but I needed to focus on the shoot.

The shoot went well. The nights that I checked the footage, I spent with her alone. She was not happily married. We talked about my life with Elaine, and what caused us to separate after fourteen years of marriage. She was considering leaving her husband. She also had two daughters. She was so vulnerable and at the same time searching for a lot of answers. I can't even remember her name. That's what is so amazing. We got very close through our talks about life, hugs, kisses and no sex. Pretty amazing for me. Intimacy was so important for both of us at the time. She made me think a lot about how intimate Elaine and I had always been, even during the tough times.

We exchanged info and believe it or not she and I wrote to each other for a number of months. She was still thinking of leaving her husband. At one point we even discussed the possibility of us together. Then it stopped.

CUT TO 5 YEARS LATER.

Elaine and I and the kids are staying in London in a small hotel off of Sloane Street, and who is there…my Swedish love.

I told my beautiful wife about my Swedish connection. I told her that I had never really forgotten that relationship. Her response. "I think you should have coffee with her." Wise wife.

We had coffee. She was very open. She thanked me for our time together, and I did the same. It was so great to be together after all those years. She stayed with her husband as I did with Elaine.

Like I said, I do not even remember my Swedish woman's name, but that chance relationship had us both get in touch with what we had lost in our very special marriages.

A mini moment off Stockholm
1977

While on the shoot in Stockholm a number of people suggest I take a ferry ride to a number of wonderful islands off the coast. I believe they are called the Archipelago group. The ferry taxis from one island to another and you can pop on spend a few hours or days and go on to the next island. There are many islands, so one day I took my two daughters for a ride on the ferry. My intention was to just ride from one island to another and see the islands from the boat and not get off. My kids had a different idea.

At the first island stop. The boat docked and maybe twenty people got off and a bunch of others got on. As the boat pulled away everyone waves at each other. Look at those little kids on the shore waving...they look just like...they are my kids.
STOP THE BOAT...STOP THE BOAT.
My kids got off and were waving goodbye as I was still on the boat.
BYE DADDY...
What followed was chaos. I ran up to the cockpit or what ever you call it. Yelled at the captain to turn around. He shook his head no. I screamed "my kids got off by mistake, turn the boat around." They tried to convince me that another boat will pick them up in a few hours.

A FEW HOURS!

I lost my cool. All I could think of my wife killing me after I lost my kids on an island off of Stockholm. Believe it or not, the captain turned the boat around and picked the kids up. He told me he never did that before.

This "ugly American" lived up to our reputation. It took a $100 bill to change his mind.

My two loves.

Pick up lunch.

One of Elaine's and mine favorite places in the whole world is Lake Como, Italy. Specifically Bellagio is a tiny town on the west bank of the Lake. We have been there a half dozen times. Each time it actually got better. The more familiar we were with the local, the more we ventured out to tiny villages that rimmed the Lake. Not just famous places like Villa D'Este which is an incredible tourist mansion to visit.

On one of our visits, my brother Stan told us about a great restaurant across the Lake...Au Velu. We totally forgot about it, until the day before we were about to leave to come home. We took the ferry across and drove to the place. As we pulled up the hill, a man came out and told us that they had just closed for lunch.

I told them we were leaving tomorrow and that this was one of my brother Stan's favorites. The man turned out to be the manager. He showed us out to the terrace and asked us to wait a minute or so. In the next few minutes her brought out two wine glasses and a bottle of their local vino. Followed by remnants of their dessert for the day... homemade pecan pie. Without another word he returned again with two cups of cappuccino. He said they were closed, but if I would give him a credit card now, we could stay as long as we wished. No hurry. Enjoy!

The sun was shining across the Lake as we downed the whole bottle of wine. It took us well over an hour. No one was there except us. How special. I am not a drinker and my wife can not hold it either, so before long we were too drunk to drive. We downed dessert and our coffee and I slowly returned to this world. Sober enough to finally go home. We were there, alone for a couple of hours. How wonderful can it get. As we drove down the hill we heard someone on the terrace above us...he was waving goodbye. It was the manager. How great is that he puts himself out for us and waves goodbye.

When we got back to our hotel the manager came over and asked...

"Did you enjoy Au Velu?" I didn't realize we had told him we were going there. I told him the story and he smiled…"the manager called, you left your credit card there."

My painting of our lunch at Au Velu

Pick up lunch.

3 Little Indians
1980

When we first bought our home in Sheffield, Mass we always wanted a large barn to add to the property. On a trip to New Hampshire we saw a wonderful cow barn sitting out in a field. We approached the owners, and much to our surprise they agreed to sell us the barn.

It was so beautiful. Had not been used for over 20 years. They originally had cows but not for years. The Wilkensons were our builders and they made the trip up to move the barn. They numbered and lettered every board and every beam and eventually moved it across the road to our property.

We bought an old blue wood silo and used the wood to make a ceiling and floor in the barn. Found two giant 200 year old doors to use on the front of the barn. We ended up with a two story barn. Red washed old boards on the outside. Added a bathroom and a two story fireplace and a stairway out of the original barn beams for stairs leading to the second floor which became my first art studio. A 1250 ft. Studio with a wood burning fireplace. Not bad. Right.

Elaine had first dibs on the downstairs. For years she had been collecting vintage Western furniture and Native American jewelry. She opened her store…**THREE LITTLE INDIANS.** We had traveled many times to Santa Fe and Elaine had made a number of contacts. Now it was time to shop and ship originals, no repros. The stock was sensational. I also got life size paper maché Indians. Three of them.

By the way, back then no one took offense with the word "Indians." We grew up with Cowboy and Indians. I flew the Indians back from someplace down south. When I carried them out of the plane, the folks at Great Barrington Airport thought I was carrying live bodies. They were so great. I sat them in the shop and when people came in many thought they were real people.

The shop was a giant success. Even though it was out of the way, really off the beaten track, in a short time we had a few write ups in the local papers and Elaine was off to a great start. Then the problem came. We were going up to the country on weekends, and it ruined our weekends. Elaine was in the shop all the time. She was selling and making a lot of money. I remember when my Uncle Sunny (who happened to be our accountant) saw the place and saw that she could not keep the inventory in stock he was blown away.

We decided it was time to hire someone to run the shop on weekends. Turns out we tried three different people. None of them worked out. Why?
Elaine. She knew and understood the history and background of every piece of jewelry and every piece of furniture. No one could sell like her.

So in about a year we closed the shop.
I had my first paint studio.

Josselyne and her birth parents. 1996

Not sure of the year, but at one point in our lives with Joss she made decided that she wanted to find her birth parents. When we adopted her there was a point when we were with the lawyer at the court and out of the blue he asked Elaine and I if we wanted to know the names of the birth parents. For some reason we said no. The names were sealed.
In hindsight I wish we had said yes.

I cannot go through what Joss actually did to find her birth mother but when she was about 27 she thought it was time. She wanted to know about their health background and lots of other things. We told her what we knew from the information that Spence Chapin was willing to give us, but she had to do the ground work, and of course she did. There are very few people I know that are more persistent than Joss. She took every avenue and would not take no for an answer.

The big break came when she was told that the birth certificate that we had, was the same number as the original birth certificate. So, it took three people six days to come up with the original. There she was…Michelle Wasson, daughter of Suzanne Wasson born September 27,1967.

She tracked down her birth mother to upstate New York. I am not sure how she did that either, but Corning, New York is where her mother lived.

Great, right? Joss tried to contact the family. No go. After some time she finally got a response from the sister-in-law. They did not want to contact her. What idiots. In fact as I remember, they did not believe that her birth mother ever had a child. Hard for me to believe that they wouldn't at least check it out. I think Joss had other contacts with the sister-in-law but they never met. So that whole side of the family never got to meet this wonderful person.

However, a number of years later Joss had a DNA test and her birth father's son Danny showed up with a match. That opened a new door to the other side of the family. Turns out her father was Leon Schneider and we think that he and Suzanne had an affair, and Joss was born.

That opened the door to a sensational group of people that were right here in New York City. When Joss contacted them they greeted her with open arms. One of the daughters of Leon, Elizabeth, had a house just 15 miles from us in The Hamptons.

Since then we have met a lot of the Schneiders. They are exceptional people and they love Joss. Who wouldn't.

She has another family. Yeah!

Josselyne's birth father, Leon Schneider

Perception
October 23, 2023

How did I become the person I am today? Oh my.
The first 40 years of my life, before I did the Est Training, I was really
focused on myself. The more stories I write about my life, that becomes
clearer and clearer. I thought I was such a good listener…but really most
of the time I listened through my own thoughts. My opinions. It is hard to
really be with people that way.

Today I read an article by David Brooks about his new book, which
will be coming out later this week. Of course, I ordered it on
Amazon. Terrible title…*How to Know a Person.* In part of the article
he labels two types of people. **The Diminishers** and **the Illuminators.**

The Diminishers are so into themselves that they tend to make
others feel insignificant. They stereotype and label others. They
make assumptions about people. They are smart rats.

The Illuminators have a persistent curiosity about others. They have
worked at understanding others. They respect others and have a
tendency to lite others up.

Guess which categories I was before and after 40.

So much of this came from my Roots as well. As I said my mother
gave me the basic understanding of who I would become. Never
an elite. More towards the "common side" of life. This was so
emphasized by my relationship with the two families as I grew up.
The Tannenbaums and the Hermans.

The Tannenbaums were romantics. They were truly interested in
your life. They listened, and were there to support you. Very little
judgment. The Herman's…all judgment. They truly fit the bill as
*Diminisher*s. They had an opinion about everything you did and
didn't do. They had assumptions based on those opinions.
Thank God I had the common sense not to follow their lead.

Writing this memoir has helped me see that I am a "common man." Nothing is elite about me or my life. I am only special to those who take the time to understand me. And that has become my goal… to find the special qualities in every person I meet.

My wife taught me that. She raised our children that way. They were always her best friends, and she never judged them. I started out like my dad. Knowing what was best for my children…until my son Bruce straightened me out.

One day in the heat of an argument…I yelled at him…"What the hell do you want from me?" He reached out and held my hand..

"I just want to know you are there for me when I need you."
He was 16.

I wish I had been that wise when I was 16. From that day on Bruce and I were committed to having our relationship blossom.

I have been blessed with many opportunities in my life. The great part is I have surrounded myself with people who supported me and encouraged me not to be afraid to fail. Time-after-time my wife has called the shots. My children have always supported us in sometimes really crazy shifts in our lives.

A few worth mentioning...

* Going from a *chemist* to a career in advertising without any background.

* Moving from a life in the city to the suburbs and then back in one year when we realized it was a mistake.

* At the age of 43, with two young kids, selling everything picking the family up and moving to LA to try my hand at the movie business.

* Having an affair with an icon movie star. After seeing the so called fame, realizing that family was the essence of life, not fame.

* After of separation in my marriage, taking responsibility for my being the reason we broke up. Transforming our married life after 15 years, so that we would be happily married for another 50 years.

* Leaving LA to open my first advertising agency, with no cash in my pocket.

* At the age of 72 selling everything and starting all over...as my wife labeled it..."repotting."

* Through it all...never losing sight of my North Star. I am an artist.

* Teaching art to kids and seniors at the age of 75.

* My first one man art show at the age of 80. Finally building my art studio of my dreams at the age of 89.

* And who knows what is next. I am 90 now.

* My wife and I have a 10 year plan, which includes some very exciting opportunities.

Time to ourselves, mostly.

I have resisted writing about our many, many vacations throughout our life. If it was up to this guy, I would not have taken half of them. After a few years married, my wife set up a separate bank account for traveling. It seemed that each year the amount we deposited was larger. Elaine was adamant that we see the world. She was so right. With the exception of Russia and South America we traveled everywhere.

When we loved a place we went back over-and-over. Florence, Paris and London, Lake Como, St. Barts, Positano and of course USA, especially Fire Island and Mass were visited many times each.

In fact, Elaine would often announce early in the week that she was going to London or Paris for the weekend, did I want to join her. Many times she went on her own. Elaine had a way of working it out with Joss and Amanda, too. She took Joss to Paris, Amanda the USA, especially Santa Fe. Now Joss and Mike are basically living in Paris and come home to visit us and their kids.

Why did we settle in on certain places? Each gave us a dimension of life that we wanted to explore. London taught us all about Vintage clothing and antiques. We went to so many auctions and shows there. Our collections enriched our lives. Sante Fe was a visit at least once or twice every year. We came to love the western culture. Many times we thought about living there for part of our lives. That never happened. But, Elaine opened her Three Little Indians in Mass to keep the connection alive.

We went to so many Islands during the winter. You name it, we probably visited it, including Mexico. However only Saint Barths became a place that taught us the value of the "easy life." This French, mountainous island was a rich combination of culture and beauty. Some of the best French food, and the beaches! One more beautiful than the next. It turns out we discovered it just before the world did. After going there a half dozen times it got too fancy, and too expensive. Basically they ruined a paradise.

BALI
Speaking of paradise…there is only one Bali. The people. The art. The culture was beyond description. And then they opened the Four Season and a half a dozen other fancy places. Our first visit we had a tented home with a fireplace and a small eating place next to a wading pool. Each night our helper would come in and light our fire and each morning our breakfast was waiting for us outside. The little birds would eat most of the fruit before we got there. It was a wonderland of peace. No TV, no entertainment which meant lots of reading and quite time to yourself. We knew this might end when we saw a sign…
ANTIQUES MADE TO ORDER.

LAKE COMO
Lake Como is by far one of the most special places we ever visited. Not far from the sophistication of Milan yet on one of the most beautiful lakes in the world…if you couldn't relax there you were in deep trouble. The food! Elaine and I enjoy Italian food much more than French. There is a certain honestly about their cooking. A great bowl of spaghetti, a salad, a simple desert with a local wine…you can't beat that. And yes, since this part of Italy is so close to the mountains of Switzerland that culture adds a dimension hard to find anywhere else we have traveled. For instance the pottery from that area is precious. We have so much of it in our kitchen today.

FLORENCE
I think we have visited Florence more than any other place in our travels. Of course Elaine visited it by herself first. She met a young man Allesandro on her first visit. He drove her everywhere. I figured there was more than just her limo there, but I was wrong. I think we have been to Florence more than any other place overseas. Yes, every time we go, Allesandro picks us up and takes us everywhere. He has become a very special friend. We have explored so many little towns around Florence. One special place is Lucca. Al introduced us to this family eating place in the heart of Lucca. Maybe the best food in the world. Sienna also became a great place to visit. One night we all got so drunk, including our driver, that the owner of the restaurant

had to take us back to Florence which is over an hour and a half away. The malls are Elaine's afternoon visits. The rich culture, art and museums are hard to match. The churches. The tiny towns surrounding this tourist city. Still untouched. I hope we have one more visit left in us.

EASTERN CULTURES

We fell in love with the Far Eastern cultures. **VIETNAM** is beyond description. So hard to believe that we fought these people. A war that almost destroyed a culture that is so rich in art. The people seemed so kind and caring. This country has been conquered over so many times that the conquered life stayed in place. Everywhere the Vietnam food is influenced by the French. A rich, sumptuous combination that is so delicious. You cannot get that food in America. They call it Vietnamese, but that is as far as it goes. We bought so many antiques in Vietnam. The art and jewelry are so special. The woman work and the men smoke. The woman run the country and the men take the credit. Our time there was unforgettable.

Because we loved Vietnam we went to **MYANMAR**, formerly Burma. I think Elaine had her first mini stroke there, but no one

knew what it was. Since she did not feel well I did most of the exploring of this country in conflict on my own. There was a deadly feeling throughout. I went down to the docks to see the water front. There were hundreds a people carrying 50 and 100 pound bags or rice on their skinny bodies. I was told later their rate for the day was $1 American dollar for a 12 hour day. There were military soldiers everywhere. The people were suppressed. Very scary. We flew out of there as soon as we could. I think we stayed 3 or 4 days in all. Turns out I was in jeopardy when I went to the docks. An American had been kidnapped the week before and no one knew where he was. Boy was I lucky.

Time to ourselves, mostly.

SOUTH AFRICA

A trip that was only once, but we would recommend it to everyone, was our trip to South Africa. It is a very long airplane trip. First you fly to London for 6 or 7 hours. Then you fly to Cape Town for another 14 hours. When we got there our room at the hotel would not be ready for 5 hours. We were so tired we lied down on a chase lounge and slept the day away. Exhausting but so well worth it.

The politics of South Africa are so complicated. There are 3 capitals, and Johannesburg is not one of them. Apartheid was present between 1948 and 1991. Most of the country is black, but for most of it's history white people were in power. The beach in Cape Town was about 2 miles wide. Yes two miles. The sands are almost pink and the water is so clear it almost looks white. When you see it for the first time it feels like you are in a dream.

We spent a great deal of our time in a Safari at the switz Forest Lodge. First class beyond belief. You had to stay in your glass cube house in the middle of the jungle during the day, all day. The temperatures at noon were around 120 degrees. If and when you went out a guard with a rifle had to take you to the dining room. You went on the safari at night and returned in the early morning around 5 or 6 AM. Had a first class breakfast and back to your house. During the day animals would come right up to the windows and look at you, like you looked at them at night. The safaris were unbelievable. You went out with the same two couple every evening. Six guests a driver and a guard who sat up front in a basket chair with a gun. The cars were 110 Defender Range Rovers which had their roof removed. It was like a convertible. We only stopped to see animals. Oh those animals. At night there were so many Lions and their mates and cubs. During dusk and daybreak hoards of running jaguars and leopards Giraffes, and herds of Elephants just to name a few.

I was amazed. Every once and a while you would slowly stop, and watch one animal tearing apart another. I was concerned that it would upset Elaine. To the contrary. She watched as the "survival of the fittest" played out. In the middle of the evening we would eat a large catered meal in the heart of the jungle. Paper bags with candles in them lite the way to the camp. It was all first class. The safaris were beyond description.

The last day I complained that we had not seen any elephants. Our guide got on the walkie talkie and within an hour we found about 20 elephants bathing in a giant pool of water. I asked if we could go closer. They accommodated me. **DON'T MOVE** the car came to a stop. **DO NOT MOVE** the guide shouted at us. Turns out we had driven into a herd of elephants. Our car was surrounded. One came up behind us, his tusks came over the top of the car. It turns out they are pretty blind. They can see shapes and only move to attack if the shapes move. It was all over in about 3 or 4 minutes, but it seemed like an eternity. How exciting.

The other two couples were both from Johannesburg. One guy and his wife were the biggest bakers in that city. He said they made 10,000 Croissants everyday. The other couple were just married. I had come on the trip with my right hand wrapped from surgery. It had almost lost two fingers on that hand when I got it caught in the prop of my Vintage J 3 Cub. I needed to have the stitches out. "I wonder how far the nearest hand surgeon is to take my stitches out." I asked since he was a local. "How about 12 inches," he replied. Yes, he was one of the best hand surgeons in South Africa. He took the stitches out that afternoon after breakfast.

And one last thing. Elaine was amazing on this trip. One night we all got drunk, and we had to pass a card around without using our hands. The card was in our mouths. You should have seen Elaine rolling around on the ground with this great looking guide. I wish I had taken pictures. She said she didn't remember anything the next morning. The guide was so good looking I would have gone for him.

By the way we also went to Victoria Falls…save your time. It is not worth going .

We went sometime after the apartheid was over, but you sensed the

Time to ourselves, mostly.

Phinda Forest Lodge in South Africa.

hostility was very present. Little remarks were made almost every time whites and blacks were together. The thing that struck Elaine and I was how fractionated the country was. There were more than a dozen different groups that fought for the right to be elected to their congress. The difference of each group often depended on the color of their skin. Yes they were all what we would say were black, but you could not use that word around them. They were browns, tans, and various other names. No one was called black. They were fighting politically all the time. Sad, they waited so long to run the country, and when we were there they were not succeeding, yet. I am not sure how it is today. My daughter Amanda went on vacation to the Lodge just a year or so ago, and she loved the experience as well.

SICILY
Another place that we always meant to go back to is Sicily. Special beyond belief. We went there many years ago, maybe 30 or so. But we recently recommended it to Sophie, my granddaughter and every place we told her to go was still extraordinary. Since we have been all over Italy it is tough to tell you why we loved it so much. We stayed in a very special hotel in San Domingo Palace in Taormina. It was at one time was a monastery for the Monks. Most of the rooms had a terrace that looked out over the Ionic Sea. It was surrounded by fruit and olive trees. You could pick the fruit off of the trees in the Italian

Gardens. The olives needed to be washed but they were special as well. We ate diners in the hotel. They featured Sicilian wines, which were very special.

But the best meal were eaten in the mountains. As you drove towards Mt Etna, there were many little towns off the beaten track. You might come upon a house at the top of one of the hills and ask if they were serving lunch. No menu. A bottle of water and a bottle of a wine, often from their vineyard were also placed on the table. The lunch was what ever they made that day. Usually started with a soup or salad, a bowl of pasta and some meat dish. Homemade pie and espresso coffee. Cost back then $10. Forget what it cost it was some of the best food we had ever eaten. The people were so friendly. We happen to go there during their Halloween. When we went to the local square downtown every child was in the same costume. They were all Zorro. Little kids dueling. Black capes, large white shirts, blacks hats and of course pencil like mustache. It was like being in a movie. So innocent, so wonderful.

We rented a 124 Fiat.
The smallest car they make. It was all they had to offer. We traveled half way up Mount Etna. I say half way, because we never made it to the top. At the bottom it was about 80 degrees that day, but half way up the mountain the road was covered with snow. We skidded and slid. And finally we could not go any further. There was only one road going up to the top and we were holding up all the traffic. I noticed a few of the cars had put on chains, and every one was honking.

What happened was hard to believe. About 6 big Italian brutes had us get out of the car and they lifted it up and turned the car around. So embarrassing. They picked the car up. Turned us around. We drove down the hill, but that little car a few days later saved our lives.

A life not cut short.

Like I said we rented a tiny 124 Fiat on our visit to Sicily. On the last day we decided to drive across the island and stay on the northern shoreline before flying out to Naples. As we were on our way we almost lost our lives.

We were traveling on the right side of the road and a giant 16 wheeler truck coming in the opposite direction made a sharp turn and came over into our side of the road. This is hard to believe but he was heading right towards us…I had no choice but to slide under his 16 wheels. That's right this tiny car slid under his wheels in the back. We came out the other side. It was not our time. Any other car would not have fit under the back of the truck. We were shook. We sat in the car for a few minutes, the truck driver had stopped to see if we were ok. He kept on bowing and shaking his head, like he didn't believe what happened. Neither did we.

We drove to the next town and got a cup of coffee. We both sat at the counter and started to shake. Elaine got on the phone and called the kids. We needed to make the connection. We needed to get home. No planes were leaving for Naples. We found out that the only way to get to the mainland was on an Italian tramp steamer that left that night and arrived in Naples the next day. No beds. You had to sit up all night. That's what we did. We sat part of the night in a smoke filled TV room that was showing Italian spaghetti westerns. Everyone was smoking. Everyone was Italian, obviously. What a night to remember. The next day we flew home. When we saw the kids it really hit us. We grabbed them and cried and cried.

It was not our time.

Obviously I love this picture!

A life not cut short.

IRELAND.

There was a time that Elaine and I decided to do a TV show…
Cook Around The World.
We were ahead of our time. There were no cable stations so there had never been a channel committed to food or travel. These were are two favorite things so we figured if we could sell the idea, someone else would pay for our vacations and great meals.

One of the first places we visited to do a demo was Ireland. Specifically we had heard about this incredible chef Myrtle Allen who had a cooking school and a restaurant and hotel called Ballymaloe. This was near the water in County Cork.

We rented a car and drove to the restaurant. Myrtle Allen said we should join her for lunch and she would show us around the kitchen. As we approached the building we noticed a number of people in various gardens around the building. We later found out that most of the vegetables and many of the herbs were grown on the grounds. Myrtle was one of the forerunner chefs that planned her menus around what was available from the earth or the sea that day.

What we were about to experience was one of the best meals we had ever eaten. We might say that about Paris or Florence, but Ireland?

She met us at the front gate and showed us around the grounds. Not only did she raise veggies, but we even saw fruit trees and a few olive trees as well. We really could have been in Sicily.

I forgot to mention what she looked like. Late fifty. She looked just like we imagined. Ruddy cheeks. Outdoor look. So healthy. She was wrapped in a white apron and wore a blue chambray shirt.

The restaurant only had about a dozen tables and all were filled already. Turns out there is a waiting list for lunch of about two or three weeks, and some months of the year you can't get in. They were serving a buffet that day. It is hard to remember specific dishes, but as we approached the long buffet table you could smell a sweetness in the air. Each dish was spectacular. Much of it came from the sea. The special of the day was stuffed crab on the shell. Myrtle told us not to miss that dish but welcomed us to taste as many dishes as possible before we would meet in the kitchen.

Every dish was light, yet seemed very rich. Small doses of the food was all that you needed. Elaine and I have traveled throughout the world, and we had to admit this meal was one to remember. What made the food so special? By the way, for desert we had a deep dish homemade apple crumb cake with heavy cream.

Myrtle showed us through the spotless kitchen and we sat outside to talk about her and the food as we sipped our coffee that Myrtle made for us personally. She did not want to talk much about herself but she gave us a book that had been written about her. We told her how much we were moved by the meal. I asked her the question that was so pressing on my mind.

"What makes your food so special?" I thought I would get a long answer. Instead she smiled and answered with one word. "Butter my dear…Butter!"

My favorite eggs à la Sophie

Whisk eggs well in a bowl and add small cubes of cold butter, don't be shy with the butter. Pour that mixture into a cold pan, and cook, stirring constantly with a rubber spatula on low heat. Continue stirring until you reach Baveuse (Baveuse is a French cooking term meaning moist, juicy, just a bit runny or undercooked). Turn the heat off and season with salt. Plate and top with chives, if desired.

love you
Sophie Saccio

MOROCCO

What an exotic trip. Fes and Marrakesh were the highlights of this trip. Watching young girls as young as seven years old, having their hands tattooed with vivid henna was the kind of visual excitement that set the tone for this trip.

The henna was so special. The mothers told us that the henna was a sign of good health, fertility and wisdom. It was put on their hands in anticipation of their marriage…and one of the favorite designs was birds…again a symbol of being a messenger between heaven and earth.

Even though it was over forty years ago some of the sights and events are as memorable as some things that happened just weeks ago.

Fes is a very old city with a unique Medina in the center.
We were told it is the oldest Medina in Africa. I believe it. The streets were very narrow, and they crossed and intersected each other. You could get lost just by taking the wrong turn. The story goes many people never returned from the Medina if they went without a guide.

The hotel set us up with a guide. He was a gentle giant. Wore a djellabas kaftan and a turban wrapped around his head. He couldn't do enough for us. He spoke broken English, but we took the time to tell him that we liked real antiques and older printed fabrics and exceptional traditional clothing.
He did not hesitate taking us to the Medina.

Stall after stall. He motioned to the ones he wanted us to see and the ones we should pass up. We soon figured that he might be getting a token payment whenever we purchased. So what Elaine said…and she was right. Turns out she was right. He had excellent taste and we filled our backpacks with item after item.

Mostly cloths and silver jewelry. He let us move around a lot on our own as well, but he was charmed by the fact that I would say to

Elaine…"Hon, look at this, and Hon isn't this perfect, and Hon come look at these…and Hon…that is what I call my wife most of the time when I am excited. At one point after watching us our guide waived at Elaine to show her a friend's stall…

He said "Hon, come with me, you will love this." For the next days as this wonderful gentle giant showed us the best places for jellabas and jewels and of course rugs…he would always waived to Elaine and say…"Over here hon." We never corrected him.

Marrakesh was mystical. Truly one special place. Where to start, there was so much to do and see. We exhausted ourselves after the first few days…and our hotel suggested we go to the Hammam.

Don't confuse this with a bath house. No this experience is like on other in our lives. They claim that when we have spent a few hours in a hammam besides having physical healing through out the body their will be spiritual rehabilitation. I thought it was over the top, but they were right.

We spent about four hours with a combination of heat, ice, water and massage, capped off with the whole body wash, including a shampoo for the scalp and then being wrapped like a baby in our own large room. No noise. No sounds at all. A deep sleep followed until they woke us. What an experience. You leave not feeling your body and an empty mind for now.

The following day or so was spent in their Medina. Much more organized. Sort of took the mystery away, but we bought some very special clothing there as well as in Fes.

The highlight of the trip was the trip across the Atlas Mountains. We hired a driver who spoke in simple phrases like he would point and say "Mountain," "Desert," "water." Before we crossed Atlas we traveled through part of the desert. I saw a group out on the fringe off the road and I asked our driver to stop. He did, but he shook his head no. What followed was total stupidity on my part. Elaine and I thought it might be a local bazaar, so I took my camera to take shots of the locals.

Within five minutes we knew we were in trouble. Two young men came running over and grabbed Elaine's arm. I stopped and did not touch him but yelled " leave my wife alone." They started to drag her back to a tent, I ran up to them and grabbed Elaine and freed her and we ran back to the car. The woman were all making this very weird sound. Turns out we were violating their privacy by taking pictures. Of course. The driver took off and we realized what a fool I had been.

It took us about two hours to drive to the base of the Atlas Mountains. It was summer and about 85 degrees because we were close to the desert. The Mercedes began to climb the mountain. It was winding roads and after about an hour and a half we arrived at about half way up. There was a small house there and within minutes we were surrounded by the most beautiful group of children. Maybe ten or more of them. Toasty brown complexion and their cheeks looked like they were wearing rouge. The whites of their eyes shined so bright against their skin. They looked so healthy. They lived high up in the Atlas range, and an adult there said that most of them had never been down to the base. We bought small treasures that they had carved out of branches. I forgot to say that they were bundled up with colorful woolen shawls. It was below freezing. The drive up the pass had taken us from 85 to 30 degrees in less than two hours. The top of the mountain was covered with sheets of heavy snow. This is where these children lived all year round. Can you imagine what it would be like in the winter. I took out a few books on the Atlas Mountains and it turned out that these children had a name…The Jalabus Children. The National Geographic had written many articles about them. Before that trip we never knew they existed.

We went through a private little house with a bedroom and living room and a porch looking up to the Atlas. It was hard to believe we had been there hours ago.

That night two men from central casting served us dinner in our room in front of a roaring fire. Both dressed head to toe in white their lean bodies shown through their kaftans. A bottle of local wine, iced water and a steak and salad if I remember right.

Elaine and I sat up in bed after the dinner. All of a sudden I noticed that she was crying. It was the children. We will never forget them.

Speaking of children.

One other small happening right outside the base of the mountain. There was a tiny village and they were selling mostly arts and crafts and silver jewelry. Within minutes 20 or more village children piled all over the car. It was so scary. They wrapped on the window and wanted money. A friend had warned us this might happen in the cities where poverty was rampant. He had given us high bouncing tiny rubber balls. I opened the window and through the tiny balls against the stone road. They bounced twenty and thirty feet into the air and the kids chased them instead of us. It was such a different experience with the Atlas Mountain children. They were poor but rich in life. They loved their lives you could tell. The village kids were in total survival. A lesson learned.

The next day we went to the village again.
This time the kids did not show up, instead the shop owners rushed the car shouting…"throw me the ball," "throw me the ball."

The Stroke.
August, 2005

Most days are just 24 hours. A few last a lifetime.

We had just moved into our new home in Hampton Bays. I was working upstairs in my new studio. It was small, but it gave me the opportunity to be serious about my painting. A place I could lay out all my paints ready for the next day.

And then it happened…I heard my wife crawling, yes crawling up the stairs. I thought she was playing a joke on me. She entered the door on all fours. Her face was contorted. She was having a stroke. All the signs were there. I sat her on the coach upstairs with me, and called Dr. Rogers. I said it was an emergency and he got on the phone. I tried to stay calm as I told him what had happened.

"Let her lie down and give her two Tylenol. She is probably over reacting to something."

I followed his instructions, but she got worse. A friend was staying with us that weekend and we finally piled her in the car. I had heard there was an injection called TPA that could dissolve the clot, but their was a time limit. We rushed her into Triage. They quickly confirmed it was a stroke. I tried to reach Rogers, he called back about a half hour later and he ordered the drug, I think just within the 4 hour limit. I think!

THE DAY THAT CHANGED OUR LIVES FOREVER.

One day your just cruising through life and the next everything changes forever. From a partner of 45 years, add a new role: caretaker.

How has it changed our lives over the past 18 years? A lot.
Forget the month at Rusk in New York City. I stayed at my brother Stan's apartment. At the hospital everyday for that time. All the fittings for leg braces. All the doctors appointments to check her

progress. No travel. No going out to dinners or lunches, at least not until she could walk again. Elaine had lost the use of her left arm and most of the mobility of her left leg. She walked with a cane or a walker. That's just the physical stuff. She was in a lot of pain from time to time, but through it all she never got negative. Never.

Thank God for our home in the Hamptons. We put in a chair lift, and put in hand bars wherever they were needed. I eventually built a new studio on the same level so that she could join me while I painted.

And to top it off, dementia kicked in five years ago. Elaine lost most of her teeth. That part has been pretty tough. Joss and her family have really put themselves out to help. Mandy too. Our five grandchildren have been very supportive, and so has my brother Stan. Our homes are only 15 minutes apart so we see each other every week. He usually buys us dinner one time per week and we eat it at home. We talk a few times every day. I am not sure if this would have happened.

Looking back…we were 72 and 74 pre stroke. Elaine is now 92 and I am 90. Stan is 95. I have been Elaine's caretaker all that time. We manage alone. So does Stan. Pretty amazing.
How would our lives been if the stroke didn't happen?

Very different. Better? I am not so sure. I learned a lot about my self over the last 18 years. I am a better husband and by far a better Dad and Grand Dad. Elaine and Stan talk every morning. They are very close. She considers him her boyfriend some days, and others her brother.

My value system has changed. Family and painting have been strengthened. My True North. The time with my great wife has actually improved as well. She is truly amazing. She drags that body around and hardly ever complains. She is as healthy as can be. If it wasn't for that day and the stroke, I doubt if I could keep up with her. We have made the best out of a pretty challenging situation.
Do I wish the stroke had never happened? Of course.
But life goes on. Each day is a gift.

EGYPT AND ISRAEL

Loved Egypt. Not so much Israel.

ISRAEL.

Sure we were moved at the wall. And because we are Jewish we looked for all the ways we could support this country that never got started right back in 1948. A country so divided and confused. It was clear that a two state solution would never happen, even back then thirty five years ago when we visited there.

They seem to always be at war. And the people seemed so arrogant. They obviously needed to be strong. They were surrounded by what they called the enemy. The children knew nothing but war and survival. What a way to live.

As I write today…Israel and Hamas are at war, again. A war that neither can win. Israel must get rid of their enemy Hamas. In doing this many people have turned against them because their solution is not working…tens of thousands of civilians, especially children have died. Hamas ravaged Israel. Killing 1200 people. Raping woman and taking over 200 hostages to who knows where. Truly an atrocity, and Hamas says they will do it again until Israel does not exist.

Biden is doing his best, but the leadership of Israel is all wrong and their solutions are blind to the need of the Palestinians. We saw a bit of this when we visited an eternity ago.

The tensions existed then, and have only gotten worse over time

EGYPT

We fell in love with this country when we visited there about forty years ago. The pyramids. The temples. The kind people, back then.

We stayed in a very special hotel, The Mena House right in the desert. The pyramids were right next to the hotel. We remember their buffet lunches. The table was over 30 feet long, filled with special dishes. Every day the food was different. Elaine would never miss it.

Talk about the pyramids. Words can not do them justice. They truly are a wonder. When the sun set on them, the simplicity of their shapes made you cry.

One morning I decided to run out to the desert and run around the pyramids. I was a long distance runner then, and I was training for my next marathon. What a special run this would be. I got near the first pyramid and a strange feeling came over me. I realized I was out in the desert and no one knew I was there.

Suddenly a car approached from the opposite direction. My sixth sense told me to turn around and head back to the hotel. I was right. The car had 4 or 5 young men in it. They were stealing pigeons and then they noticed me. I took off and made it back to the hotel . When the concierge saw me in my running cloths, he asked where I had been. He told me I was crazy. There had been two kidnapping that month. Another stupid Herman episode.

The dessert was intriguing to Elaine and I. One day we hired a guide and we all rode out into the desert on our horses. That's right we rented horses and a guide to help us ride safely in the desert. I was an excellent rider and Elaine could hold her own. When the guide saw I could ride, he said go for it. I did my Lawrence of Arabia. I felt like Peter O'Toole as I galloped over the dunes. Pure freedom. Never forgot that experience. Wonderland.

When I returned I overheard Elaine negotiating for the purchase of our guides turban. A long white soft fabric wrapped around his dark skinned head. He delivered one to the hotel the next morning. Leave it to Elaine. Shopping in the dessert. Nothing stops her.

The Temple Karnak. This is the largest temple in the world. They say it is the largest religious building ever made. I believe it. There are many temples along the Nile, but none competes with this world famous edifice.

When you enter you pass down an avenue with two rows of Ram headed Sphinxes. They symbolize the god of Amun. You soon enter into the most dramatic room. There are over 130 columns. They are close to a hundred feet tall. They are each carved with the heads of kings. And they are all stone. How did they do it? How did they build these columns? By hand. How did they get them to stand up? They dug a hole and slowly moved the base of the column into the hole by building a wall that would eventually hold the column straight up in place. What? Each column was build that way. It took our breaths away. No other place like this in the whole world. What a feat. I asked how long it took to build this masterpiece?

The answer....over 2000 years.
That's a good job, right!

Like father like daughter.

Amanda runs one of her Marathons with Irv.

Our trip across America.

Elaine had an idea. "Let's tour the country"! We had been all over the country. What did she mean?

"Let's tour the country by stopping at every Ralph Lauren Outlet." Hello…Earth calling Elaine I said.

I am a pilot. We had a small plane. A Piper Archer. It cruised at around 100 miles per hour. Pretty slow, but better than a car. Why not try it. I needed to take off 3 weeks. Spoke to Charlie and it worked it out with him. Elaine called a Ralph Lauren store and got a list of all his outlets across the country.

Yes we flew across and ended the first part of our trip in Spokane Washington after zig zagging across the USA. Our daughter Amanda lived there. We spent about a week and headed back home. There were a few special places. Redding, Pa. They had so many things sent from the New York City store. Back then they were real outlets. Today they manufacture for the outlets. Hardly any bargains. In Redding I found a three piece striped seersucker suit that I always wanted. It was in Ralph's favorite brown with a vest and all. In NY I remember it selling retail for around $300. Too much for me. They had one suit in my size. Thirty two dollars. Yes those were the days. I wore that suit for many meetings at my ad agency. Always with a bow tie and a expensive English cuff link shirt. I looked like a real ad man.

These were the kind of bargains you could find. We filled up the plane and eventually had to send back some of the cloths to make sure our little plane was not over weight.

Another great Ralph was in Steamboat Springs, Colorado. We loaded up on outerwear. I still have some of the jackets. Today I can really call them Vintage. Again they cost 10 percent of retail, usually.

But the best of the best was in a truly unexpected place. Valdosta, Georgia, just north of the boarder of Florida. We bought the place out. T shirts that were pure lightweight cotton were normally $25 back then…your choice $1. I think we bought every color. Walking shorts for $3. Nylon outerwear for $5. I think we spent a couple hundred dollars and had to send the bags home UPS.

And, the highlight was after shopping we went to a local place for lunch that our sales woman at Ralphs recommended, and she gave us a card to get 20% off. What a lunch. Hard to describe. They had a buffet. All you could eat for $5. There must have been 30 different vegetables. All home made. No kidding. Every table had a family munching away, going back and forth for refills.

There was one group in the back where we sat that had nine children with a mom at the head of the table. She was blond and slim and beautiful, and all the kids were the same. Ralph would have loved that family. Here's the thing…Elaine and I never forgot that family…They were so well behave. No arguing just helping each other. The mother let them do their thing. No bossing around. Each kid took care of another kid. Dad showed up when they were almost over. Hugs and kisses all around. We couldn't help ourselves. We spoke to the mom and dad.

"Are these all your kids?"
Yes. "How do you get them to be so great together?"

She smiled and answered. "Tough love."

We always had one.

My daughter Joss reminded me of something. We always had at least one dog. With me it started with a wonderful mutt Bongo. I have written a few stories about him. But we had so many other dogs and they played a very important role in our lives.

There was Elaine's *Corky*. A nut beyond belief. She got him when we first met. I had a wire hair terrier so Elaine got one as well. They were both pretty crazy dogs. When we adopted Joss, *Corky* would steal her cloths and take them under the bed. You could not get her out until she ripped either her diaper or her cloths into shreds. That was our last wire hair terrier.

Then there was *Ibura*. A 125 pound Rhodesian Ridgeback. She was so beautiful. We had just moved to the suburbs and it was Elaine's idea to have a large dog to protect her if I came home late from work. The dog was so sweet, but she didn't know she was big. Problem came when she would see Joss, who was about 3 at that time, she would run across to greet her and knock her over and cover her with kisses. She would also pounce on the bed in the morning to say hello to Elaine. One too many of those love leaps. Elaine got rid of him within months.

And then there was *the runt*. Can't remember his name. We got him when Elaine and I first got married. He was wire hair terrier pup. The ugliest puppy you have ever seen. Bruce picked him out. When we asked why he picked him, he said…. "nobody would want him." He was right, and also pretty crazy, too. One day we were playing with the pup in our bedroom. We had a very small window above our bed. This dog just jumped out the window…as he jumped I caught him by his back legs, and pulled him in. By the way we lived on the twelve floor. Bad, real bad. Oh, by the way when this dog saw babies he would grab the baby by the ass and we had a tough time getting him to leave go. We put an ad in a suburban paper and gave the dog away for free. We explained how terrible the dog was, but this couple said they were very experienced with dogs and took him. Two weeks later they called…the dog jumped out of a window in our home and bit the mailman. Do you want him back? Sure.

There were a couple of other dogs that we loved. *Gin Gin* was a yellow lab. Maybe the best dog we ever had. Lovable. Smart. We had her for 15 years. It was really Amanda's dog. She would use her as a pillow all the time, and *Gin Gin* would never complain. She would not die. She had cancer, we took one of her eyes out. Amanda would not let us put her down. The vet took her and Mandy would go to see her each night. Big kisses and love when she saw Amanda. The vet insisted that Amanda not come for two nights. She passed the second night. The best, really.

Amelia was our first exotic dog…a PBGV. A Petite Basset Griffon Vendeen. We were looking to replace *Gin Gin.* Elaine and I went to the Westminster Dog Show at Madison Square Garden. They have over 200 breeds in the basement. She went around one way, I went the other. When we met Elaine said she fell in love with one breed that she did not know much about…I said I loved one also. Turns out it was the same dog, the same breeder. It was a PBGV. The breeder did not have any dogs for sale, but she knew of one in California. We called and they had a 6 month bitch that they were going to show, but she did not work out, so they wanted to know if we would be interested. She sent us a few polaroids and we fell in love. A week later we picked *Amelia* up at Newark airport. I got down on the floor to take her out of her shipping cage and she ran to me and did not stop kissing me . It was love at first sight.

This breed was wonderful. Short legs, long ears, curly coat, *Amelia* was a tri-color white, black and brown. She was a love boat. Only one problem with the breed…they were runners. We had a country house in Sheffield, Mass and we had a lot of land. *Amelia* would break through the screen doors to roam the land. One day she got hit by a car and that was the end. So sad. The story doesn't end there.

We went to a show in London where this breed was started, and much

We always had one.

to our surprise they had PBGV but they also had a big version of our 45 pound dog. A GBGV. A Grand Basset. Gorgeous. They weighed in at almost twice the size. We met a breeder there...Vivian and we went to her kennel about 50 miles outside of London. She had one guy left from the latest litter. When she found out we lived in an apartment in NYC she would not sell him to us. It took a number of calls and a promise that we would keep *Alfie* (what we decided to call him) in the country. Then another trip to London. The only condition was if it didn't work out, she would take the dog back. *Alfie* was not the smartest dog, but he lived for over 15 years, and gave us so much joy. Vivian was so great we ended up getting two more GBGV's from her...*Lola* and *Lucas*.. Really tough breed in so many ways. *Lucas* died from a heart attack at 10 years and we still love and own *Lola*. When she goes we will get a mutt like *Bongo* at the shelter we think. No more fancy dogs.

By the way *Alfie* was the second or third of that breed in America. That was about 22 years ago. This year our breed won Westminster as the best breed. Talk about life being circular.

We had two Yorkies. *Max* which we had for 17 years. I bought her when Elaine and I were separated. She weighed 3 pounds. I took her home with Joss in giant container, and Joss promised she would walk and feed her. Really. That never happened.

Turns our Joss is not a dog person. She had two of her own, but never really trained them. They pretty much were taken care of by the kids or her husband Mike. She ended up with another Yorkie, *Izzi*.

About 5 years ago, Joss went away on vacation and left *Izzi* with us for two weeks. We still have this little 15 year old. Cries all the time, and fights with her food, but I have to admit I have come to love her.

That's it so far on the dogs...

We always had one.

There is only one Paris.

Elaine started this one. When Joss was 16 she started taking her to Paris. She fell in love with it. Year after year we would go over there. The city is like no other. There is no city I have ever been to that is designed for form and beauty. No mater what area you are in there are streets that belong in museums. The design of the architecture is wondrous. And where else can you have croissants and coffee on any corner that is perfect. The bread, still one dollar for a giant baguette that you can not get in the states. I personally like Italian food better, but I doubt if I have ever tasted a finer stew than in Paris. And the sweets! Forget it. I can't figure out why their sweets are so perfect. And the Challas. Nothing compares to its flavor. As much as I Iove going to that fine city, my daughter and her hubby can't live without it.

This May they rented an apartment and are pretty much living there full time. They come to the states every 7 or 8 weeks for a couple of weeks, and then back to their new home. I have never seen such joy in their lifestyle. Even Michael who is beyond a workaholic has transformed his style of living and is in heaven. And their three kids are doing so well.

**It truly is a dream come true.
So great.**

There is only one Paris.

Let's do it again.

I had my 90th birthday August 22nd, about 2 months ago. I was so special. One of the people who came is a friend of 43 years, Bob Hillman. Bob showed me his tattoo on his right arm. He wrote all of the eyewear companies that he basically started. The tattoo ran from his shoulder down to the bend in his arm. A lot of companies, and the fun part, I was involved with him, with most of the over the past 40 plus years.

I met Bob in 1980. He had opened a eyewear store in Paramus, New Jersey. It was a very special store. Ten thousand square feet of very unique eyewear. A lab, an exam area. It was like no other eyewear store. He sat with his partner Larry in the lower area, like a basement. I liked him right off the bat. We had a very hot ad agency then, and I wasn't sure these two guys could pull off opening a chain. After an hours conversation I changed my mind.

It turns out Hillman showed me through the lab and he said something I will never forget…he said that he could make most glasses in less than an hour. Most lens's were stocked in the wall. All he had to do is fit them into a frame. Up until then you got an eye exam, picked out a pair of glasses and usually waited a week or more to get your finished pair. That was it. Talk about sitting on a gold mine. We put the lab in the front of the stores and people could watch their glasses be made in less than an hour. It changed the eyewear business overnight. Really.

That was Eyelab. I help them build 4 or 5 stores, and Quaker Oats decided to go into retail and bought Eyelab from Bob and Larry. Bob was only 29 then, but he was a millionaire over night. They kept Bob on as a consultant. I remember they put him in a little office and there was a big computer on his desk. I asked him if he knew how to work it…he shook his head no.

Paul Price from Quaker said he would test our campaign against his big agency. We won every time. Our campaign which included a TV commercial showing wire animation of a store that comes to life…

with the copy…someday there will be an eyewear store that can make glasses in an hour…someday is today at Eyelab and the store would come to life visually.

That commercial plus a full color mailer of 16 pages was the perfect campaign. We ran it for 3 years and opened 40 more Eyelabs. All successful. Then like most big companies, Quaker sold Eyelab for almost 50 million dollars, and I was out of an account.

About a year later I get a call from Hillman…"Let's do it again. They never had me sign a non-compete."
We opened Hillman Eyes and that was so much fun. Long story short we built 4 or 5 stores and they were all big hits. We broke the mold by featuring designer eyewear and had a chart with all are competitors prices…ours was always the lowest. Big idea. We had life size blow ups of Bob Hillman in the front of every store. We made a giant fold out mailer that was sent to tens of thousands of people and Hillman Eyes was off and running. When we opened in White Plains we got Don Mattingly from the New York Yankees to come to the opening. They called me two hours before we opened to come up…the traffic was around the block.

We had the Midas touch back then. Hillman Eyes also got sold and Bob and I were figuring out what could be next.

Let's do it again.

China, of course.

It was Bob's idea of course. He had been going back and forth to China for years. Most of the product for the stores came from there. He knew that country way before a lot of Americans did.

Why not open stores there? Let's do it again.
Bob said he would meet us in Hong Kong. Go to the Regent and look for the guy behind the front desk with P3's. That was a style we had made for many years.
This was a giant glass hotel overlooking the water. Sure enough when I got there all of the guys were wearing his P3's. I handed one my passport with a $20 bill in it as Bob had suggested.
"No need for the $20 Mr. Herman…we will give you a high room overlooking the water." He took the $20 anyway. So much for payoffs. But it did not end there. Everyone seemed to have three hands in China. Two for themselves and the other was for doing business.

Our first store was to be opened in Beijing. We stayed at the best hotel The Sofitel. Every morning the farmers would ride their bikes into town with their vegetables on the back of the bike around 6AM. They were lay all their veggies on the floor for about an hour. Sell out by 7AM and then there was ball room dancing with the farmers in the square for the next hour. At the same time you could get a haircut and watch the dancers. It was so third world. Almost 40 years ago. Never forget it.

When we got to Beijing the store was to be finished. It was hardly started. Over the next 3 weeks the whole building and our store was finished. Must have been hundreds of workers. They put up bamboo hoarding all around the building. Each worker had a different color hard hat. Like Electrical was yellow, plumbing blue, etc. They worked around the clock. Two shifts 24 hours a day. From far away the building looked like ants with colored helmets were crawling all over the bamboo.

The store was pretty big, 2 levels about 4000 square feet. Big full color towers with pictures of eyewear, never seen before in China. We opened to mobs of people. Within a week we were on target for the year.

And then it happened. We came to work and the whole store was emptied and put on road in front of the store. They closed us down. A local Chinese company was given the space, and they offered Bob a new location. Turns out they did the same thing with McDonalds. They had the largest McDonalds in the world. The average Mac that we have in America would have about 5 check out stations. This one had 30. It was doing so much business the Chinese couldn't stand an American company doing better than a Chinese company, so one Sunday they knocked the McDonalds down and rebuilt it for a Chinese company. I am not making it up.

That was Bejing. We moved on to Shanghai. At the time there were over 25 million people living there. We changed everything. I decided we should open stores with a new name.

America's Eyes.

Grey advertising in China told Bob it was a terrible idea. The Chinese hated the Americans. We talked it over and Bob said he agreed with me and that is how America's Eyes was born. I was going to use an American flag like Ralph Lauren for the logo, but changed my mind.

From the day that we opened it was a giant success. Bob had taken on a Chinese partner so they let us do our thing. Finally got smart. I did a whole new campaign featuring Hillman throughout the stores, showing all the successes in America. The Chinese loved it. Hillman became a hero.

I will never forget the first month that I got my fee. I was back in the states and I got a fake Louis Vuitton® briefcase in the mail. When I opened it there was a package wrapped in Chinese newspaper. It was 40,000 rem and bees. There were 8 R&B's to a dollar. My monthly fee in Chinese cash. I called them and said I could not work this way. They told me everything was done in cash only. Bob confirmed. So I finally convinced my bank to turn the cash into dollars. Crazy again.

America's Eyes became the second largest eyewear chain in China. Still is today. They used my campaign to open 27 more stores. However after the first year they stopped paying me. I had a five year contract, but when I complained they said they liked the work and did not need me anymore. Thank you. Sue me. That was my almost last taste of China.

A Chinese company asked me to design and build a giant, 30,000 sq ft. Exhibit for a big trade show in Shanghai. OK, but I collected the fee up front. When I showed them the design they laughed at me. I only had 4 desk areas for their salespeople. They wanted 12 offices with doors on them and one giant office about 25 feet tall. OK. It was a weekend show. At the end the president of the company shook my hand and thanked me and then he took me too the large room up front. When we opened the door it was filled with black garbage bags, floor to ceiling. What do you think was in the bags? All cash. All cash. That was my last dealing with the Chinese. As I write this all I can think about is how dangerous their culture seems to be. And the was 40 years ago.

You know Bob and I went on to open the first Ready Readers company. We opened a company called HplusH. We financed it ourselves. It became a cottage industry not a company that it should have been. I actually went on QVC with the readers. It was fun, and in the beginning pretty successful. We got some glasses into Department stores also. Saks Fifth Avenue and a few other stores. Had Jeffery Banks design tartan frames. Did a lot of the right things, but it never took off. We made some money, but two young guys beat us in our own game. Warby Parker cornered the market and did a much better job than we did. In the end we closed it down and donated about $200,000 in product to third world countries for people that could not afford eyeglasses. In all it was a fun project. Even got my son-in-law Michael to actually run all the inventory. He actually ran the company. He was priceless.

Here's the thing about my relationship with Bob. Through all of our companies we never had paper or contracts between us. We trusted each other. To this day I feel the same about him and his need to be in the eyewear business. Last year he bought out a 20 year old company…Fabulous Fanny's in New York City. They have some of the very best vintage, I mean real vintage eyewear anywhere. It is in his blood. He knows product better than anyone I have ever met. Whatever I can do to help him, I will be there.

But if he were to say… "Let's do it again Harvey." I am pretty sure the answer will be thanks, but no thanks, Bob.

Our honeymoon
1963

How stupid can you get Herman. It only took you five years and finding an
apartment to get married. Where do you go on your honeymoon?
Bar Harbor, Maine.

It should be called Barren Harbor. I rented a tiny cottage on the
beach. It was away from everything. The beach was so rocky that you
could not walk on it. Forget swimming. The cottage was called The
Thimble. It looked so cute in the pictures. It was down right ugly.

On the second day there I asked Elaine…"How do you like Bar
Harbor?" She asked me if I liked it. I told her I hated it. She was
honest and told me that it was terrible. We had paid for 10 days, and
left after just two. The lobsters along the roadside were great. The
people were pretty good too. That was it for Bar Harbor.

We got in the car and drove down to our favorite place, Massachusetts.
I think we stayed at the Lee Cabins again. Ate at some wonderful
restaurants in Great Barrington. We were meant to be there.
We have traveled almost everywhere in the USA…
but nothing ever talked to us like Sheffield, Mass.

Our honeymoon 1963

Money, just follow it.
November 12, 2023

Elaine was a great rider.

I put in the specific date because it relates to this morning when I read the review for Barbara Streisand's memoir in the New York Times. And last night Sophie and David, Sage and I got into a series of stories that all focused on Money or the meaning of it at the time. When things happen I very rarely had a perspective on how they were connected. But now as Barbara says in her memoir, all of a sudden events that seem to be unrelated are not.

Time gives you the distance to see the patterns in life sometimes.

Leon and Rose Herman and their grandchildren.

A dollars worth of nickels!
1945

The whole Herman family worked on weekends in Herman Brothers Silk Shop. My father, Sidney, was the oldest boy of the seven brothers. My aunt Anna was the only girl in the bunch. And my grandmother Rose, who was about four foot eleven sat at the cash register and checked every receipt for addition. None of the brothers were very good at adding and subtracting except my dad. She made sure every penny was accounted for as her feet dangled in the air as she held court while on her high chair.

My brother Stan and I worked in the pattern department. Vogue, Simplicity, Advance, Butterick were just a few patterns that we carried. Woman would sit on a long table and pattern books were opened to many designs. The ladies would carefully turn each page until they fell in love. "Look at this dress. Isn't it perfect!"

They would write down the pattern number and bring it to either Stan or myself or Jean who worked there as well. (*By the way Jean who was 10 years older than me became one of my first sexual flings in life.)File cabinets were lined up on every wall. We would search for the specific pattern and then ring it up and call one of my uncles who would lead the customer out into the store to find the perfect fabric to fit the design. Eventually they let Stan and I work with the customers…especially when we were very busy.

The store had many tables filled with rolls and rolls of fabric. Cottons and satins, velours and velvets. Prints and solids. Thousands of choices. What to choose? That was the fun part. You would open a roll and the customers would either swoon over it or reject each choice. Once chosen we would measure out 3 or 4 yards enough for their dress. There was a yard stick on every table.

Then we picked out zippers, buttons and thread to match. We helped design their treasures. Then we had to write up the order on a small pad. One copy to Grandma Rose. At the end of the day we had to meet with her and she would review each sheet and order with us. If the math was wrong she would deduct the mistake from my $5 per day salary. If I overcharged she kept the difference. Here's the thing. I could understand her doing this with me..I was a kid…but she did it with each of my uncles too. How embarrassing. She was tough. She never smiled or had fun. She expected perfection all the time. And god forbid you did anything to improve her system!!!!!!

As an example, one day it was pouring and business was very slow. I had an idea. I took 20 nickels out of the cash register and figured I would put the dollar back at the end of the day. All even, I thought. I walked up and down Monroe Street. If a meter was about to run out I put a nickel in and put a card on the window by the door.

"Your meter was about to run out so we put a nickel in.
Compliments of Herman Brothers Silk shop."
My idea.

About an hour later a lady came in with the card in her hand and went over to Granda Rose to thank her. She then proceeded over to pick out a pattern and ended up being a pretty nice sale. I was so thrilled I went over to Grandma so proud and told what I had done. She called on the house phone, and my dad came down.

"Harvey went into the cash register and took a dollar out."
No mention of the card or the lady.
I have to admit my dad handled it very well. He took me aside and when I told him what I had done, he smiled…and said…
"Always ask."
"Never do it on your own." A harbinger of things to come.

A dollars worth of nickels! 1945

Door to door.
1950

I was in my senior year of high school. I never had money. I needed a summer job. Oh what to do. I heard that Life magazine was hiring part time sales people to go door to door selling Life in Newark, New Jersey. Why not.

It was a pretty good offer. If you bought Life for three years they would give you Colliers, and The Saturday Evening Post, two more mags for free.

As a sales person, our manager would drive us to a block…drop us off, and then you were on your own. Five or six hours later they would pick you upon the same corner that they started that day.

I schlepped to door-after-door-after-door for hours on end. Took half hour off for lunch. More doors and more doors. In the first 3 days zero. It was a commission job. No sales. No money. I was going to quit but I had a brainstorm.

You got to understand…each order was worth $36 in commissions. The week that followed I wrote on average 2 orders per day. $72 in commissions. The next week 4 orders per day. And that continued for the eight weeks that I worked there. I was the top part time salesperson! Everybody thought I was doing something illegal . But each order at the end of each day was confirmed by my sales manager. They were all good. What had I done?

First I have to admit I was a real cute guy at 17. And I dressed so great each day. And almost every sale was made with a woman. What was my secret? Why was I so successful? Listen to what I came up with.

Each day, after they dropped me off I would go to the local news stand and buy 3 or 4 copies of each Life, Colliers and Saturday Evening Post. My out of pocket investment. I would walk to a door.

Ring the bell and if it was a woman, I would smile a cute smile and put all three of the magazines in the woman's hands and turn and walk away. Most of the times this is what happened.

"Wait, what are these magazines," or something like that.

"Do you have a local newspaper delivered to you daily, well starting this month if you buy Life Magazine you'll get the other two magazines absolutely free." I would answer, and I would start to walk away again.

At that point they either closed the door and I was out the magazines…but enough of the time it was something like…

"You mean if I buy Life I really get the other two free?"

I would say…"Yes, and they are delivered right to your door each week just like your local newspaper."

That was it. I signed them up for three years. It worked a lot of the time. Like I said, I lost a few sets of mags each day, but in the end I made over $5000 that summer in commissions.

The free mags did it time after time. My sales manager couldn't figure out my method, so at the end of the summer he pleaded with me to tell him my secret.

I sold the idea to my sales manager for $500 when I left.

I don't think he was cute enough.

So much in Sweden
1977

When shooting the Sindy film for Marx Toys, one of the countries that we traveled to was Sweden. So many important events happened in that country.

I had never been to this part of the world before. It was summer and what I could not get used to was the length of sunlight each day. There was only about 2 or 3 hours of darkness, the rest of the day was daylight.

It was a nocturnal world. Weird. It meant that most people there sleep very little. That helped to understand what seemed to be a curtness or the very short sentences of the people. It made them feel cold to me.

As I describe more fully in another story, we only spent seven days in each country. Travel. Settle in, pre-pro the first day with a pick up crew, except for Bob Steadman, my cameraman. Location next day. Shoot two days and the next two days vacation with my daughters and Bob's two daughters, too. We were both separated from our wives then. Travel the last day.

Sweden was are next to last country, so we had the shoots pretty well organized. When we arrived at each country a limo would pick us up. My kids got used to that luxury right away. Especially Amanda. When we landed in Sweden there was no limo, just a stretch Volvo. "Where's the limo" out of the mouth of Amanda. She was six at the time.

We got to the production office and "thunderbolt." The production manager for the shoot blew me away. She was beautiful. Blond. Middle age like me, in her forties. We were going to spend the next week together. How was I going to handle this, without screwing up, again. Yes, Elaine and I were separated, but I needed to focus on the shoot.

The shoot went well. The nights that I checked the footage, I spent with her alone. She was not happily married. We talked about my life with Elaine, and what caused us to separate after fourteen years of marriage. She was considering leaving her husband. She also had two daughters. She was so vulnerable and at the same time searching for a lot of answers. I can't even remember her name. That's what is so amazing. We got very close through our talks about life, hugs, kisses and no sex. Pretty amazing for me. Intimacy was so important for both of us at the time. She made me think a lot about how intimate Elaine and I had always been, even during the tough times.

We exchanged info and believe it or not she and I wrote to each other for a number of months. She was still thinking of leaving her husband. At one point we even discussed the possibility of us together.
Then it stopped.

CUT TO 5 YEARS LATER.

Elaine and I and the kids are staying in London in a small hotel off of Sloane Street, and who is there…*my Swedish love.*

I told my beautiful wife about my Swedish connection. I told her that I had never really forgotten that relationship. Her response. "I think you should have coffee with her." Wise wife.

We had coffee. She was very open. She thanked me for our time together, and I did the same. It was so great to be together after all those years. She stayed with her husband as I did with Elaine.

Like I said, I do not even remember my Swedish woman's name, but that chance relationship had us both get in touch with what we had lost in our very special marriages.

The Georg Jensen Doors.
1980

When the famous silversmith Georg Jensen moved from Fifth Avenue to Madison Ave. They put up these 14 foot wide doors for the entrance to the new store. Many articles, pro and con had been written about them. They were made out pewter and carried the Jensen logo across the whole opening. So impressive.

Jensen is a Swedish company and is still in business today. The problem was when you left and opened these massive doors they could hit into people that were standing outside the store. In any case many articles were written about them. They became famous.

About five years later Jensen ran into financial problems and they chose to close the Madison Avenue store. One day, on my lunch break, I walked by the store and 4 burley guys were lifting each door off their hinges and walking them to the back wall of the store. A sight that was hard to believe. They were emptying all the lighting fixtures and display cases too. Two seedy looking guys were sitting in the center of the store and checking off everything as it was moved to the back.

I entered and introduced myself. Don't ask me why. I made up my mind that I was going to own those doors. It started with small talk. And then I realized these two guys had purchased all the fixtures including the doors. Our office was right around the corner just 2 blocks away. I asked Charlie to bring down a couple of blank checks to the Jensen store. When he got there and I told him what my plan was, he said I was crazy and he left.

It took me over four hours of conversation. Starting with the doors belonged in a museum ending with what are you going to do with them. I will take them off your hands and they will be out of your store tomorrow. A few minutes before five I presented them with a check for $2500 and the doors were ours.

A day later a moving company had them installed in our offices at 59th and Park. I think it cost almost as much as the doors to move and install them. Charlie couldn't believe that I got them for $2500. He said...."I pay more than that for my suits."

Georg Jensen's doors.

We loved those doors for a lot of years, but we moved to larger offices in The Kaufman Astoria Studios in Queens and I decided to put them up for sale. Christies, the famous auction house came up to look them over and said they thought they would sell for between $150,000 to $200,000 and they would move them at their own expense. But they would only sell them with a no reserve, because they did not want to send them back. I agreed. At one point they were considering putting them on the cover of the catalogue, but it did not happen.

I was so excited that day. They had displayed the doors near the entrance and people were surrounding the doors. Touching them, and looking at them with such love. Just like a piece of art, which they were.

When they started, the first bid was $7500. And that was it. No one bid on these famous doors. They sold for $7500. Is there a pattern emerging here? Remember the silver saddle.

The Georg Jensen Doors. 1980

The silver saddle.

My dad called me one day. He was so excited. Turns out a good friend of his was short on cash and owned two silver saddles. He wanted $1500 for both and my dad bought them for me. That's right he said that they would look so good with my furnishings.

This was around 1979. We had just moved into 19 East 88th Street and he was so right. The whole apartment was Art Deco. And, silver saddles would make the living room. It took us a few months to move in and get the apartment set up. I called my dad and said I could come out next weekend and pick up the saddles. I had a special place for both of them.

"I's only one saddle now," my dad said. He had sold one of the two saddles for the $1500 he paid for both. He got his money back.
Oh well, it was a gift.

I picked it up that weekend. What a saddle. The whole saddle was covered with pure silver Indian heads. Even the bridle and the martingale were covered in silver. The boot holders were covered in the silver heads. It was sensational. I bought a saddle holder stand from Millers saddler, and had it painted matte black.

The saddle was just stunning sitting in our living room with all the art deco furniture. I loved in for almost ten years, and then paid about $3000 to have some of the leather replaced and repaired. It needed that work to keep it special. About a year later I decided it was time to sell it. We needed the money. The market was hot, so I called a dealer in Santa Fe and after seeing pictures he said he would give me $25,000 or he could put it up for auction with no reserve. I was happy to get the $25,000. The dealer was so pleased as well. He had bought it sight unseen, which was pretty rare for the price of the item, but he loved it and thanked me.

About a year and a half later I noticed in the Antique Bee paper that we got each week that there was a giant auction in Santa Fe.
The listing was long and the estimates seemed out of site. And there she was, our saddle. No mistaking. There could not be two saddles

like this one in the world. I called the dealer I had sold it to, and he confirmed it was our saddle. The estimate in the catalogue was $25,000 to $50,000. Oh well had I made a mistake?

Of course we did not go to the sale but about a few days after the auction I called to see how the saddle did. The lady said she would get back to me, but she thought it did very well.

Later that day she called. It did not sell for $25,000 or even $50,000. It sold for $250,000. It was one of the best selling items in the sale that day.

A quarter of a million dollars. A quarter of a million.
What can I say. You win some…you know the rest.

The silver saddle.

Service Fabrics
1958 or so

After I left my job as shift chemist at I G Farben Industries my dad had a plan for us. He knew a guy by the name of Werner Klaus who had a company that according to my dad was making a fortune. He supplied skeins for dye plants throughout the country. I know you are wondering what is a skein?

At the time their were very few knit plants in the country. Most fabrics were woven. And they were most often dyed as yarn, not fabric dyes. In other words, before they wove the fabric they dyed yarn to make the fabric. And in order to assure that each yard of fabric matched the one before it, they had to test the batch of yarn with these skeins that Werner Klaus would sell to them. Each skein had to be perfect in denier and weight otherwise the dye lots would not match. That would be a disaster.

There was a society that as a chemist I was a member of, The American Association of Textile Chemists and Colorists. A square T C Square as it was known in the trade. Werner was also a member of this group. It was a pretty closed fraternity. No one dared to by fabric or skeins from you if you were not a member.
Really. Talk about trusts.

My dad wanted to go in competition with his friend Werner. How could we know how he operated? My dad had an idea. Why don't I and a few other Philadelphia Textile graduates pretend to be checking out his company as Textile graduates? In other words spy on him. I couldn't believe he wanted me to do that on his friend Werner. But we did.

Werner loved the idea. A buddy of mine called and within two weeks he welcomed us to his offices and labs. It was a great set up. About 40 people weighed the skein lots. They even had a closed room to control the humidity, so the skeins would always stay the same. It would take some money to replicate and possibly even improve but it definitely was doable.

Dad was thrilled. That is how Service Fabrics was formed. I came up with the name. After doing some research I was told that Werner was very expensive and he was often late in his deliveries but since he had no completion what could you do.

On the surface it looked like we could really do well with our new company. I prepared a brochure and we sent it out to a number of local dye plants and I followed it up with calls. Amazing. No one would see me. No one. I explained that although we were new we guaranteed on time delivery and we were almost 30% less expensive. Finally someone told us they could not buy from us unless we were certified by A square T C square. OK I was a member but the company had to certified.

After numerous calls and no appointment, Dad got pissed and called a few friends he knew in the dye plants. I do not know how he found out, but he told me that Werner had an exclusive with the organization. Others had tried to knock Werner off but it was impossible. Figured it out yet? Yes he was paying them off to get an exclusive. Dad thought we could do the same….but guess what, not that I was a boy scout, I just didn't want to start a company like that.

Dad used the name Service Fabrics for his business.
My brother Mitch was his partner for about the next forty years.

Religion
2023

Stan and I would both go to the same schools. Passaic Park had the famous PS 3. Right next to the school was the Ahavas Israel. The temple or synagogue my dad attended. He put me in Hebrew school at about the age of 6 or 7. I went to Hebrew School five days a week after PS 3 until my Bar Mitzvah, when I turned 13. I became a man, and got my first fountain pen. I think Stan went through the same process.

Why didn't it stick. I became a man, and that day stopped going to Hebrew School. I never understood how important it was to be a Jew in this world. Not back then, but I do today.

Going back to studying for the Big Day. Rabbi Silver taught me. He sold shoe polish when he wasn't being a Rabbi. He was tough. He was physical with us. If we didn't do our assigned readings that week he would lose his cool. One time he didn't mean to, but he pushed a kid down the stairs, and almost lost his job as rabbi. It's a pity, but those are the days I remember most.

Also I had very little to do with my grandfather Leon, my fathers dad. But he questioned my reading Hebrew all the time. He would take out his bible and turn to my part that I was to deliver that big day, and test me. I was pretty bad most of the time. My favorite answer was…"we didn't get to that part yet." In the end when the big day arrived I was ready.

Evelyn had really been looking forward to that day. She dressed me in a camel colored cardigan jacket that my dad manufactured. A wonderful patterned vintage tie, and brown leather and suede shoes. She had a gold tie pin made for me with my initials on it. A gold key chain made out of my whole name, and the best…a Bulova watch. This was 1946, and believe it or not I still have the watch, tie pin and gold key chain with my name on it. The watch is engraved August 22, 1946 my birthday. These were the highlights of that day.

Today, I am a man?

As far as practicing my faith, the only time I went to shull was for the high holidays with my dad. We would never miss Rosh Hashanah and Yom Kippur. I did that every year until my dad died at that age of 105. And for a few years after that, I went with my wife to temple on my own. I also fast every year on Yom Kippur. It reminds my of one of the few close ties that I had with my father.

This is one of the few regrets I have in my life.
I have always been proud of being Jewish, and I never passed that down to my kids. Not at all. What a missing.

The Jews are a proud people.
The culture is so rich, and as a parent I did not pass that richness along to my kids or their children.

With the war that is happening between Israel and Hamas, there is a terrible uprising of antisemitism. It has always been there, but now more than ever the survival of our Jewish culture is being tested, again.

Wings & Roots
2011

About 10 years ago my wife and I wrote a book called Wings and Roots.
For years so many people complimented us on our children.
Mandy and Joss turned out so special. They couldn't be more different
in so many ways. But both are strong, independent successful moms and
daughters. They both are very happily married and although they raised
their kids so different, each has turned out to be very special and self
sufficient as well. A great accomplishment in todays world.

We take some credit for that…especially my wife. That is why we wrote the book. Why not let people in on why our families turned out so special. It took about a year to write. My dear talented friend Charlie Rosner put us in touch with an art director, Jen Gaily. She has turned out to be a very close friend. She took our words and gave them life with many pictures from the early years with our children. The book turned out to be a true reflection of our lives together.

Roots are usually related to background. That part is true, and what we meant by roots is a much deeper meaning. It is a true understanding of life with and without it's faults. The chance to develop self esteem. The promise that dreams can come true, and they are worth pursuing especially embracing your failures. It encourages young people to take risks. With a strong understanding of life, anything is possible.

Once we have established strong roots we are ready to fly. Use those wings and take chances especially when the prospects are questionable.

Elaine and I are the lucky ones, so we thought we would pass it on.

New York City, again not a word was spoken. I dropped the kids off. Brian's parents blasted

him, in front of us. We spoke, and told them I would call tomorrow. When we got to our house, my wife greeted Mandy. A lot of crying. My daughter Joss was wonderful. She was really miffed, *to put it mildly*, that she had lost her wonderful car, but she too said nothing mean.

Mandy waited to talk. She tried to hold back her tears. The first words out of her mouth were

This is a big one for a lot of people.

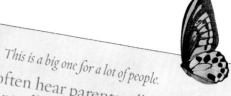

I so often hear parents talk about controlling their children

Control is generally not a good thing in relationships. Save it for driving a car, or flying a plane. I can remember when I was bringing up my children, this one came up time after-time. I guess you could have called me a "control freak." This would show up in simple life examples.

Want to BUILD TRUST?
HERE'S HOW! Answer these questions:

Can you remember a specific time when you stopped trusting your child?

There must be a specific time & circumstance, pick one.

What happened?

Don't embellish it. As they said on Dragnet, "Just the facts, ma'am."

What actually happened?

What did you say?

What did they say?

Where did it go from there?

YOU WILL SEE WHERE THE TRUST WAS LOST IF YOU HAVE AN OPEN MIND.

HOW TO STAY SANE WHILE RAISING YOUR KIDS!

WINGS & ROOTS

After reading this book, you'll never have more fun raising your children and strengthening your family roots.

ELAINE & HARVEY HERMAN

Don't we all hate to fail?

The Est Training and The Landmark Forum 1977

I tell you a lot about what our family got out of this work in another story. But I wanted to make sure that I include the seventeen years that I was a Seminar Leader for Landmark.

After completing the Est Training I attended a few follow up seminars. I got in touch with a different dimension of this work. I realized that I wanted to learn to lead Seminars. My daughter Joss and I both trained to lead at the same time. We watched so many Werner tapes as part of our training. It was so good working with her. She got the distinctions so quickly. I worked my way through them, also.

Just to clarify Seminar Leader. The Forum and the Advance Course are usually lead by Forum Leaders. There are only about 50 of them in the world and only about a half of them actually are qualified to lead the main courses after many years of training. Joss went on to be one of those Leaders. I did not.

After you complete the entry program…The Landmark Forum you have the opportunity to go into various follow up seminars. Those are the programs I led for many years, as well as being an Introduction to the Forum leader.

It took a lot of work, and it was worth it. I led about two or more seminars every year. I led to thousands of people. It was so rewarding to see people participate in having their lives and their families lives turn out with joy and freedom. Did that happen for everyone. No. But most people got so much out of the work and passed it on. Sort of like a stone in the water and the ripples that it sends out.

I have so many examples of how the work works,
but I thought this one was worth telling.
I flew my family to Nantucket for lunch one day, and we stopped at a yogurt store to get our dessert. When I checked out, the guy behind the cash register said…"No charge Harvey."

I looked at him…but had no idea who he was. Before I could say anything he said…

"I am sure you don't remember me, but I remember you. I came to one of your introductions to the Forum one night. I was the last guest in the room and everybody had either signed up or left. You came over to me and you told me that the intro was over, and you wanted to go home. You asked me if I was going to do it. Before I could answer you asked me what would I like to get out of the Forum if I did it. I laughed and said I would like to stop procrastinating, just like tonight. And you didn't leave it there you then asked me what would I do if I stopped procrastinating. I thought for a moment and said I would probably give up my job on wall street, it pays a lot of money, and open a bunch of yogurt stores."

True story. Just one person who transformed his life.
That's why I loved being a Seminar Leader.

Our Grandchildren

What can I say. We have five grandchildren. I must say they are each as unique as can be.

Joss has three incredible children. Not so *children* anymore. Sophie is 27 and is married to a wonderful Irish guy…David. They are happily married for about one year. She is an accomplished person for her 27 years. Been a chef and now works with her dad as a prop master on Law and Order. Whatever she has taken on in life she has accomplished. David, her husband is from Ireland. He moved here about 8 years ago and is a very successful part owner of three restaurants in New York City and Brooklyn. David is ten years older, and the relationship really works. Sophie is the glue that holds the family together. She is smart beyond her years. When she and David visit us they can't do enough for us. Just wonderful.

Joss's second child is Sage. He is 21. Brilliant. He could be considered a nerd, but he is not. Great at school. Wonderful artist. He is gay. Has a sweet partner, James. He knows so much about everything. Really. He is going to have a complicated life, I think. He thinks everything through, over and over. Lately he is taking more risks, but he thinks too much sometimes before acting. A good soul where it counts. Once he has accomplished somethings in life he will strengthen his self esteem. He hops on the Jitney some weekends just to get some time with us. Can't get any better than that.

Skylar. A very special human being. She is 17. She is going through a transition in her life. She was born a he named Shane, and over the past year in a half she is a woman. A beautiful woman in every way. She loves film and probably will try her hand at that business first. She is so much more as a woman then she was as a man, in my opinion. She is a happy soul now. She is so great with Elaine. When we are in Paris she wheels her around in her wheel chair. She comes out many times to spend time with us. We love her.

Amanda has two children.
Her oldest is *Samantha*. She is 27 years old, about 6 months older than Sophie. She is a unique person. I must admit over the past few years I have not been too close to her. Sammy has a wonderful partner...Iris. Iris is a singer and is part of a band and Sammy represents the band and works with them. Not sure more than that. I want to get closer to Sammy and intend to work on that. I am not sure if they are going to let me. We will see.

Her second child is *Max*. He just turned 23. He is a body trainer. He is working on his masters to be a person that will work with people on a whole body. He is in excellent shape. He works at it all the time. When he was younger he was a bit of a pain in the ass. Arrogant, and knew it all. Over the past few years he has matured and is coming around. He loves vintage watches. At some point I will gift him one of my special watches to start his collection. I already gave him a Panari watch from the fifties. He intends to go out on his own next year. That will be really good for him.

Like I say...five grandchildren all very different. They have really enriched Elaine and my life. Hard to understand the difference they make unless you experience it yourself.

They were all here two days ago for Thanksgiving.
Our family is so rich because of them.

This is more or less a description of my grandchildren. I think it is important to know how this group of five have impacted my life. I can not speak for Elaine but I know that this group have taught me how shallow I have been looking back just 25 years ago.

My son Bruce was gay. He died from AIDS. He was brilliant and his life was cut short by that horrible disease. I met him when he was just 6 years old and for the next thirty years I did a lot of growing because of him. I had mishandled the homosexual part of our relationship for the first five years or so. He helped me to see how my biases were holding me back in life. I was missing out on this young man's beauty.

I must admit I was hardly prepared to pick up where his father had not done the job. He did very little to support him in life. Elaine raised him completely. He was so creative. He was a working actor and wrote a play with Sheri Felt his dear friend, and got it produced off broadway. He was a teacher. In fact, he ended up being Amanda's drama teacher in high school. He accomplished so much in his 37 years. He was so smart and worldly beyond his years. He was witty and wise. He helped me to grow up, so that when Joss and Amanda came along I had developed some muscle as a dad.

At the same time my relationship with my brother has shifted dramatically since we moved out to Hampton Bays. It is not just the proximity, it is my understanding of how he has developed a special rare appreciation of how his life has turned out. He too is a homosexual.

A very special time for Stan now. When he turned 90 he had a series of articles written about him. He was truly acknowledged for his many accomplishments on and off the fashion court. It opened a whole new arena for him to play in. This 90 year person was not ready to wind down. The business world opened up again to him. Many new beginnings, and the great part is he stepped into all these new openings and you could see how much he enjoyed it.

Stan just had his memoir published. It is an important statement of his role in the fashion world. He truly is an icon in the world of fashion. They did his life story on the *Sunday Morning Jane Pauley Show*. I am very proud of him.

At his age of 95 that is remarkable. You know the 90's are really a time for most people to start winding done. Not him. Not me either. There is so much to do, and not a lot of time left to do it.

Sophie & Sammy

Michael, Josselyne,
Sage, Skylar and Sophie

Our grandchildren are each unique.

**My wife and I
are *so thankful*
that each and
every one of them
is in our lives.**

Skylar and Sage

Max and Samantha

Our Grandchildren

Two sensational, but different!

Michael...

When my daughter Joss told us she was going to marry this guy Victor, I flipped out. I tried over- and- over to talk her out of this ridiculous relationship. They had met at Landmark and he was from Utica, NY. Here's all I will say about Victor. Joss asked us to fly her up to Utica to meet the family. We piled into my Baron and on the way up I joked with Elaine that they probably had a truck tire painted white on the front lawn... that was my attitude about Utica and Victor.

When we arrived at the house...you got it...not just a tire painted white, but a plastic flamingo sitting inside the tire. What can I say.

When I finally gave in, I looked for a giant loft on Fifth Avenue that could add a rich feeling to this wedding. I found a vintage loft that was so beautiful. When I showed it to Victor he said..."it's so old and dirty." Oh well again..

As two hundred guests were waiting outside and my beautiful daughter sat with me in her white lace gown I pleaded with her... "Please let's call it off, we'll have a party, please Joss."

Four years later, how she hung in was shocking to me... my first son-in-law bit the dust.

Some time went by and Joss was thinking of running an ad in New York Mag to find her soul mate and my daughter Amanda said she was working on a film and there was a guy Joss should meet. She was working with Michael Saccio.

"Ok, I will have a cup of coffee with him, that's it."

Yesterday they celebrated their 28th wedding anniversary. That's right a lot of coffee later Joss and Mike are married and as happy as can be.

Joss, Sage and Michael in South Beach.

Two sensational, but different!

Michael Saccio

Who is Michael Saccio? What makes him tick?
Let's put it this way…here's a guy who was adopted like Joss, and although
I did not know him back then…he has shared the fact that he was a
drug addict and an alcoholic by his teen age years. In fact he and his older
brother Mathew were both hooked at an early age. Mat is still suffering
and has not been able to break that bond. Mike on the other hand not only
got clean, but he turned his life around in such an amazing way that it is
truly remarkable.

They got married in our apartment on 88th Street. A tall, good looking down to earth human being who has become a great husband and spectacular father to his three kids. On top of that he helps Elaine and I every day. You can depend on him. He is a propmaster. He has been on numerous films with his dad Tommy and has been the prop master on Law and Order SUV for I think 20 years.

He is one of the most detail conscious persons I have ever known. Some times he drives me crazy going over- and- over and over details until it is drilled into your head. But that is his strength.
His Dad Tommy had a reputation as a lovable pain in the ass. A real tough guy who was a marshmallow inside. He died in a plane that he built from scratch. Part of me felt a little responsible. I helped him become a pilot…but he loved every minute of flying until the day it ended abruptly.

At Tommy's funeral Barbara Streisand sent a note saying how much she loved him. He taught Mike his craft. He was so tough on him, but it worked. He has a career that brings him respect.
Mike has been working since his teen years. When I say working, he may have given up alcohol, the drink, for life but not when it comes to work. I think they have replaced most groups on Law and Order, but not Michael's. To make sure he has position covered
Mike trained his daughter Sophie to work with him, and to handle the department when he is not available.

Me and Mike in Paris.

Last May Joss fulfilled her lifetime dream…to live in Paris. As it worked out Mike was able to go with her…all production was closed down because of a strike. I was amazed. Here is a guy who's whole life was a commitment to long days of work, all of a sudden he is living in Paris, not working a job and taking on the household chores with Joss in Paris. He loved it. He flourished. Shopped in the markets for fresh fruits and veggies and cooked up a storm every night. Joss would complete her coaching calls by 9 or so and they would have dinner. He planted all the flower boxes on his terrace and has learned to enjoy down time. Quite an accomplishment.

And on top of that, their three kids all handled their lives on their own. A little help here and there, but they found they could trust the kids to make their lives work. A parent can't ask for more than that.

Joss and Mike are very happy and contented.
I guess she got it right this time.

Irving

I had been a Seminar Leader for quite a while and time after time I had been responsible for getting the team together to assist. I had asked Amanda so many times to help me, but she never did. One Sunday I was so short on my team I finally talked Mandy into working one day with me. She arrived and within an hour she came over to me and asked...
"Who is that hot guy running the mics?"

At the end of Sunday she called home and asked if she could go with Irving to Detroit.
"Who's Irving?"

A couple of days later..."Dad can I go to Fort Walton Beach this week with Irving, he is stationed down there?"
"Who's Irving?"

About a week later..."Dad, Irving and I are in Florida,
can you come down for the weekend?"
They had rented a boat and took us out that weekend in Florida. Then they had planned a lunch and at that lunch she announced that she was getting married to Irving.

I left the table and told them I didn't want to be sorry for what I was about to say. I sat outside on the curb to cool off, and then Elaine and I saw they were serious and I said yes if they would wait six months and if they still felt the same we would make a big wedding in our country house in Mass. They agreed.

Two weeks later they changed their mind and said they wanted to get married soon instead. After much talking they won. We gave them a great wedding in the Burdon Mansion in NYC.

Here we are almost 30 years later, and it lasted. Not just lasted. It got better with time. Two kids later and lots of moves they are now buying a great coop on the water in Brooklyn and both of their kids are turned out to be very happy.

But who is Irving?...

Irving turned out to be a pilot in training in the Air Force. He has a sister Lori who still lives in Detroit where Irving is from. Irv's dad still lives in Detroit, too. He brought the kids up because his wife left him and moved to Hawaii. Marvin did the best he could to raise the two kids.

When I met Irving I had been a private pilot for over 20 years and I was thrilled that this young man was being trained to fly jets. They got stationed in Oklahoma and we went down to visit them a number of times. They got a house for around $150,000. Big backyard and lots of rooms. We hated Oklahoma, but they made the most of it.

In fact at that time Irv was having a tough time with his flying. It sometimes happens that way. He was struggling at the bottom of his

class but he hung in their and made it happen.
He did not give up, no way.

Turns out that is one of his core strengths. He works at it no matter what. I know I flew with him a number of times in my twin, and he went from being nervous pilot to total joy over time.

His mom left him…but he hung in there and made it work.

He came out to our house one time on his own to discuss why he was having such a tough time in his marriage.
He hung in and made it work.

He had a tough time getting his first job as a commercial pilot. He wanted to work for Jet Blue. My brother Stan put in a good word for him, but they took over a year to get back to him. In the meantime he could have gone to work for NetJet, but he hung in there.

Turns out that is one of his core strengths. He works at it no matter what. I know I flew with him a number of times in my twin, and he went from being a nervous pilot to a total joy over time. And now, he's actually building his own plane! It is turning out beautifully. Today he is a captain at Jet Blue and has flown for them over 18 years. He also flies intercontinental to London, Paris, Amsterdam and Rome.

Mandy is very successful, and so is Irving.
It pays to hang in.

On our beach in Hampton Bays.

Stupid chances.

Like I said previously, I am so proud that in my forty years as a private pilot. I must say most of the times I never took chances. I said most of the time. Taking chances as a pilot is stupid. John Kennedy, Jr. never should have taken a chance that night to fly IFR into Martha's Vineyard. It cost him and his wife and sister their lives. Stupid and pilot are like oil and water. They do not mix.

I was thinking the other night, and I remember three stupid times that I put myself at risk. All of them turned out fine, but why I chanced them is worth talking about.

SHELTER ISLAND
Elaine's cousin Lori had a house on Shelter Island. Long before we moved to Hampton Bays, Lori invited us to visit her. The ride from Great Barrington seemed too long, so I looked on my VFR map and found a small private landing strip on Shelter Island. I had to call ahead and get approval to land there. The guy was so sweet. He told me that the strip was not easy. It ran up and down a hill and if you got there on a day where the winds were on your tail, it would be very difficult for most planes and their pilots to get off the 1300 foot grass runway.

I assured him I would check the winds that day, and if they were wrong we would not come. I also told him I was a tail dragger pilot and I had a lot of experience in my Archer on short runways. He gave me approval to fly in and out.

The flight down was uneventful. In less than an hour we landed safely on the tiny grass runway on Shelter Island. It would have taken us about 6 hours driving and a ferry to get there. I was so proud of myself. The winds when we arrived were perfect. I landed into the wind going up hill, and had no problems.

We had a great day with Lori and arrived back at the runway around 5PM to take off. He had a small windsock at each end of the runway and here's the issue…the winds had changed by almost 180 degrees. This meant I would have to take off with a tail wind not a head wind. That meant adding at least 10% extra to roll out. When I did the weight and balance it said that we needed 1350 feet to take off that day.

Those extra 50 feet. What to do?

We should not have done what I did next. I decided to chance it. I taxied to the very end of the grass and let the plane warm up. I put my feet on the brakes and ran the motor up to the red line for take off… let it stay at that high RPM and finally let her roll. We were running down hill, but I could not take off until I reached 65 knots or I would have to abort. 50, 55, 60…still no lift…65 the trees at the end were coming up I pulled back slightly on the yoke and she started to stall… pushed the nose down and picked up a few knots and pulled the yoke back again, and we cleared the trees by a few feet.

What a stupid thing to do.

ST. BARTHS
The second one was even worse.
We had gone to St. Barths many times. The airport at St. Barths was famous. To say it was challenging would be misleading. You had to approach the airport quite high because of two hills. We called them the "women's breasts." They stuck up on the hillside and once you passed them you had to dive to the runway to land. There was a marker painted across the runway. If you did not touch down by the time you reached the marker you had to take off and do a go around and try another landing. At the end of the runway was the bay with almost no beach. Every month or so a plane would go off the runway and into the water. If you were lucky the beach would stop them and the plane could be taken apart and towed away. If it landed in the salt water, all that could be saved would be all the avionics. Oh well.

I decided I wanted to test my short field skills. They rented Archers at the airport and I had brought my logbook with me. I took a lesson with a great looking French pilot. He was so cool. He was based there and he made everything look so simple. He never hurried. He would make all the right moves and he took us up three times, before letting me sit in the pilots seat with him in the right seat. I did two excellent landings and he signed me off to solo land at the airport.

You so often forget that when you are flying and have another pilot with you it gives you a lot of confidence. Anyway, I taxied out to the runway and took off over the water. It was so beautiful I was tempted to fly around a while, but since I was not familiar with the area, and had no maps I stuck to the plan. Land once safely and they would sign me off to fly solo anytime.

I got my self set up to land going on the downwind. Called out my position for any traffic that might be coming to the airport…no one responded so I lined up the plane base to final. The two giant breasts came up so quickly…I checked my airspeed…too fast…too fast, I flew past the line on the runway and knew I had to go around. Full power and off to 1800 feet for pattern altitude.

I realized I was nervous. What had I done wrong? What should I do different? Do not panic I told myself. Back on the radio I announced my pattern altitude and set my self up for the final approach. Here is where I used my skills…I had many hours in a tail dragger, my J3 Cub…when your airspeed is too high, bleed it off with a side slip… point the plane into the wind and push the rudders in so that the plane is slipping into the wind. When I got to the "boobs" I pushed the plane sideways and she slowed down so much that I had to push her nose down so as not to stall. A perfect 3 point landing.

My French instructor was so impressed.
He said he couldn't do it much better.

He had no idea how much I was sweating.

AEROFLEX

There is a tiny airport in New Jersey called Aeroflex. 1200 ft runway with water at each end. And only 30 feet wide. From the air it looks like a piece of licorice. I had flown my Cub in there a number of times, but one day I was flying with a friend Harley Carnes. He was an instructor and had many hours in all kinds of planes. He was also an acrobatic pilot. He was out of my league.

We were flying around in my Archer and he asked if I had ever flown into Aeroflex with this plane. No never. After some talk he said let's fly over the airport and see if it worked for me. We flew around the airport and Harley assured me I could do it. We had flown together a number of times so I figured he's right, give it a try. Lesson number one. When you are pilot in command it is your responsibility to fly the plane even if you have an instructor next to you.

"Let's do a full stop. Have a cup of coffee and go somewhere else," Harley said.

Never do anything you are not sure you can't handle as a pilot. I remember my first instructor telling me this. What was I doing that day. I was showing off. I lined the Archer up on the downwind, turned base and then to final...perfect set up. Slowed the plane down to 75 knots. Perfect airspeed. The approach couldn't have been better. I checked the wind sock. The wind had shifted it was almost 20 degrees off the runway, which meant I had a cross wind and that I would have to slow it down even more and point the nose into the wind.
Did all that.

Harley said..."looking good."

I put in full power...took off and didn't land.

Harley said..."wise move Harv."
"What? You told me it looked good."

He responded..."your the pilot in command."

Stupid chances.   313

65 years, but who's counting?

My wonderful wife and I are together over 65 years. We met in 1958 at a horse show in Madison Square Garden. Even though it was like thunderbolt the minute I saw her, it took five years for me to propose. I must admit I was a baby when I met her. She had been married and divorced and had a child. She had been working as a model since she was 15. She was so advanced in her life, and I was a baby. What did she see in me?

Recently I asked her that question. She smiled…
"I liked you just the way you were, and still are today."

If I look to see why we have flourished over all these years I think that is the major clue.

When I first met Elaine, I loved her just how she was. The only time that our relationship has fallen on bad days is when I decided to change her. Make her better. To improve our marriage by making her more like me.

I sometimes have lost sight of the fact that she has always been the source of our relationship. She has better instincts. She very often sees beyond the day-to-day.

She has taught me a lot. Especially in the raising of our children and our grandchildren. She has always been their best friend. She never sees the need to change them, also. They are perfect just the way they are and aren't. Sound familiar?

When I think about it…what freedom she has had in our marriage. When we got separated, for good reasons…even though she was hurt, she did not allow herself to be the victim. She picked up her life without me and made every day count for her and the kids. Which brings up another reason our marriage is wonderful.

Elaine is selfless.

In writing this memoir, I have learned a lot about myself. I have rarely been selfless. A quality I so admire in others.

Left: Elaine and Nina Fineberg
Center: Elaine in Vietnam
Right: Elaine and her partner, Linda Lipson.
 Their casting company was the
 second largest in NYC,

However, I also realized that one of my best qualities is I am usually open to taking risks. Being a risk taker has been so essential in our lives together. Some have worked out and others have not. One thing for sure this baby has gotten better at life as I have grown older. I have always had a wonderful support system in my family. The truth is I have usually loved my life, my wife and my family. They have made me a better person.

So many people have so much, and don't appreciate it.
How unfortunate. What a waste. Elaine taught me early in the game to appreciate what we have.

I guess down deep I always knew I was lucky to meet this lady. These 65 years are my reward.

A frustrated architect!
2019-2022.

All of my life I have aways wondered if I could have been a successful architect. I had always enjoyed renovations of each and every house and apartment we lived in. But I never did the whole job.
Design something and then follow through on it.

About four or five years ago, we were not making much money in the market so my daughter Joss and her husband Mike sat down to see how we could get extra income. We decided that I had always done well in real estate, so perhaps we could find properties that needed work and flip them for profit. I loved the idea. So we started looking for the right property to develop.

We chose to work on the North Fork of Long Island. We lived on the south shore which was really developed and the prices usually were out of our price range. So off we went to the North Fork. It is so lovely there. Still lots of farm land and open fields yet so near to the water. We looked and looked and could not find anything worth investing in. Until one day we saw an ad for a mission style house that had been started and not finished in Mattituck, one of our favorite towns.

Good thing we were beginners. We fell in love with the place and put in a bid for $615,000. It was accepted. We wanted it so bad we decided not to have a pre-purchase buyers inspection. No one should buy a house without one. What followed was amazing.

The house was started ten years ago. That's right, all those years they started and stopped. Time after time. It was owned by a family and they did not agree on anything when it came to the house. We discovered a lot of issues. The house had sunk on one end and we had to run steel beams in the base to support it. The inside had been started. Some construction but all the plumbing was done wrong and parts of it had been destroyed. The electrical had also been done half ass.

And here's the big one. They never got permits from the city to do any of the work. No permits. Everything that was done had to be inspected. Like siding had to be taken off the outside of the house to check if the strapping was done properly. Changes had to be made in order to pass inspection. And boy, we were neophytes. Innocents. In a way it was best not to know what a mess we were in.

The bottom line. We fixed everything. I designed the interior with Mike and Joss's help. We installed a magnificent kitchen. All the bathrooms were done in Italian marble. All the fixtures were Italian glass. The flooring throughout was stained a whitewash. Great fireplace. Lots of decking and a salt water pool. The landscaping made the place. A winding road up to the house turned out so special. In the end we built a mini mansion on the North Fork. It sold for around two million. On the South Fork it would have been double that. And we made out financially, in spite of all the surprises. And we met the best real estate broker ever. Sheri was so helpful in advising us on this project. What a great beginning. I got a chance to test some more of my design skills. But still no real architectural test.

The market got tough. Hard to find unique homes. We had been looking on the North Fork exclusively, but we checked out a house in Southampton on the South Fork. Not your usual home. It had a French look to it. It was part of an early development, and very different. It had over two acres. Came with a pool and a tennis court. There were a few issues. First we were not blown away by the neighborhood, but our property was outstanding. Second the house was tiny, only about 1300 square feet, and needed substantial work. The design was very special for the neighborhood. It was overpriced, asking over a million. The pre-purchase inspection was good. We got it for around $900,000.

The challenge was to build it out to over four thousand square feet and keep the French mansard look. I sat down and turned the house into an L shaped home, with a massive room over 1000 square feet with 3 skylights and about 20 foot ceilings. Add two more bedrooms, 2

Southhampton. Turned a 1300 square foot home into 5200.

more ultra modern bathrooms while also redoing the two main house
bathrooms and expanding the kitchen to almost twice it's size.
I designed the whole place and an architect rendered the drawings.

In addition we had a 1700 square foot basement part of central air
with 10 foot ceilings. That area could be used for anything. So the
house was really close to 5300 square feet when it was complete.
We priced it at 2.2 million and got just under 2 million.
Again made out pretty good.

I loved the work and it proved to me I could have been an architect,
but I was satisfied not being one.

The real estate market has gone through the roof.
Right now no bargains to improve and flip.

Patience Herman.

The end result of our project: The Mattituck home.

Antiques and Watches

From the time we first met over 65 years ago, we both fell in love with antiques. We didn't have much money when we first met, but we went to our favorite auction in Kingston, New York. Cal Smith and his father had auctions almost every weekend and we drove up there and bought as much as we could afford.

When we got married and moved into Sheridan Square in the Village we had no furniture. We rented a U haul it and drove up to Kingston. We furnished the whole apartment for about $600.
A velvet Victorian couch was $25. A Mott table and 6 Mott chairs were $75. Rugs, two Chinz soft chairs were $38. And on and on.
A whole apartment costs us around $600. We filled the trailer and drove back to the city with our treasures. Those were the days.

We collected Early American and Western Antiques. When we got more money to spend we went out to Sante Fe, New Mexico. This was back around 1985, way before Cowboy outfits and Native American Jewelry from around the 1920th became popular. In the 90's Vintage places throughout the country caught on. Two friends of Elaine's opened up What Comes Around Goes Around back then. In fact this week they had a big write up in The New York Times. So we were all ahead of our time.

Elaine opened her own shop in Sheffield, Mass. in a big barn opposite our home. It was an immediate success. It was called Three Little Indians. We couldn't keep the merch in stock. Elaine ran the shop and she felt that her time on weekends was special, so she started to feel that the shop robbed her of her free time. We tried a number of people running the place but it was not the same. Elaine was great at it, we never found anyone to run the place, so eventually we closed it down.

During that time we met a great couple who ran the Vintage clothing and jewelry for Ralph Lauren. Bob Mellet and his wife became close friends. We were even god parents to their daughter Sunny. They had one of the best Vintage stores in the country. We made friends with Bob's boss Doug. He ran all the Ralph Lauren Vintage stores, including furniture and especially jewelry. We loved Early American. We had so many wonderful Blue pieces throughout our country home. When we moved we called Doug and he bought many of our best furniture. It ended up in Ralph's Tee Pee's on his ranch in Colorado.

I guess you get the picture by now. We were really into the right stuff way before it got popular. This was especially true with our jewelry. Every year we would go over to London a few times and Elaine would buy silver and enamel pins. Mostly animals. Horses and dogs were our favorites. Elaine still has a wonderful collection. One year Ralph Lauren's group saw Elaine buying the wonderful pins. The next year when we went around the shows in London they were all gone. Our friends at the shows apologized and said that Ralph's group had cleaned them out on the pins. They bought them all. Wiped the market clean.

We used to buy them for around $10 each and sell them for $25 in Elaine's store. Ralph had them on sale in his Madison Avenue store for $150 each and they all sold out.

Same thing happen with my Breitling Watch collection. I had been buying these great watches in London for around a thousand dollars. They were just for myself. When Bob Mellet saw them, they cornered the Brietling Vintage watch market. Most of the great watches ended up in the Madison Avenue Ralph Lauren store. I still have around seven of them, but the prices now are out of site.

When I think back on our love of antiques I tend to realize that we loved to play in the business of antiques.
We were just collectors

Never Florida!
9/11/2001

Most of us can never forget that date. We lived just North of Canal Street on Broadway at the time, and on that memorable day I was flying up to Rochester, New York with a client Bob Hillman.

Elaine watched the second tower come down from one of our windows. It was hard to believe. We had just moved to this new apartment, and we were renting for the first time in 30 years. We sold a giant apartment on Union Square and couldn't decide what to buy now.

A few months after that horrible event Elaine and I were having dinner out and she amazed me. "Let's buy in Florida." I asked her what brought this on. She thought that people were panicking and that we might find a good deal in the South Beach area. Unbelievable. She was so right.

We called a broker we knew in South Florida…Massimo, and asked him how the market was. Elaine was right. Lot's of people were selling. It was a great time to invest in South Beach, an area that we loved and believe it or not was still pretty reasonable.

We were on a plane the next week, and Massimo showed us a number of places but none of them were right for us. A lot of good investments, but we wanted to be right on the water in a new building. On the second day of looking Massimo said that he might have the perfect place. It was a new building that was not quite ready to move in yet right on the cut where the cruise line ships came in and out. It was called the Murano.

We feel in love. There was a two bedroom with a giant bath. A very big living/dining room and a very large terrace that surrounded the unit. All the rooms had a door to the terrace and it was right on the water.

It turned out you could watch the massive cruise line ships go in and out. When they came in at around 5AM they could not run their engines, so they floated down the cut with their lights on. It was like a Fellini movie.

Their was almost no one in the building. It was due to be completed within the next few months. Turns out the owner had invested in four apartments and he was panicking. We knew he paid around $500,000 per apartment so that is what we offered him, even though he had it for sale for $700,000. He accepted our offer. We had to put in flooring and paint the place but that was simple. We were the second person to move into the building.

We loved Florida in so many ways. I started painting again.
I did a few paintings that were really perfect. One ended up being our logo card that I send out. It is a portrait of Elaine and I and our two dogs. Amelia a PBGV and Alfie our first GBGV. I was so relaxed being in Florida.

They opened a restaurant right across from our apartment. La Piazza. One of the best French and Italian bistros in South Beach. It also had a pool and as owners in the building we belonged to the beach club there. We swam almost everyday.

Our apartment turned out perfect. We used Italian stone throughout. And we put up flat screen TV's in both bedrooms…way ahead of the times. It was a really easy way to live.

As the building filled up, it turned out that really wealthy young people discovered the Murano. Rolls, Bentleys and Ferrari's filled the garage in our building. My 69 Chevy convertible was loved by all. So many Hip Hop or R and B groups I think that's what they were called. They all wanted my red 69 Impala with a white leather interior. I ended selling it to one of them when we left.

Nina and David Feinbergs, two of our closes friends owned right on 5th Street also in South Beach. We were only a 10 minute walk from each other. We spent a lot of time and a lot of money on Lincoln Road. Every. Sunday they had wonderful antique shows on Lincoln road. Nina was into leopard and plexiglass. Not us. We found so much Art Deco at fair prices. We ended up furnishing our whole apartment from the antique Sundays on Lincoln Road.

My brother Stan put us in touch with a close friend of his…Charlie Cinnamon. He was a PR guy for events in South Beach. He hooked us up with tickets to many concerts and theatre. That was so special. One night Charlie called and said he had two tickets to a burlesque show in Fort Lauderdale…were we interested. We drove up there and got in but missed the opening. It was a strange show. After about a half hour Elaine turned to me and said…"hon…they're all so old." She was right all of the actors were in their 80's and even one in her 90's. That was the idea of the show.
Once we understood we were so hysterical. Just on of the many, many highlights of our stay in South Beach.

We sold the place for $880,000 after about two years. Our agent said to hold off another year and she would double our money.
She was right.
We needed the money to invest in our big move to Hampton Bays.

South Beach was fun. We tried renting the next year in the same area, but it was not the same. The beach, the sun, swimming, running, good friends and great meals.

What could be wrong.

The Brothers in Hampton Bays.

Never Florida! 9/11/2001

Union Square

Union Square was so special. We decided buying a tiny apartment when we also bought in South Beach. We found a studio right on Fifth Avenue and 16th Street. 108 Fifth. Top floor. Nice 300 sq. foot terrace. Three little balconies, a fireplace and a nice bathroom. The apartment was tiny. The kitchen was very tiny, the bedroom was tiny, too. But it had charm and there were only two apartments on the floor. Very special. We turned the one bedroom into a studio. Took the walls down and put up vintage glass doors that slide into the walls and also closed to form a bedroom.

I wanted an Italian modern kitchen. Had it built in Florence, Italy and shipped in a container to NYC. It turned out sensational, and cost half as much as it would to build in the states. Like everybody said when they came to the apartment, you made the very most out of the space. We did. It was fun. Even got a green marble fireplace mantel to make the fireplace a real point of interest.

Union Square was wonderful. The best restaurants. The park had a farmers market each week. Still there many years later. And, one of our favorite places was the Union Square Cafe. Every Monday we would have dinner at the bar. Oscar would make our favorite drink. We would each have a ice cold Cosmopolitan. And, we would share a Lobster Pot Pie. Then finish with each having a second Cosmo. That's when we could drink. If I tried that today, I would be under the table.

We bought the place for $633,000. After the buildout we had $725,000 invested. This is an unbelievable part of the story. I found the perfect home in the Hamptons, but didn't have enough money to buy it without selling our apartment on Union Square.

We had to come up with the money in 48 hours and close on the home in less than 30 days. Impossible. I called Julie Johnson. I told her if she could sell our apartment within 48 hours she would get a $20,000 bonus. She sold it in one day. One day. 24 hours sold at our asking price, $1,450,000, almost double what we had into it.

It turns out she had taken pictures of the apartment when we told her we may be selling. She put it on her website, and it turns out a woman from Chicago had bid on an apartment in our building earlier that month and lost out to someone else. When she saw the pictures she had a friend run over, and her friend fell in love. Said it was better than the one she lost out on.

The next day the lady from Chicago flew in, saw it, and gave me my asking price. Really.

I guess it was meant to be.

My brother Stan
December 10, 2023

My brother Stan went into Lenox Hill Hospital today, after four days of suffering with throwing up and loose bowels. Sorry to be so graphic, but Stan is amazing. He is 95. Lives on his own. Still plays tennis a bit. His business is sensational.

He completed his memoir a few months ago and it is being published by a prestigious company. He was to have a book signing with Fern Mallis at the YMHA and another with the CFDA also but they are canceling it for now.

The memoir is extremely well written and is enhanced by timely pictures and some of his sketches. He is very pleased with the way it turned out.

A lot of people want to take on their memoir. Very few accomplish it.

When he turned 90 they wrote a number of articles about him and that launched his career again. So great that he has become an Icon in the fashion world and is being acknowledged for his exceptional career.

A new plateau at 95. Very encouraging. Stan and I have become so close over the past 20 years. We speak multiple times most days. We very often fill the gaps in our lives…remembering our versions of the past. He is a good soul. We have chosen very different paths…yet they often lead to the same results. I so enjoy his relationship with my wife. It's sort of like a boyfriend and girlfriend. They really enjoy each other. To say the least it makes me very happy.

Get well soon.

I ♥ this picture!

My brother Stan

We traveled

As soon as I started to make money my wife grabbed a portion each year for travel and vacations. Again, who's the wise one here. If it up to me in the beginning I was happy just to be in NYC.

I am going to set down a number of places. Some we loved and went back over and over like London and Florence, Italy. Others we went once and that was enough.

BUDAPEST. A bit of a disappointment. Loved the fact that it is two distinct cities, one on each side of the river. We found the old city quite beautiful. The more commercial side was mostly hotels. Reminded us a little of Shanghai,China. Can't remember which side is which. I guess that says it all.

PRAGUE. It reminded us about Paris, but not as good in any direction. When I asked Elaine today what did you like about Prague…she said all she could remember is wanting to get out of there. I found the fashion shopping very good. Again, not like Paris.

Turkey. The terrible poverty turned us off. Some of the architecture was worth seeing, but every place in the cities there were people riding on top of buses and begging. Begging and Begging. We couldn't take these poor children being used by their parents to get money. How sad it is that is what we took away from Turkey.

ISLAND VACATIONS.

We went to so many warm places. The best for us was St. Barths.
We wrote that one up already.

ARUBA WAS OUR FIRST. Elaine hated to lose at gambling. I asked her to put $20 down on the black jack table and keep the bet there for five times. Twenty turned to forty. Forty to eighty. Eighty to one hundred and sixty. One hundred and sixty to three hundred and twenty. Only one more draw and she would come away with six hundred and forty. She did not want to go forward…I insisted. She lost her money and wouldn't talk to me for the whole day. That is what we remember about Aruba with the trees all bent away from the winds. I thought it was funny, Elaine thought it was stupid. As she put it…"I don't like losing, it's very uncomfortable."

Like I said we went to so many warm islands…one that stands out was Anguila…we went there for New Years on the bicentennial in 2000. The whole family came. We rented a house close to the beach, and on New Years Eve we watched the fireworks on all the islands that surrounded ours. It was like no other New Years Eve I can remember. Sure beat the ball and Times Square. Also Joss found a local place that had an outdoor grill and we ate chicken and ribs every night. Superb.

On one of the islands we all rented horses and rode with our grandkids on the beach. We never forgot…Michael rode with Sophie in his lap. She fell asleep as he rode with her. Talk about relaxing. That was the important part…we took the whole family and our grandchildren very often. Those were the best vacations.

SANTE FE. We took the family to this wonderland many times. Our favorite place was Bishops Lodge. We would all go out every morning before breakfast and horseback ride through the hills and valleys. Then we would all devour an all you can eat South Western breakfast. We loved shopping throughout the town. Our favorite was Canyon Road. Every Sunday they had an antique market out by the

Opera House. We bought more Native American than you could imagine. By the way the Opera House is world famous. It is half indoor and half outdoor. One a month the biggest Native American crafts and antique show in the town square. We had a lady friend make us hand stitched shirts with authentic Indian (that's what they called them then) designs.

They had one of the best American Spas we ever went to. And, the real estate was so depressed when we first went there back in the late 70's early 80's. There was a period of six months that nothing closed on in the whole town. Six months nothing sold. We saw an exceptional home at the end of Upper Canyon Road. Pristine condition. Fireplaces in most bedrooms. Peach orchards. Views overlooking the city. A separate art studio building. It was on the market for $675,000. We made a firm offer of $425,000. They accepted and we chickened out. Oh well. That house today is worth 3 to 4 million. Obviously a big mistake Herman. We loved Santa Fe. It is truly one of the most magical places in America.

ST MARTIN. By far the worst trip in our lifetime. We rented two houses and took the whole family. The first night we went out to diner and someone got into our house and stole everything of value including all my camera equipment. We were told buy the police that the house had been broken into on a regular basis. The island itself was a big problem. A lot of poverty. Big resorts for the white folk. Very little art or culture. Not a place we would go back to. Turns out Elaine fell and hurt her ribs. She was not doing well so we cut the trip short.

On the way home Elaine got very sick on the plane. She was throwing up and running a high temp. The doctor on the plane felt she was in real trouble and we landed in Bermuda. They took her in an ambulance to the hospital. It was a disaster. After many tests they discovered she was dehydrated. They gave her a couple of bags or saline, and they wanted to put her in a ward for the next few days. No way was this going to work. We both said we wanted to leave and go back on the next American Airlines flight the next morning.

They would not sign us out, so we can not get on the plane. We needed the paper work.

We left the hospital the next day. I had made the reservation to go home and American Airlines asked if we were signed out, and please bring the paper work. When we got there we went through all check in and went directly to the front desk to board. They asked for the paperwork. I said sure and started to go through my bag. "Oh my god, I must have left it at the hotel, this has been the trip from hell, what do I do?" I should have been an actor they let us on the plane and the trip home was uneventful. *Hated St. Martin.*

POSITANO. Elaine took Joss there when she was 16. I had to work so they went alone. They loved it and we went again the following year. What a special place. All carved out of the side of a hill. The food, the people and wine, oh my. The owner of the hotel fell in love with Joss. Paulo was his name. He couldn't do enough for us. We traveled to all the towns in the area. This part of Italy was one never to forget.

MEXICO ZIHUARENJO. This town became famous many years after we visited it a few times. It was featured in the Shawshank Redemption movie. Right on the beach and totally unique. At the time it was not a resort, really.
We stayed in a home right on the water and ate at small bistros. It was like going back 50 years. We loved it. Don't know what it is like today.

STEAMBOAT SPRINGS TO SPOKANE. Elaine and I ended up on one of our vacations in this famous town. President Clinton had been there the day before us. We went into a local store that sold everything from yogurt to sensational outerwear. We bought the place out. Bought two green nylon jackets that Ralph Lauren would die for. Gave one to my brother Stan for his green Range Rover and we still have ours today. We rented a car to take the trip north to visit our daughter in Spokane, Washington. The car they offered us was terrible. We made a deal to drive a giant Ford Expedition directly to Spokane. It was from there originally.

The open spaces, the mountains, the fields of yellow flowers…this was straight out of National Geographic Magazine that you find in the Dentist office. By the way, no speed limits. Reasonable and Proper read the signs. Which really means go as fast as you want. That car did 100 miles per hour a number of times on that trip.

We stayed with Mandy for 10 days. She actually left us with our granddaughter Sammi. She was two at the time. What a cute two. Mandy had set up her high chair in the kitchen with a giant piece of plastic on the floor under the high chair. Here's how Sammi ate…"one for me, one for the floor." After each meal we emptied the plastic and Sammi would laugh. We taught her how to sit in a chair on that trip. She was so cute. We would put the chair against a wall and she would back across the room into it, and then laugh and laugh and do it again. What a happy child.

We did the trip to Spokane a few times. Once when Mandy was pregnant. Oh my was Mandy pregnant. She was the size of a house. She called us in New York to rush out, she was having the baby. False alarm. We went back to New York only to be called the following week again. This time she delivered Sammi.

We did the same thing with Max. Irving was stationed in Cambridge, England. They rented a house and we went out there when Max was being born. We got there just in time.. He was in a massive room. Mandy was the only person at the hospital on the base. So cute with his stocking cap. We followed Irv and Mandy all over except to Korea where he was based for a while. Oh well isn't that what Mimis and Poppas do!

VALDHOUSE/SILS MARIA. My brother Stan loves this hotel in the Alps. If you love the mountains it does not get more beautiful. We stayed at this old hotel. They had a quartet that would play chamber music every evening before dinner. Can you picture this in todays world. It is like stepping back into the 20's and 30's. Our favorite part was hiring a horse and buggy and traveling to the top of the mountain through the snow. Hot chocolate and sit on the bannister and look over the mountain. Cross country skiers travel along the frozen river for miles and miles. A very special place. They would send us a CD of the chamber group each Christmas. And it was addressed to: Doctor Harvey Herman and wife. I have a feeling that everyone was a Doctor. Made you feel special, from a special place.

LONDON AND FLORENCE. My daughter Joss has had her dream come true. She finally has rented an apartment in Paris. She and Michael are in love with this city.

We love two cities. Our first love was London. I think we went there over and over. I opened an office with Charlie there. He discovered Saville Row and spent every dime we made in that city on that fancy street. Every store owner knew him. Oh Charlie.

Elaine and I would go over just for weekends and stay extra days when we could. We always stayed at small hotels in Knightsbridge off of Sloane Street. At the end of Sloane was a long street filled with vintage clothing and antiques..Kings Road. We made many friends there. Pippa and David Schwartz lived in the Cottswalls. Richard Hall became a dear friend as well. He was a client in the toy business and remained a close friend forever.

London was like a second home to us. Who could forget the Basil Street Hotel. The best English breakfast ever. Fresh orange juice from Sicily. It was deep red in color and until we went to Sicily we never tasted anything like it. The breakfast plate had bacon, sausage, grilled tomatoes, potatoes and all the bread you could eat, and we did. The rooms were so tiny, but the food made up for it.

Our wardrobes came from Vintage stores only. Over the years we made so many friends in that business. Every weekend we would go to the markets Friday was Bermondze…Hot baked potatoes filled with beans, coleslaw and anything else you desired. It was a breakfast or lunch. Some of our best jewelry came from that market. Saturday was Portobello. So many dealers. I bought most of my Rolexes there. Today neither of these markets exist. What a pity.

At one time we thought seriously about living there but the kids came first.

FLORENCE We have toured almost every place in Italy. Florence is by far our favorite city. Some cites have some things you can not match…like Naples and their pizza and Rome's pizza is on the same level but very different. And nothing can compare to the sight and scenes of the Almalfi coast. But overall there is almost no place in the world that is more lovely and loved by us than Florence.

The museums and art galleries have some of the best art in the world. The food is very simple and delicious. A bowl of spaghetti can not be matched anywhere. And the fruits and vegetables are beyond comparison. That's the food. The architecture can not compete with Paris, however each street in the city has a richness. Even downtown in the heart of town there are small but spectacular gardens and homes that enrich the Florence experience.

For us the malls are less than an hour out of town. Elaine loves that shopping. And Lucca and Sienna are right around the corner. Each of those cities are magical on their own.

On her first trip there on her own, Elaine made friends with Alesandro. He owns a limo service and he has become like part of our family. We speak all the time. He can not do enough for us. Good friends are hard to find.
He takes us everywhere.

We love him and we love Florence.

Paolo in Milan with Pretzel.

Florence Prime Meat Market.
1967

On the street right off West 4th Street in the heart of Greenwich village was and still is a local and fabulous meat market. Florence on Jane Street. There really was a Jack Ubaldi and his younger partner Tony. Every one called the market Jack's. This tiny store was the talk of the town. Not just Greenwich Village, but the whole of New York City and beyond.

We would only buy our meat at Jack's. It was an experience to shop there. First of all everyone was on a first name basis. They knew you and they knew what cuts you liked and the ones you never tried. We had our apartment right around the corner. And, my brother Stan was literally next door. This market was an institution. You didn't just ask for steak, he knew we loved New York strip steaks and he would make sure he did not sell out of them until we got ours for the week.

Our daughter Joss was just 3 when she discovered Florence Prime Meat Market. She would go with us each week and the minute we entered the store Jack would stop what ever he was doing and take out the baloney and slice a two inch piece off and hand it to Joss.

"Thank you for the banonie...Mr Jack." No matter how hard she tried she could not pronounce her gift..."pernonie."

When we moved to the suburbs Jack would fill our order and we would drive to the city each week to get precious steaks.

I told this story to my new son-in-law David. He was so thrilled to hear about Jack and the Florence Prime Meat Market. He Googled it and found out they were still in business. Jack was gone but it was still Florence Prime Meat Market and they had just written a book about this famous place. David gave me a gift of the book.
There was Jack on the cover, beaming in all his glory.
It brought a tear to my eye.
Some things you never forget.

There was only one Jack.

Florence Prime Meat Market.

If I can't paint now, I am in trouble.

Where an artist paints is so fascinating. For years I would study different artists, their work and their studios. When my wife painted she would only paint in the bathroom because it was easy to clean the tile. By the way, she only painted in the nude. Again, after painting would jump into the shower. I would come home from work and there she was covered with paint, head to toe, her brushes in one hand and the biggest smile on her face that you could imagine. I wish she still painted today.

I have researched so many artists and their environments. I have been a painter most of my life. I always found a small space to call my own, but I am such a neat nick that I must clean up after painting and set up my pallets for the next time, so when I got to my paint space I was ready to go. When I looked at other painters it was amazing how messy some of them were. I wondered how they could work. But, the work space is so personal, almost like the work we produce. I learned a lot from the research and always had an idea of the kind of studio I would work in someday.

Except for the time we lived in the suburbs I never had an official studio until we converted an old barn that we found in New Hampshire and brought it to our home in Sheffield, Mass. It was a wonderful studio with a giant fireplace. Sometimes I would paint right through the night and have a cup of coffee the next morning as I surveyed the nights output. When we sold the place it was back to finding a corner somewhere to paint. Not complaining, but sometimes it was frustrating.

When we moved to Hampton Bays, I converted a small bedroom upstairs into my studio. A compact space, but great light and a wonderful view. I started to produce some excellent work, some of my best. I was retired and had the time now, and the right space. The work got much better over the next couple of years.

Then my wife got a stroke and she could not join me while I painted. I was on the second floor and she could not navigate the steps.

Time for my next step. I needed a studio on the same floor as Elaine, so she could join me as I worked. This was the opportunity to have the studio of my dreams. I went back to work reading and studying other artists and why they designed the studios they worked in.

I started by making a list of all of the areas that I would need and what each area would look like and function. Beauty and function. Function first. Within a month I had my first set of drawings done. Good, but not great. The light was all wrong. Not enough wall space. An area where I could finally work large. At least 5 by 6 feet and room to plan. Also great storage space. Why not have it all.
Back to the drawing board.

If I can't paint now, I am in trouble.

In another few months I had drawn the perfect studio, to me at least. It was on the same level as the rest of our home. I would break through the hallway at the back of our house, go through a long gallery hallway, where I could hang some of my work, have a separate room that I could turn into a bedroom off the hallway and at the end of the hallway it would open to a 20x25 giant room with 16 foot ceilings, two massive skylights, a storage area that had a John in it and a sink to clean up after working. When it was all done I thought it was perfect.

I found an architect to draw up plans and then got our builder to give us costs. My son-in-law Michael and I and my daughter Joss had built two homes together so we had all the people to do build it, but when I got the estimates from Mike it was too expensive. Mike and Joss said no. They would help me pay for it. It was my dream and they wanted to help make it possible for me. How great is that.

I am not going to go through all the stuff that we had to change in order to afford my dream. And, my grand daughter Sophie looked at the drawings as we were about to start the foundation. "Where's the fireplace Poppa," she asked. Right again, and about an additional $15,000 later we had a brilliant fireplace in the center of the largest wall in the studio. Perfect.

Yes perfect is how I would say it turned out. Even better than I had planned. There were two giant windows that faced North to get the great light and above those windows two massive skylights. This is where I would do most of my drawing and planning my work

But I needed an old architect desk about 8 feet wide that would tilt up an be deep enough to work on. I finally found one in antique shop in Southampton. It was as if I designed it. But they wanted too much money. I bargained with them, but me being the cheap skate I can be, stupidly passed on it. I told my brother Stan about it. He said go back and buy the desk you fool. It sounds perfect. I went back the next day to buy it and believer it or not it was sold. It was sold. I was pissed at myself.

I went to the owner and complained that I was such a good customer how could they sell it without calling me first. They apologized, but my being cheap cost me again.

About a week later the antique shop called to say that they had a desk that was great. I should come in to look at it. When I got there I was shocked . It was just like the first one I had lost. In fact it was the same desk. My brother had been the other buyer.
He had bought it for me.

That was about a year ago. I now have started working large and the work is the best I have ever done.

**It only took 40 years to have my dream come true...
but who's counting.**

If I can't paint now, I am in trouble. 343

Rutt's Hut

I can't believe I almost forgot writing about this one. It played a very important role in my life. If you do not know this place Google it. You will find out what a "ripper" is. If Clifton, New Jersey is famous for anything it just might be the best hot dogs anywhere.

When we got our drivers license the place we most went to was Rutt's Hut. Ken Berman got his car first. A two tone green 1952 Chevy. On Friday nights we would drive our dates over and devour these giant dogs. This will sound terrible...these hot dogs were unique. They cooked them in boiling oil. If you wanted it well done they would keep them in a few minutes longer until the skin popped open and revealed the pure beef. This was called the "ripper." Then you would top it off with the best. Homemade yellow relish. A secret recipe that they eventually packed and sold in large plastic containers to take home. They also made their own mustards. Two or three different ones. Each hotter than the next. And there was also home made baked beans and their own sauerkraut. You could pile all of these on top of your ripper and eat as many half sour pickles as you could fit in. If you ate two of them, you were a hero.
There was only one Rutt's Hut.

I dated a bunch of young ladies and judged them by how much they could consume of these wonderful dogs. I only knew one who could eat more than any of the guys.

George Feifer of Herman Berman and Feifer ended up living in Russia for ten years. He missed home so I sent him a Rutt's Hut sweatshirt. You would think I bought him a Rolex.

I talked so much about Rutt's, my son-in-law drove out to Clifton and bought us a half dozen dogs and each of us a Rutt's Hutt T shirt.

We devoured them for lunch yesterday...the dogs, not the T shirts.

The "ripper."

I almost left this one out
1943 to 1949

This is a tough one. My dad remarried about a year after my mom passed away. He met Evelyn at the Congress Hotel in the Borscht Belt on Sacket Lake. Single Jewish ladies very often went up to the hotels in that area to find a great mate. My dad fit the bill. He was making money and his wife was gone for around a year. Sure he had two sons, but that didn't seem to deter Evelyn from pursuing my dad.

She found out that he was single and loved horses. So she rushed to Kaufman's Saddlery in New York City and outfitted herself from head to toe in the best riding outfit around. Dad was not fooled, but for some reason they hit it off, and cut to the important stuff...he did not hesitate getting married. We were not invited to his ceremony...he told us he would tell us when to call Miss Jacobs mother. That's it. A pretty bad start.

We moved to a small house in Passaic...64 Kensington Terrace. Dad was starting to make money because of the war. He was selling a lot of fabric to the Army. It was 1943 and it was not long before Mitch came along. Up until then, Stan and I were not that happy with Evelyn or Dad, but it was manageable. When Mitch came it was all changed. The next 8 years were pure hell. To put it bluntly Evelyn could not handle raising Mitch and the two of us at the same time. Looking back on it now, she was way over her head and could not tell my father. He was so busy making a living for his family.

This story is important because those years had a lot to do with my attitudes about life going forward. Those years were the most miserable ones in my whole life. Turns out Evelyn was tough beyond belief. Stan went off to college and she turned into a very aggressive punishing person. I was the one she took it out on. I was scared to death of her. She would squeeze my arm and shake me until her nails ripped my flesh. She punished my all the time. I must admit I was not easy, but looking back on those years all I needed was love. I complained to dad from time to time but he refused to believe me. I did not know who to turn to. I was young and life was not working out. Dad said if I could not get along with her that he would send me off to Military School. I remember how lost and alone I felt at that time.

One day really stands out in my mind. I argued with Evelyn about something and she lost her cool. I don't remember how old I was, but I was pretty young and small. She grabbed my arm and pulled me down the stairs to the basement. We had a giant refrigerator down there. It was just a big box that the overflow of food would be stored in. Most of time it was empty. This is hard to write about, but she put me in that icebox. It was one of the most frightening moments of my life. I screamed and cried out. "I'll be good, please let me out." I am sure I was only in there for minutes but it seemed like I was going to die.

From that time on I did whatever Evelyn told me to do. She had won. She broke me.

She was much better with Stan. He ended up designing dresses for her when she gave out trophies at the horse show at Madison Garden. He said he was shocked when I told him about all the beatings. I was quite surprised that he was surprised.

When Stan was in puberty she took the doors off our bedrooms so that we could not masturbate. Really.

Stan was on the David Suskind television show many years later when he was successful and told that story. People found it tough to believe but were hysterical with laughter.

A day came when I was about 15 that everything changed. Evelyn cornered me in the front hall and hit me on my arms and chest. I don't know what made me do it, but I hit her back for the first and only time. My fist hit her in the side of her head and she went down like a ton of bricks. She was a giant of a woman. Tall, big breasts and very scary. I knocked her out with one punch. I thought I had killed her. She got up and started to cry…"I am going to tell your father. I am going to tell him. You are going to get it now."

She never told dad. She never mentioned the punch and she never, yes never hit me again.

Why am I including this story? At first I decided it served no purpose. But recently I changed my mind. I realized that I painted my problems with her over my relationship with Mitch. What a lose. How stupid can you get. Not only did I not have a mother I could have lost a brother too.

Mitch is now 79 and I am 90. In a seminar I am in I got to see that this is why I have never developed anything with my younger brother. The issues I had with Mitch's mom clouded our relationship. I am going to make an effort to correct this. It is never too late.

I also have found myself complaining a lot about dad. I had always felt that he loved Stan more than me, and he got all the attention. Possibly true…but so what. He did the best to raise all three kids, and by the way he stayed with Evelyn until the day she died. He told Stan and I that she was the "love of his life." Dad passed away a few years later.

Why bring this up at all?

I realized that dad was not very nice to my wife until she had her stroke. Before we married dad tried to talk me out of it. He said to her, believe it or not, that she was married and divorced and she was dead wood. Why would I marry someone with so much baggage. I deserved better. She never forgot that. Every time I bad mouthed dad my wife would chime in and she felt great that I felt the same way about him.
That is over.
I love my dad. He did a good job. Not the job I would have done but who am I to be critical. No more looking for agreement from my wife.

No more being judgmental of my young brother Mitch, too. He has a family that he loves and they love him.

After all isn't that what really matters.

Evelyn and family minus Stan.

The Herman boys.

I almost left this one out 1943 to 1949

The Tannenbaums.

Thank god for this wonderful family. Starting with my mom and continuing throughout my life this group of people gave me the roots and a wonderful set of values in life. They have always been there for me. Always.

When Elaine and I married in 1963, sixty years ago, she painted a special picture of my Tannenbaum family. My grandma and grandpa and their eight children. The shot was taken 100 years ago in 1923. What a special shot. Grandpa sat in the middle with my Aunt Ellen on his lap. She was a baby of two. My uncle Sunny just off to his left and all the others surrounded this 300 pound giant of a man.

To celebrate our first year together in marriage Elaine painted a picture of all ten Tannenbaums. It is so special. The reason I say "is" is because it hangs next to our bed out in the Hamptons. I wake up each day to this fabulous group that has meant so much to our family.

This year I found the perfect person to print this painting as a limited edition of just 10 and sent it out to the daughters and sons of everyone pictured in the painting, with a letter from me telling them how important their moms and dads had been in the lives of me and my brother Stan.

I asked that their families keep the love alive. The response has been so special. The Tannenbaums survive.

Stanley and Grandma Tannenbaum.

Some of the many Tannenbaums.

The Tannenbaums.

Those Mad Men Days!

I was a late bloomer. Didn't have sex until I was in college. But I made up for my lateness over the years. In college I dated a lot and most of the dates turned out to be intimate and sexual. I really found that I liked sex and yet there was a part of me that felt that I was preforming, and I rated myself from time to time. I am not sure if that is natural, or if others do the same.

I went back in my memory to review some of the sexual relationships that I had. Most were just sex for the sake of sex. Some stand out as being very important. Certainly my engagement to Boots Orlanis was very special. Our sex was sensational. No performing as I remember it. She and I hit it off. We loved to have sex almost all the time. She was a true soul mate.

When I got into the advertising business, that is when things changed for me. I was happily married and yet I still felt the need to have outside sex. I remember when I was at Smith Greenland, I think I had affairs with at least 3 women. Each was an assistant to one of the principals of the agency. I had to have all of them over the 3 plus years I was at the agency. They were seductions. Pure sex, no real involvement. This went on for the first 14 years of my marriage. I never got the effect it had on my relationship with the world, and certainly my family.

When we lived in Hartsdale I met a very young lady. She was 20 at the time and I was 43. I carried on that affair for over a year. I was such a cad. I lied all the time to my wife that I had to work late. What was I doing? I even had a fling with my wife's best friend. And the biggie was my five month affair with Elizabeth Taylor.

Looking back on all that sex I still wonder why was it so necessary? Was I so insecure? Why did I need sex so much? Was it all just my need for love?

This is one of the very few regrets that I have had in my life. Who was this man? How blind could he be?

There came a time when my two daughters sat me down in the living room at 19 east 88th street. I remember it was a Sunday.

 Joss and Amanda were very serious. They told me they knew that I was cheating on Mom and it did not work for them. If I continued cheating, they would not see me anymore. You had to be there. They did not say it in anger. They wanted me to know that they were with Mom and I had to shape up or get out. I was shook.

I did not say anything. They left me sitting alone in the living room. I only remember that feeling of losing everything all at once.

I stopped cheating on my wife and family that day.
That was over 45 years ago.

Those Mad Men Days!

The Stroke
2005

It was eighteen years ago that Elaine had her stroke. How has this effected our life together? I was thinking about that over the past few days, and thought I would write about the relationship today and how it has been over the period since she crawled up the stairs to my studio with her face twisted…"My god honey, you are having a stroke."

Life changed that day for Elaine and I. We rushed her to the hospital and she was left with a left side pretty well paralyzed. We spent the next 30 days in Rusk hospital on 34th Street and the River in NYC. My brother Stan lived on 35th and Madison. I stayed with him during that month of rehabilitation. I was with her everyday. She worked so hard to learn to walk again. She was amazing. No kid here. She had the stroke when she was 72. Most people don't make it at that age, I was told.

A little progress. She could eventually walk with a walker and if she worked her left arm she could use it a little. Slow progress if any…but through it all she never complained. She dragged that body over and over to therapy and fittings for braces. You name it. No complaints.

How have we managed these last eighteen years? We made up our minds that I would become her caretaker. We would have help cleaning the house but other than that it is me and my bride at our wonderful home in the Hamptons. I asked Elaine how she would describe these years together

Her response…"very, very good." And she is oh so right.

If you ask me that question I would tell you they have been very tough but in many ways the best years of our lives together. There are days I would like to throw the sponge in, but those are recently since Elaine has come down with dementia.

I have had to give up many things, especially within the last two years…like flying. I could not get enough time to be safe at that passion. I am 90 and I just sold my plane and gave up flying for now. I still have my pilots license and who knows, but for now others will fly me when I can get away. I flew with a good friend Sally last week to Hyanis to bring one of my paintings to Bill and Ronnie. There will be times like that, I hope.

But back to Elaine…I am so sorry she had the stroke, but our life is deeper and more meaningful since that event.
We love each other, and how we are handling life, proves it.

Kaufman Astoria Studios.
1982

We had opened our agency in 1979. We moved to a great location at 110 Park Avenue at 59th Street. Lot's of wide open space on a high floor. The agency was booming. We were hot. Marx Toys had turned into a cash cow and we were doing such great work for them. In the first year Charlie and I took bonuses of $200,000 each on top of our excellent weekly salaries. I used the money to invest in an apartment in New York City and also a home in Sheffield, Mass. Charlie spent it on clothes.

A good friend of Charlies...Judy Stockman, an interior designer helped me design our apartment at 19 East 88th Street. A splendid art deco building that we raised our kids in. Life was so good and easy... could it get any better. We then got Eyelab with Bob Hillman and that put the icing on the cake.

Our lease was about to come up after two years and a good friend of mine was doing the publicity for Kaufman Astoria Studios out in Astoria. They had the two giant stages and were making a lot of movies and television programs. George Kaufman, one of the nicest men I had ever known wanted to open up the business and get other media and creative companies to move into the studio. A tough one for most. Although Astoria was only about 15 minutes away from Manhattan it was a world apart. Who would move to Astoria? Would clients come there? It was a little like Siberia at that time.

I went out there was Charlie. We went to the stages. Saw Woodie Allen shooting and Sidney Lumet as well. When we went to the cafeteria for lunch with George he introduced us to the cast of the two movies being shot there at the time. We talked and talked and by the time lunch was over George had offered us $250,000 in cash to build and 6 months free rent. I was sold. Even Charlie thought it might be exciting.

I called Judy Stockman and she came out to the space. She was so excited. She drew this very dynamic, tasteful layout. A two level office with a suspended showroom in the center to show our work. We fell in love. We showed it to George Kaufman and the deal was done. It took 3 months to build and George bought a special black van to take clients back and forth from Manhattan. Everything was done with the best taste.

All of the clients loved coming out and being in the movie business for a day. Especially the MTA. And the office was such a pleasure to work in. Even Charlie really liked it. He was not sure that it would work out.

Astoria was such a mixture of Italian, Jewish and so many other kinds of people. It was affordable. And there were a number of very special restaurants. We fell in love with it all...for the first year.

Then we realized that we had a big problem running the agency out there. We thought getting clients to come out would be the big one... but we were wrong.

We never realized that creatives would not want to leave Manhattan. We couldn't get good talent to leave the city for Astoria, Queens. No one would come at any price.

Charlie and I were feeling the effects of working overtime, especially me. It started to backfire. And then out of the blue the world opened up for us again. I was sitting in the office early one morning and who should walk in. It was 7:30.

"Let's have breakfast together, you big bum."

It was my buddy George Kaufman. I loved the guy. He was one of the most successful real estate people in the country. Up there like the Rudins. Besides the studio he owned or ran over 30 buildings in Manhattan. And, here's the thing...he was as nice a human being as I had ever met.

We loved to talk about our affairs with our movie stars. He had one with Gina Lolabridgida and I had been with Elizabeth Taylor.

Kaufman Astoria Studios. 1982

We talked about what it was like to run with the big stars. We loved each others company.

I thought he was going to ask us for more rent. He would show our space to people who wanted to move out there. It was like a showcase for the studio.

He took me to his favorite breakfast place…the cafeteria in the studio. He ordered his favorite blueberry pancakes with Italian sausage. I started to get a little nervous. He was all smiles.

"OK George, what's up?" I finally blurted out.

"I need your office space. Don't get excited. I know you did a great job building it out, but Lifetime just signed a 2 year contract out here, and they love your space."

Oh my god. He was saving our ass. Charlie and I were trying to figure out how to get back to Manhattan and here comes our savior.

"I will build you new space and charge you less. I will make it worth your while."

Here's the wonderful part about this gentle giant of a man. I told him the truth…that we were trying to figure out how to get back to the city. He hugged me and said he would pay for the move, pay for us to build a new office and pay for the first 6 months rent. It cost him over $500,000. He could of taken advantage, but instead he made our lives supreme.

What a guy. George Kaufman.

215 Park Avenue South.   Back to the city.

Kaufman Astoria Studios. 1982

The Older, younger brother.

What can I say about this younger, older brother. He has alway been five years older than me. That's because he was born five years before me. Neither of us were supposed to be born. Mom and Dad were warned that her heart was not strong enough to have children. But they did it anyway. She died when I was just 7 and Stanley or "Stash" as many called him was only 12.

When we were very young I hung on every word of his. He put up with me. He usually got everything. Piano, tap dance, great outfits. I didn't. Oh well, don't make that mean anything, right.

It was so great having an older brother. I really looked up to him. Whatever he tried, I tried. He jumped off the high diving board in the borscht belt and I followed him, even though I could not swim at the age of 4. He tumbled from one bed to the other and I followed but didn't make it to the other bed, instead the cedar chest punched a hole just above my right eye and 12 stitches closed that one out. How can a kid half his age compete!

As we got older and he went off to the University of Cincinnati he came home to find that Dad had told me that since I was going to work with him I did not need to go to college…instead he put me in a commercial course in High School. I was learning how to type when Stan found out and talked Dad into sending me to college instead. Don't know how he did that.

In those years he was like my "trim tab." The smallest adjustments kept me on track. That's the way I remember it.

He went from college to the Army in Germany. He finally allowed his life as a homosexual to enrich his life. We grew apart. He fell in love with Gene, his lifetime partner, and we grew even further apart. Our life paths were so different. Still there were times that he helped me manage my life.

Stan and his 30 year partner, Gene.

I graduated college a textile chemist, and worked that career for just two years and decided it was not for me. I wasn't sure what was next. Dad was pissed that I was not going into business with him. He had to wait for my other brother Mitch to join him a number of years later. Mitch worked with Dad for over forty years. I couldn't make it for forty days.

Stan and I sat down one day and he casually suggested that I liked working with people and people seemed to like me, why not try PR or advertising. It made sense. Again that "trim tab" at work.

When I married at the age of 28 in 1963, we had already created lives that were far apart. A few years later in 1969 he won the Coty award, ahead of Ralph. His life had taken off, and again. I was working for seven different ad agencies learning the business so that I could start my own ten years later in 1979.

He was in Southampton with Gene and our family had discovered the Berkshires. Our family now included Bruce our son and two sensational daughters….Joss and Amanda and two dogs of course. Stan had his standard poodle…Moe.

I took a break from advertising in 1975 for a few years to try my skills at being a movie director. A five month affair with a movie Icon while

Stan had become the King of QVC and the Icon of Career Apparel. In 1979 I finally got my dream...my own ad agency. It was a giant success until I got bored in 1990. That year Stan's life with Gene ended and so did Bruce's. A lot of ending and new beginnings.

Stan became the president of the CFDA. A really big deal. And he and Fern Malis started the tents in Bryant Park...another big deal. Stan was in the limelight for the next 16 years and he finally got recognized as an Icon in the fashion business.

I was a consultant in a number of businesses for the next 15 years until Elaine and I retired to Hampton Bays, right around the corner from Stan in Southampton.
I have become a full time painter and although Elaine had a stroke our lives out here have been some of the best years. Stan and I and Elaine have grown very close. We speak everyday...perhaps a few times each day over the past ten or more years.

Stan just had his memoir published. It is an important statement of his role in the fashion world. I am very proud of him.

I just started my memoir. Again that "trim tab" at work.

Stan and my granddaughter both encouraged me to tell the story of my life, and this is one of the stories in that effort.

Stan is 95 and I am 90, of course.
He is stepping into the future every day.
A good example to follow.

Let's hope we can enjoy the following years together.

Try and pick Stan and me out!

The Older, younger brother.

My life on a horse

Throughout my life, horseback riding was always there. I never would have met my wife if I did not show up that night at The Garden. Truth is, Dad put me on a horse when I was just five. I do not mean a pony, a horse and I loved it from the first minute. He did the same with Mitch and Stan but it did not take. Dad always wanted one of his sons to follow in his footsteps as a rider. It looked like me, but it never really happened.

Did I ride? You bet I did. And I was a natural. I had great hands. I could feel the horse and be one with it. But I never showed. I never made it to the ring. According to Dad I "was not ready yet." Now, now be nice.

Let's go back to beginnings again.

We had a horse before we had a car. Dad had learned to ride when he was a young boy in Vienna. He had something to do with the famous White Lipizan. Dad kept a horse in the garage in Passaic, New Jersey on Palmer Street. What fun to ride around the neighborhood. Not the usual sport of a Passaic kid. I loved riding.

As soon as he could afford a stable he brought the horse to Allwood Avenue in Clifton. He brought his three boys there to ride almost every weekend. What fun This was when I was around five to twelve or so. Many years of fun riding.

Dad had regular saddle horses and he also started jumping. He didn't get into 5 gaited horses until much later.

One story I remember was we all went to a show to watch dad jump this great horse that was supposed to be a winner. Every time dad would get to a jump the horse would stop and not jump. Over and over, until dad dropped out of the class.

Turns out Joe Brown who took care of dad's horses was supposed to have the horse shipped down to the show. Instead he pocketed the shipping money and rode the horse about 10 miles to the show. The horse was too tired to jump. Oh well.

Another story happened when I was about 10 years old. I was riding with a friend Louie Klienman next to the airport in Caldwell. (Where I would have my first flying lesson forty years later). Louie and I rode out about a mile or so ahead of my dad and his friends. We galloped and rode like nuts. Faster and faster, until my horse stepped into a hole and I went flying over his head and the horse went over as well. We both were laying there. I thought I had killed the horse. I got up slowly and Louse helped the horse get up on it's four legs. All seemed well. "Louie, don't tell my dad, he will kill me." That's all I worried about. Funny how that event sticks in my mind.

Through my teenage years I rode a lot with dad. After college I continued riding. Never showing. I was so good at it.

You see there are a few things you either get right or you never master becoming a special rider. Your feet were first. You had to fit your feet in the stirrups so that you always posted off the ball of your feet. The second most important one was your hands. So important. You could feel the mouth of the horse if you were good. It was all in the hands. The horse knew when you had this right and when you didn't . And finally the knees. These were so important. You could direct a horse without your hands, with just the pressure from your knees.
I learned this very early and my knees we're so strong.

I often took a horse out and rode it bareback, no saddle and just a halter around the head. This meant you were riding without reigns. You would hold on to the horse's main and control him with just your knees. What joy. Dad watched how I did this with such pride, but he preferred that I use a saddle.

You can tell how much I loved riding. When l got older my uncle Bruno got a horse but he hardly ever rode it. It was a dapple grey. Beautiful horse, but it didn't get worked out enough. So dad asked me to drive up to work out the horse when I was in my last year of high school. Wow that was great. But I had to make sure after I worked the horse out that I would walk her until she was dry and then wash her down and dry her before putting her in the stall. I always did.

One day dad came up and he really gave it to me. You see I really worked a horse out. I always rode hard. The dapple grey would lather up, but I always walked her till she was cool, and washed and tried her before putting her away. When dad saw her so lathered up he made me stop riding. I never rode that horse again, and I believe that was the end of my show chances. Dad never lathered his horses, when they started to sweat he cooled them down. I felt they never got to their full potential. But he was the boss, and he felt I did not care about the horses. I did ...I felt you had to push them sometime, especially in a class if you wanted to win.

Dad, to my best of memory, never won classes. Later when he had a trainer ride in the shows we would occasionally win.
As I write this I can see how stupid I was to resist dad. It was just the way he ran his life. He did not need to win, he enjoyed the ride.

He taught me how to enjoy riding.

When Elaine and I went to Egypt we got horses and a guide on his horse to take us out to ride in the desert around the pyramids. When the guide saw how comfortable I was on the horse he told me to go and "ride the wind." I did. I felt like Lawrence of Arabia. What a day. Total joy. Elaine loved the head dress the guide was wearing. The next morning he showed up at our hotel. Seemed Elaine had negotiated a good price for the headwear. She could shop anywhere, even in the desert.

When I turned 50 I stopped riding. I changed passions. I started flying. I gave all my spare time to flying. No more riding. Turns out I learned to fly Piper cubs. You flew the plane like a horse. Stick and rudder...just like hands and knees. I got real good at that, too.

When dad turned 90 and I turned 60 dad sat me down and made a request. "Please start riding again" he asked. He wanted his legacy to continue in the family. He wanted my grandkids to ride. I agreed. But what happened...? I had lost it. I no longer had the strength in my knees and my hands were so bad and weak. I tried for a few months but the touch was gone.

I don't know how dad rode into his nineties. He was special.
I thank him for teaching me how to ride.
It really was a passion.

No ponies for me!

One Sheridan Square.

This address played a very important role in our lives. Elaine found this apartment on the top floor. It had a terrace all around it. In fact there was another apartment next door that shared the roof. An old lady, whose name I cannot remember, rented that one.

When Elaine found this Shangrila we were not married. She was going to move in without me. We had been going together for 5 years but I was too scared to make the commitment. She found this apartment and I proposed. "Let's get married." *Some proposal.*

But it worked. Bruce, Elaine's son from her first brief marriage, lived there with us. It had two bedrooms, a giant living room dinning room with a fireplace and a closet for a kitchen, but a terrace surrounded the whole apartment and looked out on the whole of The Village. We loved it. I think the rent was $255 per month. Stan lived just down the block on West Fourth Street. It was in the heart of our favorite place in the world...Greenwich Village. A block away was the Park.

By then we had moved out of the North apartment on the roof to the South apartment, which was a tiny bit bigger. When we finally adopted Josselyne we had to cut Bruce's room in half, which was pretty small already. He was pissed, and rightfully so. We had one dog then...Corky. He was originally Elaine's dog. He would steal anything that Joss would wear and rip it to pieces. I wonder what that meant. I really got into painting at night, although there was very little room to paint.

We only lived at this apartment for less than 4 years, those years were some of the best in our lives. We grew up there. We saw theatre in the neighborhood. I painted and so did Elaine. We both took courses at The New School.

It opened our relationship to the world of culture, and we grabbed the golden ring.

One Sheridan Square.

QVC

Like I said in another story, Stan has become the King of QVC. As of this writing he has been on there selling his loungewear plus for over thirty years. What a record. Hard to believe.

He is so loved down there in Westchester just outside of Philadelphia. When he comes on, the world of QVC ignites and his customers who give him his 5 star ratings can't wait to phone in and tell him how important Stan Herman is in their lives. It is really amazing.

So what does that have to do with me. Well every once and a while QVC entertains taking on new vendors. Bob Hillman and I had started the first fashion Ready Reader eyeglass company and I decided to take a shot at QVC. Twenty companies were interviewed that day. They reviewed your product line and gave you an introduction to why QVC was unique. If you passed that part you had to go in front of the cameras and make a presentation offering your product line, not selling... offering. Big difference.

Twenty two companies started that first day, only 5 survived the first part. I was one of them. The five went in front of the camera. A part I loved. I wore red glasses that day, and red shoes to match. They loved the ready-reader line. It was the first they had ever offered. It was new to them. I don't know if being Stan's brother helped, but I suspect it did not hurt. Two of the twenty two became new vendors. Our great line of fashion ready-readers and John Maddens shoe line. Pretty impressive. The new venture began.

I made a lot of mistakes working with QVC. First of all, I did not understand that they could return any part of an order with no reason. Stan was on so long that they Grandfathered in the fact that they could not return any of their purchases. Once they ordered, they owned it. We were just the opposite. So when they ordered with us, I should have kept the quantities limited. They loved a lot of the product, and they ordered too much most of the time. It meant going down over and over to finish selling the product. And from Hampton

Bays it was 4 hours each way. Eight hours round trip for about 5 minutes of air time.

It was fun being on. They wanted me to wear my red shoes all the time. A signature idea. And, here was the biggie. When would they put you on? Sometimes it was in the middle of the night, or other times it was very early in the morning, and they wanted you there at least 2 or 3 hours in advance for make up and meeting the host. All for around 5 minutes of air time. The glasses were beautiful and unique. We priced them right too. So the first 6 or more times we were on, we did very well. It was working.

Then Bob and I came to them with a special set of very thin glasses. Very special, but at the same time not everyones cup of tea. They also liked them and ordered twice as many as usual. Also that evening I was not feeling well, so I was not up enough...the result was the glasses hardly sold. They had promised us 4 or 5 showings because they ordered a lot more than we wanted to sell to them, but after that one selling they returned about $100,000 of glasses, without even advising us. Wow.

There was another set of glasses, the Filigrees that was selling great, so the next day they reordered the filigrees again. I did not want to fill another order unless they gave us another shot at the ones they returned. That was it with QVC. It was fun while it lasted for a little over 2 years.

It taught me a real lesson. Because I always wanted control in business I never really wanted partners. Hillman and I were first with fashion ready readers...before Warby Parker. It took Warby over 20 million in investments before they caught on, but today they have a billion dollar company. Bob and I would never do that.

I did the same with our ad agency. At one point Arthur Fat, the chairman of Grey Advertising offered me a partnership and close to a million dollars a year to open a division of his agency, with a seven year contract. I turned it down. I never regretted it.

Some great friends from my ad days.

In 1960 I opened a company called The Promotion Centre. I wrote a whole story about sending apples out to get clients. One of the apples went to Crossway Motor Hotels. This was a group of motels around the New York City area run by a few aggressive young guys. They loved my work and hired me. I decided the best way to get to know the account was to visit each and get to interview the motel managers. This is how I met Dawin Bahm. That was 64 years ago and we are still very close friends. He was a motel manager and he did not fit. "Why are you in this job"? I asked after meeting with him. He hated what he was doing, but he said that he had no idea of what to do…that is when I introduced him to advertising.

He was unbelievable. He loved art and wanted to use that in his career. I suggested he be an artist rep. "What is an artist rep"? I explain that he could discover illustrators and other artists that could be used in editorial for magazines and advertising. He was so excited. He knew a few sculptures and illustrators and signed them up while still on his job for the motel. I gave him names of three magazines and their art directors to call. He took a day off from his work and traveled to Philadelphia to Curtis Publishing. All three mags were there. He called me that evening. "This is great. I booked three projects in the first day. This is easy, I am quitting the motel. Thanks for all the help". That's the way I remember it.

I couldn't believe he booked three jobs the first day…but he didn't book another one for the next 3 months…but he was in love. He became one the most successful out of town artist reps in the ad business. He paid no attention to New York City where most of the reps toured. He went out of town to smaller agencies and built a business no one since has ever done.

Dawin is married to a wonderful woman Joan. She is a very special primitive artist. I love her work. We have spent so much time together. We both had our homes in Sheffield, Mass. We both loved it so much up there.

I met Joan on my first job in advertising. When they lived in The Village in the city we did too. I'm not sure who followed who. They had one of the best art collections around. Mostly from artists he represented. They are both retired living in New Mexico with their daughter. They too are in their 90's. Ninety five if I am not mistaken. I met both in the business and they made our life better.

Jerry Lieberman is another incredible creative I met .He had a show of his Play Systems in the Pepsi Cola building on Park Avenue and 59th street. Life Magazine gave him 6 full color pages of the exhibit. It was beyond great. He used reusable materials to make playscapes in the park instead of those predictable swings and seesaws. Pure genius. But we became good friends for many years. We worked on toys together. The best I think was a baseball hat that transformed into an action hero, or any other kind of character. Still a great idea. But again we never got it sold. He deserved better. A really good guy. Very creative.

I also met John Baeder in the ad business. John, in a lot of ways, influenced my life as an artist. John worked at Smith Greenland as an art director when I joined them. He was a very special guy. Talented and very smart. I loved his style not just in his work. He often talked about leaving the business and becoming a painter. One day he did just that. Walked out…and decided it was time to paint.

He opened a tiny studio in a walk up on 56th and 3rd Avenue. About three months later he asked me up to see his work. I was blown away. He was painting diners. Real life diners all around these United States. The painting were so real and gorgeous. He brought a dying life style that was made famous in America back to life. Look him up. His smarts for the world around him shows up in every one of his paintings. He had the balls to do what he loved. I admire him for that step in his life. He lives in Nashville for many years. We talk from time to time. He is struggling with his health now, but he made his mark in this complicated world as an artist that is unique and very special. He is an inspiration to me. He helped me see that I had something to say in the world of art as well. Thank you John.

Some great friends from my ad days.

When I worked at Smith Greenland I met Nina Feinberg. She turned out to be one of our closest friends. She was married to David. A wonderful guy as well. Turns out we hit it off immediately. We had two girls the same years that they two boys. The kids became fast friends. We each became each others god parents. The kids went everywhere together. They lived on the Westside we lived across the park on the Eastside. In the summer the kids went to the same camp. Our lives became totally intertwined.

Nina was a good copywriter at Smith Greenland. She was offered a job in Chicago and they said that they would only work at Foote Cohen for a year or so. David went to work there too. That turned into close to 50 years. They never came back to the Big Apple. Chicago was easy and they needed easy. Nina always wanted to write musicals for the stage. David always talked about writing novels for a living. They dabbled but never took the leap. With it all they were as close as any of our family. In fact they were family. We miss them. David passed a couple of month ago and Nina had left him a dozen or so years ago. Of course we talk to their kids from time to time. One of them is very close to us. He is like another son. Hard to lose friends like these

Another couple that have been important in our lives. Carol Case was married to Ira Lieberman. He was our chiropractor for many years. Carol and Ira were in one of my seminars when I lead for Landmark. They got a lot out of the work. Ira had a beach house in Westhampton and Carol was a very successful rep for a few commercial directors. We spent a good deal of time together over the years. Ira passed away after a tough battle with Parkinson's for a number of years. That was about 3 or 4 years ago…and Carol has found a new love in her life. I must admit in the end I had a number of issues with Ira. Perhaps it was the disease that made it difficult for me to continue our friendship. As I look back I wonder if I could have done more to repair the rift. It certainly was up to me, and I did not do it. There are so many other people that we knew over the years, that I realize I did not include in my memoir. Sorry if you are one of them.

A late bloomer?

Bruce was cute at 5 when I first met him.

When I look back on my life I started out late on most important things.
I was a virgin until my first year in College. I lived with my parents until I
was 25. I opened my agency at the age of 46. I ran my first marathon at the
age of 43. Wow. I just realized that I left out all my running…
10 Marathons and one Triathlon. They were so important in my life.
Well I am going to write about them now.

Some great friends from my ad days.

Running keep running.

How did I get involved in running long distance? A good friend of mine, Norman Tannen decided to do a film about the New York City Marathon. He shot it, and asked if I would help him edit it. I did. I think this was around 1973. They ran around Central Park 6 times and never left Manhattan. I looked at about 500 people who ran it and said…"I can do that". Then my cousin Lloyd ran his only marathon and I said "if he can do it so can I". Not that I am competitive or anything.

I was living in California, it was 1976. I started training for my first marathon with two friends from LA. Jan Berfin and her friend I can't remember his name right now. They wanted to run one in New York. We found one in May of 76 that was in Plattsburg. I had never heard of it. It is on the border of Canada. Why we picked it, I don't remember.

We all traveled from LA on Thursday and arrived in Plattsburg late that afternoon. The marathon was on Saturday, very unusual. We rented a car and rode the route, marking off all the mile markers and a band that we could keep on our wrists. We were being so creative. I had bought a whole new outfit for running including new sneakers. The marathon started at 9AM Saturday. Turns out there were 600 people entered. It was hot. In the morning it was over 80 degrees. The race started and I went out much too fast. It got really hot. The water stops were too far apart, usually 3 miles or so. They should be every mile, but who knew. I soon realized that the mile markers were not the same as the ones on my wrist. I was so confused. Turns out the car was Canadian and the car was in Kilometers not miles. . Anyway around 15 miles or so I realized I was running alone. No one in front or back. How could that be? Was I running the right course? They had painted the mile markers on the pavement. I just passed 16 and I was not sweating. Bad sign. And my sneakers were killing me. It started to feel like I was going to throw up.

I stopped and a little boy on the side of the rode asked if I was OK.

Joss with my Barry Kielselstein.

I asked if he could get me some water and ice cubes. His mother came out with both. The cubes went under my cap and the water went down my parched throat. At around 20 miles I started to feel like I was done. I could not move my legs. Not a soul in site. I had hit the famous wall. Foot over foot they said to keep going...

The next and final six miles were pure torture. I had gone out too fast. Ran the first 20 in under 7 1/2 miles per hour. Much too fast. The temperature now was 90, in May. I dragged myself over the finish line in 3 hours and 42 minutes. I think I was 16th in the whole race. 285 finished that day over 300 in the hospital. It was a slaughter. I took my sneakers off and every toe was bleeding. New sneakers. How stupid can you get. I will never run another I promised myself. My two friends finished in well over 5 hours. They were wiped out also. We played on the grass and watched each person come across the finish line at lie down near us.

We got back to our motel, and a group of guys showed up in a car from New York City. They thought the race was on Sunday. Lucky them. Turns out the warmest May on record in Plattsburg was our Marathon day.

Running keep running.

London Marathon.
1982

I ran the London marathon with David Schwarz. There were 25,000 people in that race. It started out in Greenwich and ran throughout London and finished on the other side of the Westminster Bridge.

It was tough. When the canon went off we all had to get through a small area, so it took us 25 minutes to get out of the park. And they counted that on your time It was only London's second marathon, so they did not know that water stations should be every mile. It took us 4 miles to the first water station, and people were fighting for a drink. Pure insanity. Much of the route took us over cobblestones. So tough. I ran it for World Runners and I ran with a young guy who was a professional deep sea diver. I was almost 50 at the time the kid was in his twenty, and he couldn't keep up with me. He was stopping at pubs and drinking beers, and around 13 miles he threw up and quit. Really wild. I ran it so easily and ended up with a 3 hours and 29 minutes, even with the stopping to help my friend from time to time. Here was the though part. We all ran across the Big Westminster Bridge and there was no way to get back. We were all stuck on the wrong side of the water. David finished an hour behind me, so I didn't mind waiting for him. When we finished they gave us mylar capes and Hovis drink. The drink was so thick you couldn't open your mouth. Every one was throwing it up. It was a disaster. It took us 2 hours to get across the bridge back to London.

By the way a guy ran almost all the way with me. He was dressed as a waiter and carried a tray with 4 martini glasses filled with who knows what. Everyone figured the glasses were glued down to the tray. When he crossed the finish line he picked up each glass and drank away. Also there was another wild one that ran almost the whole race with me. A vaudeville horse. Turns out the front was the son and the back was the father. They ran the whole 26 plus miles bent over. Amazing.
It was a great Marathon and I finished with my second best time.

Pippa and David

London Marathon. 1982

Eight exciting New York City Marathons. 1982-1990

That's right, I ran eight consecutive marathons in New York City...and that was it forever. I ran all eight with three close friends. Joe Mathew, Lou Cooper and Beth Friedman. Joe was a priest for 12 years until he met Carol and married this delicious woman. Lou Cooper was the head Doctor for Children at the Roosevelt Hospital, and Beth used to work for me at my agency and she now owned her own promotional company. Beth had a brother Sandy who was a heart doctor and a great runner also but he was not part of our group. The four of us trained together for those eight years, running around the reservoir almost everyday. We became very close. We ran all eight marathons together.

When Joe Mathews decided to get married we held the ceremony in our apartment at 19 East 88th Street. You got to get this. Joe was this soft spoken gentleman and Carol, his soon to be bride, was so outgoing and by the way black. They so complimented each other in almost every way. We set up about 30 rented white folded chairs with a aisle down the middle. Elaine and I were so busy making everything perfect for the two families that had never met, we were hysterical when we finally went inside.

We discovered that one side was all white and the other all black. No planning, they did it on their own. How funny is that. The next morning was Sunday and Joe, Beth, Lou and I met at 90th street to take our usual 6 mile run around the park. I made up a sign and without Joe noticing I was able to put it on his back...*Just Married.* As we ran around the park as people would pass us they would shout out..."congratulations"...Joe was flipping out..."How do they know?" Eventually he found the sign, but that was an example of how much fun we had running together over all those years.

What were the marathons like? Truly the best. Millions of New Yorkers cheered us on. Every borough was so different. We started in Staten Island and ran across the Verrazano Bridge (of course the men stopped to pee off the side of the bridge). Down to Brooklyn and it's tiny stores and closed in roads. All the way through Brooklyn and up to the 59th Street Bridge and up First Avenue Lot's of bands and cheering, starting the trip through Manhattan. That took you to about the 15th mile and the serious part of the run. Most people drop out here. We are running away from the finish line to The Bronx, across a bridge in Manhattan and turn South down towards Central Park. You enter the Park at 102 Street. Still 6 miles to go.

At this point many hit the wall and either stop, throw up and continue or drop out completely. The next few miles are like running another marathon. Many walk the rest of the way to the finish line. Not me, never. I usually turned on what ever I had left around 90th Street where the family would greet me, since it was only a block away from our apartment. The finish is so exciting. You are outside the park again and enter it on Central Park South. Millions cheering for the last mile. One time I slipped and fell at this point, people came to help me up, I made them go away, I was afraid I would be eliminated if they helped me get up. *(Made that up).* When you finished across the line you checked your time. Wrapped yourself in the Mylar cape, got your giant gold metal hung around your neck, and tried to get as much water down as possible. Total Joy. Total Passion to finish.
Every one was different, and the same in so many ways.
What an accomplishment to finish.

The last one I was cooked. My wife stopped me on the run up 1st Avenue. The 15 mile mark. She looked at me and shook her head… ran around the park as people would pass us they would shout out… "Have I ever asked you to stop…please stop you are green." She was right. I finished, by dragging myself home in 4 hours and 2 minutes, my worst time ever. When we got home, she took my temperature…104.5. They got me in a bath of ice.

I could have died. But I finished. That was my last one.
I loved them all.

Eight exciting New York City Marathons.

From Bar Mitzvah to College.
1946 to 1951

Dad and family in his office.

Last night I woke up around 2AM and realized that during the years in High School I wrote very few stories. A few about selling magazines door to door and working in the Borscht Belt as a bus boy. But, not much about those precious adolescence years. My first girlfriend...Sandy Racheski, who married a pharmacist and stayed in Passaic. Or Paula Puck who wanted to marry Kenny Berman, or me. Why would I leave these out?
So I am adding just a few to fill in the blanks.

The Cousins

Dad's 90th

The Herman Family)

The big green Nash.

When I turned 18 I got get my drivers license. My uncle Sunny had really taught me how to drive when I was 13, so I got a friend to help me get my license, but my Dad had never driven with me and I wanted to borrow his cars.

Dad owned two cars. I believe a 1947 Fleetwood Cadillac that was automatic, that he bought from his brother Bruno. And a new 1951 Nash. It was a big boat in bright green but was a shift car and looked like it was pretty tough to navigate. Kenny Berman had gotten his license a few months before, but his 1950 green Chevy was in service and I had a date with Linda Pashman that night, and I wanted to take her out on my own.

Dad had a plan. He would have me drive the Nash with him for an hour or so that afternoon. Everything went well. I did everything perfect and then it happened. Dad took me to Van Houten Avenue, which was a very steep hill. We waited and then I started up the hill.

"Stop the car half way up the hill and keep your foot on the brake. Remember to keep your other foot on the clutch or you will stall." I did just that we were half way up and we stopped.

"Let the clutch out and give her gas" he said pretty calmly…"The clutch…give her gas." We were slipping and I jammed on the brake. She stalled. He stopped being calm. "Start the car and give her gas and leave out the clutch slowly" The cars in back of us were stacking up. I started to panic. "Start the car now" he shouted. I did. "Add gas he shouted, I started to slip back again, and the horns started to blare at us, and I let out the clutch and revved the gas and we flew up to the top of the hill. "Pull over, pull over" he shouted.

"I'm sorry, I'm sorry, should we do it again.
"He was shaking his head. "No your OK, just stay away from hills." Amazing. "Can't I take the Caddy tonight?" No take the Nash your will be OK, just stay away from hills."

Here's the thing about the Nash. The front seat folded down to the back seat to form a bed. Really, a full bed. I had an idea for my date with Linda. We would go to the outdoor Drive-In Movie in Clifton. You got it…During the first of two B grade movies I put the seat down. I convinced Linda I was just going to show how it worked. Sure enough I used the lever on the drivers side of the seat and the front seat went all the way down to meet the back seat. I promised her I would put it right back up. I pushed the lever back up and the seat didn't budge. Over and over I tried to pull the seat up manually. It was jammed. It would not budge.

It is no easy job driving a car without a seat to support your back. We got home, and when I told Dad, I thought the world was going to end.

Turns out, it was not my fault.

The Nash dealer was hysterical when he heard the story… tell Harvey I am sorry I ruined his date with the Pashman girl.

That's what is was like living in a small town.

Bruce on the Corvair. Couldn't find the Nash picture.

The big green Nash.

This one is a killer.

I went to college in Philadelphia...Philadelphia Textile it was called at the time. I hardly ever went home the first year. I loved college. I got my first taste of culture. A good friend in the fraternity, Bob Sarafran introduced me to the Philadelphia Orchestra, and Ormandy their conductor. I had never been to a concert in my whole life.

I weighed 200 pounds when I started college. I lost 40 pounds the first 6 months. I stopped eating. My parents thought I had cancer. I used to go out every weekend, so I never went home. Evelyn didn't care, but Dad started to worry that I might be doing drugs or traveling with the wrong people. He wasn't totally wrong.

I had met Mona. A real seductive blond. She was a friend of a friend. A Lolita type. She was my first serious sexual relationship. She taught me so much. She just loved sex. We would go out to private bars on weekends. Philly was a blue town. No drinking on weekends so the rich guys had private clubs. Marty Zeldin's Dad belonged to one, and Marty would get his membership card and we would go to the club.

One night Marty and I and Mona went to the RDA club. Mona got a little drunk and started to act silly and seductive. A good looking guy at the end of the bar came over and sat with us. He seemed OK at first, but then started to make a move on Mona. I said let's go. I can't remember how it happened but he convinced us to go back to his apartment on the Drive. Mona kept on playing up to him. I must admit it was a little scary, but Marty loved this game and Mona did too.

The apartment was on The Drive. A very rich part of Philly and his apartment was a killer. We had a drink and he put on some music. I tired to convince Marty to go...but they loved teasing this guy. You could see he wanted to get Mona in bed. She kept on teasing him. All of a sudden he went inside and came out in his under wear. He ducked under the bar to get something and we all ran out. Yes, we left there and laughed all the way home. Stupid young kids. I went out with Mona for the next few months, but she was so grown up compared to me. Eventually she stopped seeing me.

My Dad wondered who was I dating at school. I told him about this wonderful girl I had met, obviously cleaning up my Mona. Dad felt I should meet the right kind of people. Mona did not fit the bill. My Dad was a member of the Ahavas Israel, where he went to temple. A member there had a brother who was a big shot Cadillac dealer in Philly. They had a young daughter and Dad felt that I should meet the family and if I liked, I could date the girl. A good solid Jewish Philadelphia family. These are the kind of people you should associate with. What harm would it do. They invited me over for the first night of Passover. I called and introduced myself and they told me where they lived. It was only one night...I better please my father.

The house was in the suburbs. Big with a lot of curb appeal. In the driveway two brand new shiny Caddy's, of course. I rang the bell and wondered what the hell was I doing there. The door opened and a good looking guy smiled...and the smile turned to fear and then anger...he stepped outside and slammed the door behind him...

"You bastard, I've got connections in this town, I'll call the police"...

I blurted out "I'm Harvey Herman, Sidney Herman's son...
I'm here for Passover."

He stopped and hugged me...and I realized he was the guy in the private club who hit on Mona...*this was the good Jewish guy...
the right kind of people.*

This one is a killer.   387

The Borscht Belt.
1952

The Concord, Grossingers, The Pines, Kutshers, The President and about 200 more hotels made up the Borscht Belt. They say that there were over 1000 Jewish resorts in the Catskills...The Mountains... or the Borscht Belt, whatever you wanted to call it. From the fancy Hotels down to the Kuchalayns (rented rooms with a shared kitchen). It was the favorite escape for the Jews in the 50's and 60's. No where else could you get..."all you can eat" and free star entertainment at night. Milton Berle, Joan Rivers, Jackie Mason, Henry Youngman, Red Buttons to name a few. Free tennis. Free work out classes... everything was included in your star studded stay.
It was all on the one price plan.
I was a busboy there in 1952.
And do I have stories to tell.

Did you have to be Jewish to go there? Not really. Many gentile women, so called Shiksas went there to find a wealthy Jewish husband. But it was mostly Jewish families, with lots of kids. The husbands worked in the garment industry. During the week the husbands would leave their wives to go to work, only to return on the weekends. They would give us handsome tips to make sure we took care of the kids and the wife.

As a busboy you worked from 6AM till 8PM. Three meals everyday, with about 3 hours off between lunch and dinner. At night, we would get calls to go to the dance hall to dance with the lonely wives. And we did just that. Some evenings no sleep. Stay up all night and go right to work in the morning. It was a trip that a teenager could only dream of. We were 18 and life couldn't get much better.

I made a small fortune that summer. Over $500 per week. The season was 10 weeks. For instance...I took care of Tito Puente and his family for the summer. His band was booked for the whole summer. The first week he took me aside and pulled three $100 dollar bills out of his pocket. He told me his wife had a room in the main building, but he also had a small bungalow that he rented for some of his lady friends. I had to make sure no one knew about the bungalow, and make sure both rooms got whatever they needed. He then ripped the bills in half and said I would get the other halves at the end of the summer. He was a man of his word. In fact he gave me another $300 bonus for doing such a great job. Don't forget this was 1952, and I was a teenager.

Ken Berman and I lied to the owners, The Roth's, that we were on the tennis team in college. The tennis courts were over grown, and needed weeding and rolling and in exchange we would offer tennis lessons during the hours we had off, and split the fees with the hotel. They agreed. We made a bundle, but it backfired one afternoon near the end of the season. This lady wanted to hit balls with me for an hour. Turns out she was a professional tennis player. Half the hotel showed up to see me not be able to hit back a single shot. I never saw the ball. She went easy after a while. I had gotten pretty good playing a couple of hours most days, but after that the Roth's hired a semi pro player to play with the guests. It was embarrassing. I thought he might fire us as busboys, but he didn't.

I grew up that summer. I never worked so hard in my life. Most of the waiters were professional waiters. That's what they did for a living. Most were monsters. There was one guy who went by the name of Killer Joe. He hated me. He would trip me when I would go by his station with a full tray of dishes. Once he did it on my way into the kitchen and I fell and broke a dozen or more plates. The other busboys helped me quickly clean up before the owners came in. I could have gotten fired. I had to get even some how, some way.

I found out Killer Joe was often at the pool, but here's the rub, he did not know how to swim. Really. I followed him around for a few days until one day he was at the pool and you guessed it... I pushed him in the deep end. He almost drowned. Never touched me again.

Also the first few days, I had a tough time getting food from the chefs.

The Borscht Belt. 1952

My orders would go in, but it took for ever to get them out. I quickly learned that a bottle a week of Johnnie Walker Black Scotch made those orders come out in minutes. It was a included in the "cost of doing business."

Oh I forgot, how did I get this lucrative job? I had never bused a table in my life. My best friend Kenny got me the job. He taught me how to load and stack trays. How to serve on the correct side when I had to. How to take away dishes, and clear the tables. No live stock (food left over) with dirty dishes. We did it all in one night. Told them I had worked at two other hotels before and another lie hits the dust. In two days I was a pro.

Just one more short memory…
One day this beautiful woman shows up at my table. Like I said sometimes women would come up searching for a wealthy Jewish guy to take care of them. Most of them had no idea of what the Catskills were like. Most were shiksas. She ate her meal, and I went over to see what she wanted for desert.
"Can I get you coffee?"
"Yes, I would love some with milk."
"Oh I'm so sorry, you had meat so I can't give you milk with your coffee."
"That's OK…I' ll just have milk then." she said.

Working in The Borscht Belt was so special. So Jewish. I loved it.

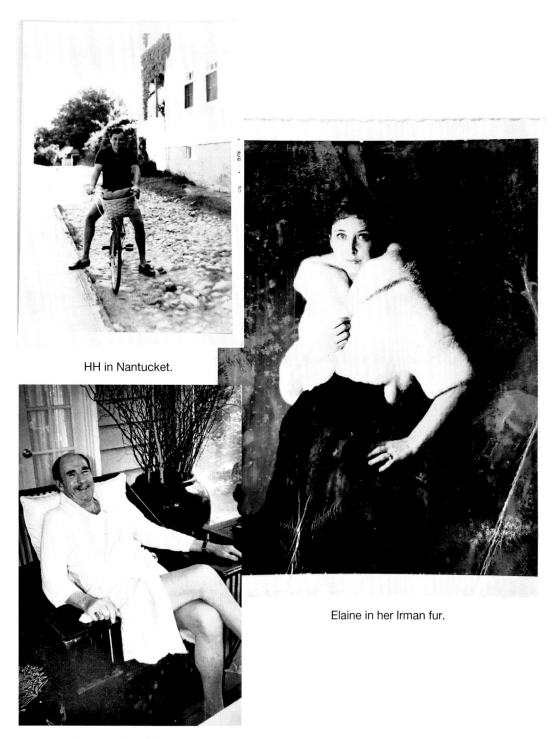

HH in Nantucket.

Elaine in her Irman fur.

Our dear friend David.

I didn't play golf with Greg Norman.

When I was engaged to Boots Orlanis, her uncle was a golf pro at a golf course in Trenton, New Jersey. I worked at the plant, just down the road. The Orlanis family gave me a new set of golf clubs and her uncle wanted to teach me the game. I never played it before then.

We would meet almost every morning and play 9 holes of golf before breakfast. He was determined that I play the game right. He taught me how to play with only three clubs. A driver, of course to drive the first shot off the tee. A five Iron only. One iron for my approach shots...the middle game as he called it. I would open and close the head of this mid iron. And a putter for putting on the green. In less than 6 months I became a 9 handicap . I was good. Better than good. When I broke up with Boots I very rarely played the game. I gave my fancy clubs to Jimmy who worked for my Dad. He really appreciated them.

I was 22 at the time. Some 35 years later, golf came back into my life. Greg Norman was one of the best golfers in the world. I got an assignment to shoot a number of films with him as the star. He had just sold a golf club company to a Japanese group, and the story goes that he personally netted 30 million after taxes.

He showed up every morning to the Jupiter course in Florida in a helicopter. He flew it but he did not have a license, he flew with a licensed pilot. They called him "The Shark." We hit it off immediately. I liked his bravado and he loved the fact that I never asked to play golf with him. You see he got $100,000 per 18 holes if you wanted to play one on one with him. The Japanese booked him as often as he made himself available.

When I told him how I learned to play golf and that my handicap was just 9 after 6 months...all he wanted to do is see me play. I never did. But what I did do is bet him, every time he had a line to deliver in the film, he would muff it. We bet $100 each time. We shot for 8 days, over two weeks. At the end of the two weeks he owed me $16,000.

He was a great golfer, but he could never remember his lines. He got so pissed when he messed up…I loved it. I was pretty embarrassed that this betting game we started got out of hand. I never intended to make him pay up. Here's how he got out of this debt.

On the last day, when we finished shooting, and everyone was wrapping up he pulled me aside and said…
"Let's play double or nothing for the money I owe you."
I tried to tell him it was OK, he could forget it.
"You put your camera down there about 250 yards away."
"Put a piece of plexiglass over the lens."
"I bet I can hit the plexi 3 out of 5 shots."

This was getting out of hand. If he lost he would not be happy and I would be pretty rich. But he insisted and we set up. He on the ridge ,and me with the camera 250 yards away. He did not hit the plexi 3 out of 5 shots. He hit it 5 out of 5. Every shot was perfect. Amazing.

This from a guy who would wake up every morning, and he could not touch his toes until he did traction.

He gave me the shirt off his back that day, literally, and signed it…
To Harvey…
the only guy who would not play golf with Greg Norman.

I didn't play golf with Greg Norman.

Dad at 103

Twelve years ago, around 2011, Dad was 103. He had only been at our house in The Hamptons once, when we first moved in 7 years ago.
We asked him to come out and make us his famous pickled onions. They were made in a rich white cream sauce. Usually he made them with herring, but I just liked the onions so he said that is how he would make them.

A few days later I received a handwritten note outlining each of the items that he would need to make the recipe. You had to see this note. I should have kept it. He always wrote with such flair. And the manuscript was perfect. This from a guy who never finished third grade in school, because he had to go to work when he was just 10 years old.

It took me hours to get the exact ingredients. He drove out with my younger brother Mitch that weekend. He hadn't been at the house for a long while and he liked all the work we had done on it. He always evaluated real estate as an investment.
"You should resell this place, you would make a big profit." I assured him that we were not selling. His one word response…"Pity."

Anyway on to the fun of the day. Like I said he was 103. He took all the ingredients out and lined them up. Shaking his head yes to everyone, until he got to the White Vinegar. He shook his head no…"this is night right, this is not Heinz. I will not guarantee it will work out. No I cannot guarantee without Heinz." That was dad.

I took pictures of him slicing each onion with such care. Each slice exactly the same as the one before. He let me sample taste the sauce. I told him it was perfect…"It's not Heinz". It turned out perfect, and dad was so surprised. I was so happy he made a few extra jars.
We enjoyed them all week.

My brother told me about two weeks later that dad hated the sauce, but didn't want to tell us. That was my dad. He did everything his way. In fact at his 100 birthday, Mitch played his favorite song…
Frank Sinatra singing…I Did it My Way.

Dad's Gefilte Fish

7# yellow pike
7# whitefish   filleted

wash & clean fish. cut in pieces, then grind (use both metal pieces)
grind 2 large onions along with fish (intermittently)

add 7-8 coffee measures of sugar
Make 2 full passes all over bowl with salt.
Make 2 full passes all over bowl with pepper.

Mix well.

Beat to froth 9 egg whites. Then add in 9 yolks and beat again.

Dad at 103!

Add eggs to fish mixture. After egg is all absorbed make 2 full passes all over bowl
with Matzo Meal (when fully absorbed, if not firm enough, add a little more matzo
meal). Pour a little club soda around end of bowl & work in. (I think about 1/2 small
bottle)

Shape fish. Keep hands wet.   1 1/4 - 1 1/2

Put fish in cold water. Bring to boil, then lower flame. Cover. Cook about 1 & 1/2 ho

WATER

Fill pot about 1/4 - 1/3 full with water. Add cut up celery (full chopped handful), and
carrots. 2 teaspoons white pepper, 3 teaspoons salt, few fish bones, & 5 scoops sugar.

Family, family, family...

So if you are still with me, you can see how crazy my life has turned out, and it is not over yet. I just celebrated 90 years on this planet.
And it is important for me to know that what ever time I have left...
I know that I want to spend as much time as possible with my family and pursuing my passions.

As I reviewed my stories I could clearly see a pattern. From the moment I kissed my wife to be on the nape of her neck...I took that risk knowing that it could be a big mistake. That has recurred throughout my life. Taking the family to Hollywood to become a director of film. Selling everything at the age of 70 and starting all over...or as my wife put it "repotting." Risks, yet at every turn my wife and my family had my back. Pretty great.

It is tough to travel now. Although my wife and I feel that we have at least one trip to Florence left. We want to see our dear friend Alesandro and have lunch in Lucca and do a lot of shopping in our favorite mall stores and possibly make it to a gallery or two. Lot's of spaghetti and at least one Osso bucco. It doesn't get much better than that. I would love our whole family to join us on this trip if possible, including my brother Stan. It is worth asking...as my wife says. Perhaps another risk worth taking.

Way back when we were shooting commercials it was a family affair. My wife did the casting, Joss was my producer and Amanda started in the early years as an actor in my toy commercials. I wrote and directed all the spots. It was a windfall for all of us. We had so many great times together.

On our early trips both in this country and overseas it was usually a family affair. Elaine split these up. Usually Amanda went on the USA trips and Joss on the International ones.

All of us have developed family ties. That is the simple, but important message that this memoir has left me with.

As they say in the finale of one of our favorite movies...Moonstruck...

ALLA FAMIGLIA...

Family, family, family...

Mom

Dedication

I did not write this memoir to find out more about myself.
It just happened.

Story-after-story I realized that my life has been special. And it has become quite clear to me how it all started.

My wife and I wrote a book a number of years ago. Wings and Roots. It was meant to be a book about parenting. Raising your children and giving them the deep knowledge of their roots. Not just genetically but building a strong foundation that will support you throughout life. The knowledge that your roots are deep and supportive can allow you to take chances, risks, and not worry about the failures in your life. A chance to fly. Elaine and I wrote the book for others, but in writing this memoir I realized it was for us as well.

It all started with my loving mother who only lasted 37 years. My dear, loving mother that wasn't supposed to bring me or my brother Stan into this world. But, for some reason she did. It was a very unselfish act. A brave act to chance having children, in spite of all the advise to the contrary. It is her roots that have given me this life.

The Wings belong to my wife. At every chance, every crossroad in our lives together, she has been the one to encourage me to go for it. When I look back over our 65 years together she never said no, and in most instances she was the one who had the vision and I followed. Thank you hon.
I dedicate this book to Helen, my mother who gave me my roots.
To my wonderful wife who taught me how to fly.

To my daughters Joss and Amanda, and their kids especially Sophie who encouraged me to write this book, my friends, and my brothers Stan and Mitchell. And to Jen Gaily, she took my words in pictures and made them fly. She's a magician.

Made in United States
North Haven, CT
26 August 2024

56598019R00220